Alternative Spaces/
Transformative Places

Mitchell S. McKinney and Mary E. Stuckey
General Editors

Vol. 41

The Frontiers in Political Communication series
is part of the Peter Lang Media and Communication list.
Every volume is peer reviewed and meets
the highest quality standards for content and production.

PETER LANG
New York • Bern • Berlin
Brussels • Vienna • Oxford • Warsaw

Joshua D. Atkinson and Clayton Rosati

Alternative Spaces/ Transformative Places

Democratizing Unruliness in an Age of Austerity

PETER LANG
New York • Bern • Berlin
Brussels • Vienna • Oxford • Warsaw

Library of Congress Cataloging-in-Publication Data

Names: Atkinson, Joshua D., author. | Rosati, Clayton, author.
Title: Alternative spaces/transformative places: democratizing unruliness
in an age of austerity / Joshua D. Atkinson and Clayton Rosati.
Description: New York: Peter Lang, 2020.
Series: Frontiers in political communication; vol. 41 | ISSN 1525-9730
Includes bibliographical references and index.
Identifiers: LCCN 2019020972 | ISBN 978-1-4331-5756-1 (hardback: alk. paper)
ISBN 978-1-4331-5757-8 (ebook pdf)
ISBN 978-1-4331-5758-5 (epub) | ISBN 978-1-4331-5759-2 (mobi)
Subjects: LCSH: Cities and towns—Political aspects. | Cities and
towns—Social aspects. | City planning—Citizen participation. |
Communication—Political aspects.
Classification: LCC HT151 .A775 | DDC 307.76—dc23
LC record available at https://lccn.loc.gov/2019020972
DOI 10.3726/b14149

Bibliographic information published by **Die Deutsche Nationalbibliothek**.
Die Deutsche Nationalbibliothek lists this publication in the "Deutsche
Nationalbibliografie"; detailed bibliographic data are available
on the Internet at http://dnb.d-nb.de/.

The paper in this book meets the guidelines for permanence and durability
of the Committee on Production Guidelines for Book Longevity
of the Council of Library Resources.

Printed in the United States of America

CONTENTS

Part IV: Exploring a Hidden Geography in Detroit

FIGURES

FOREWORD

Crisis, Austerity, & the Pleasures of Cruelty

In late–2011, Steven J. Baum PC, a legal "foreclosure mill" operating in the suburbs of Buffalo, NY, issued a public apology. Not long before, an employee had leaked photos from the firm's previous year's Halloween party featuring other employees dressed in costumes mocking foreclosure victims, foreclosure rights attorneys, and a judge critical of their unscrupulous practices. In a 2012 legal settlement, New York Attorney General Eric Schneiderman noted that the Baum Firm "cut corners in order to maximize the number of its foreclosure filings and its profits" (New York State Attorney General, 2012a). According to Schneiderman, "From at least 2007 through sometime in 2009, Baum Firm attorneys repeatedly verified complaints in foreclosure actions stating, among other things, that the plaintiff was 'the owner and holder of the note and mortgage being foreclosed,' when, in many securitized loan cases, the Baum Firm did not have documentary proof that the plaintiff was the owner and holder of the note and mortgage" (New York State Attorney General, 2012a). In other words, the firm had been taking advantage of the massive housing crisis by collecting fees from huge banks and foreclosing on homes under false, shaky, or incomplete rights to do so. But there was no soul-searching by Baum PC employees.

One of the most noteworthy pieces of the Halloween carnival of contempt for those evicted by the crisis was its construction of a "shantytown" within which the costumed foreclosure processers (most not lawyers) held signs reading: "*@!$%^&(* Foreclosure! I'm current!!" and "3rd Party Squatter. I lost my home and I was *never* served!!" The signs displayed a perverse pleasure in cruelty, which was still abhorrent then and is revoltingly commonplace now. If not an admission of guilt, carnivals of this kind at least trace the complex contortions demanded by systems of debasement rather than simply reflecting poor taste.[1] Not only did the 2007 economic crisis bring to a head the contradictions of key trends within millennial capitalism, it transformed homes and communities across the United States (and the world) at the hands of eviction officers armed with papers processed by firms like Baum. But, even further, the crisis forced an ideological reckoning with a set of assumptions about the free market, responsibility, and economic ethics. In this new impoverished environment, some acted to resist and restrain predatory capitalism, and some found even greater resonance with democratic socialism. In other instances, however, people confronted this reckoning with additional contempt for the poor, as well as people who were different or marginalized. Illustrating the latter, part of the Baum firm's temporary house of horrors was a row of mock "foreclosure sale" properties. And, they weren't alone in their heightened reactionary contempt. While nationally, blame for the crisis was often leveled at the poor themselves (Gross, 2008), it was the foreclosure mills, state austerity policies, real estate developers, and those who were evicting them, that extended the crisis, rigging foreclosure auctions, transforming the shape of communities, and getting rich in the process (see Desmond, 2016).[2] To look at transformations in the city is to see, not just bureaucratic evils, but in many corners of that seemingly banal system a sadistic devotion to it, to unfair rules, to social inequality, and to pain-by-bureaucracy. In many cases there was no banality to speak of—only lenders, developers, hedge fund managers, foreclosure processers, and others conspiring to wrest as much money and as many assets as possible from the socially vulnerable.

The impetus for this book came a few years earlier, seven or so hours west of Buffalo by car, across the US "rustbelt." We had both started our new jobs at Bowling Green State University in 2007, just south of Toledo and Detroit, when we encountered a landscape twisting under pressures from connected forces. We found our shared interests in the material-ideological dimensions of cities and urban landscape piqued by the various struggles that were developing over the redefinition of places, over the contending claims to their popular meanings, and over the physical re/construction of neighborhoods and communities as part of those contending definitions. Detroit also seemed to have a kind of artificial distance from our (relatively) rural campus, just one hour north of us on I-75. At that time, it seemed like another world, where few in northwest Ohio seemed to go or commit research efforts as a matter of rustbelt solidarity or otherwise. In Detroit's struggles, we found a chaotic spectrum of kindness and frustration, which engendered different versions of hope and long-term imaginations of the past and future.

Since the formal crisis and our research on the city, the Detroit landscape has transformed wildly in some places (e.g., Corktown's gentrification, the new "Chinatown," the Little Caesar's Arena, state imposed "emergency financial management" and municipal bankruptcy) and has stagnated in others (e.g., nearly triple the national poverty rate, almost double the eviction rate, housing at hyper-vacancy rates). When we started our writing on cityscape, Detroit was popularly seen as an "unruly" place, as out of bounds or a frontier to be tamed, explored, and developed. Alistair Bonnett (2014), in his book *Unruly Places*, marshals this term to describe disorganized sites that people feel are peculiar, scary, or different. But Bonnett, like many self-described psychogeographers and urban explorers, approaches unruliness from a rather sentimentalist and exoticizing starting point. For instance, echoing popular and scholarly criticisms of suburbanization, sprawl, and corporate urbanism, Bonnett explains: "The rise of placelessness, on top of the sense that the whole planet is now minutely known and surveilled, has given this [pervasive] dissatisfaction a radical edge, creating an appetite to find places that are off the map and that are somehow secret, or at least have the power to surprise us" (p. xiv). But one need only be a foreclosure processer to see that simply finding "off the map" places is a relatively dull edge for radicalism.

This was something intimated to us early in our Detroit work, the world doesn't need more ruin pornographers. Coverley (2009) looks at things similarly in his *Psychogeography*, in which he notes:

> If psychogeography is to be understood in literal terms as the point where psychology and geography intersect, then one of its further characteristics may be identified in the search for new ways of apprehending our urban environment. Psychogeography seeks to overcome the processes of "banalisation" by which the everyday experience of our surroundings becomes one of drab monotony. (p. 13)

But Coverley doesn't stop there. Channeling filmmaker Patrick Keiller, he critically notes:

> ... psychogeography [is] increasingly preoccupied with its own practices as an end in themselves, no longer the tool of any larger political or even cultural project but simply a self-contained and self-immersed movement with little significant impact on the environment whose redevelopment it has so vocally denounced. (pp. 28–29)

Was it possible to simply wander (anymore or ever) in the city or explore urban ruins for the satisfaction of personal "surprise" or excitement? After the financial collapse? After gentrification? After the Detroit water crisis? After the lead crisis in Flint?

In a similar timeframe, Wark (2013) writes rousingly in the *Spectacle of Disintegration* about some of the main popularizers of wandering, drifting, dérive, or exploring the psychogeographies of cities, Guy Debord and the Situationist International movement:

> Debord's sometime comrade Raoul Vaneigem famously wrote that those who speak of class conflict without referring to everyday life, "without understanding what is subversive about love and what is positive in the refusal of constraints, such people have a corpse in their mouth." Today this formula surely needs to be inverted. To talk the talk of critical thought, of *biopolitics* and *biopower*, of *the state of exception*, *bare life*, *precarity*, of *whatever being*, or *object oriented ontology* without reference to class conflict is to speak, if not with a corpse in one's mouth, then at least a sleeper. Must we speak the hideous language of our century? (pp. 4–5)

And perhaps we might say to those simply seeking excitement in the city, without contemplating the violence of capital's circulation or of class conflict are engaging in a kind of celebration of suffering—though, certainly not as conscientiously contemptuous as the Baum firm's Halloween party or as naively "self-immersed" as ruin porn. Still they are, so to speak, walking on corpses that were immiserated under capitalism by homelessness, food insecurity, and "austerity suicides" (Mitchell, 2018). Between 2007 and 2011, the Baum foreclosure mill filed over 50,000 New York cases (Morgenson, 2011). The New York Attorney General's (2012b) office reported that, "an average of 1 in 10 mortgages [was] at risk of foreclosure. The approximate number of individuals living in homes that [were] either in foreclosure or at risk of foreclosure [exceeded] the populations of Buffalo, Rochester, and Syracuse combined." The stakes are high in our urban landscapes and we must always see the brutal within the banal.

This is the post-recession world. Poor. Put out. Pissed. Prone to verkakte saviors. Admittedly, it's not too different from the pre-recession world. The rules of this current world are bound to austerity, to diminished public services, to forced municipal bankruptcies, to more privatization, and even to the criminalization of private debt (i.e., return of debtors' prison, see ACLU 2018). Austerity must not just be seen mathematically (granted, at times actual math would be a treat!) or philosophically. Rather, austerity has to also be understood emotionally, as a visceral impulse to tough love—like the conversations one hears at strange family holidays, full of hidden grudges, disproportionate hostility, and proud recollections of long-past suffering as the rationale for the torment of a new group of children.

Blyth (2013) notes in a *Foreign Policy* feature that "Austerity is a seductive idea because of the simplicity of its core claim—that you can't cure debt with more debt. This is true as far as it goes, but it does not go far enough" (p. 43). In his book, *Austerity: The History of a Dangerous Idea*, Blyth (2015) invokes Quiggin's notion of "zombie economics," or "economic ideas that will not die despite huge logical inconsistencies and massive empirical failures" (p. 10). Blyth explains this in the following:

> [Austerity] is a zombie economic idea because it has been disproven time and again, but it just keeps coming. Partly because the commonsense notion that "more debt doesn't cure debt" remains seductive in its simplicity, and partly because it enables conservatives to try (once again) to run the detested welfare state out of town, it never seems to die. (p. 10)

Indeed, beyond the evidence that austerity doesn't work, the inequality, the instability, and the asymmetrical burden it places on the poor, have, as Blyth notes, dangerous implications. As a case in point, amid the ongoing horror of Flint's toxic water supply, to remark of austerity programs' fiscal savings is not only obnoxious but misleading, given the additional health and infrastructural expenses it caused. And this is the key. Whatever impulse there is to tally up the balance sheets betrays the idea's most dangerous play: its incessant rationality (e.g., how much money is a life worth?). But, the idea of austerity also *feels good* to certain segments of the capitalist world, or segments of the capitalist "mind" (whatever that might be). As we starve one beast, we feed another (Bartlett, 2007).

Despite the delight contemporary populist politics seem to take in cruelty, mass movements sprout against that tide: The Arab Spring, Occupy Wall Street, the Detroit Water Brigade, Black Lives Matter, the national Incarcerated Worker's Strike, Me Too, Standing Rock water protectors, Medicare for All, and the list goes on. The contest for the future will implicitly be urban, as it is now, struggling to redefine the social meanings of common resources, pollution, debt, inequality, public speech and protest, and develop-ment in so-called poor and rich countries alike. The contested cityscapes of the future will be implicitly devoted to what many urbanists call "the right to the city" as a political question: who has the right to control our social prod-ucts and, ultimately, the production of our own social nature (e.g., Harvey, 2013; Lefebvre, 2003; Mitchell, 2003, 2018). This is a technological, legal, and ideological problem. It is also implicit in contemporary considerations of democracy.

One of the key ideological contradictions of the neoliberal era, of the era of austerity and cruel pleasures, is the mismatch between the physical capacity of the world economic system and the deprivation experienced by so many. Why less, given our productive capacity? Who makes those choices? The National Conference to Defeat Austerity, held in Detroit in March, 2018, recently defined their counter-narrative as the following: "defeating the war being waged by the banks, corporations, and government against the work-ers and oppressed" (Ikonomova, 2018, np). When we look at the delight in contempt and cruelty that the Baum firm's Halloween party represented, its mockery of destitute lives and its crass cynicism, we see the depth of the polit-ical crisis at hand. But perhaps we might even hold some sympathy for the employees whose livelihoods are beholden to making people homeless. Should we hold those office workers in a contrary contempt? Or do we see carnivals of that kind as expressions of the emotional repetitive stress injuries of neolib-eral capitalism? Beyond marking enemies, it is out of austerity's and neoliberal capitalism's contradictions with concepts like dignity, equality, the commons, and even democracy that we find new meanings built for and into our urban resources. And it is on that platform *against austerity* and against the *pleasures of cruelty*, for abundance *and* sustainability, for equality *and* innovation, that new struggles for meaning can find the city as something to be remade along the path of their aspirations. That platform must target the force of the pre-vailing systems of cruelty—the rights to the city and to our very nature that banks, corporations, and political budget mongers currently occupy. It is on this platform that the struggle for democratization must proceed.

All of which leads to our collaborative research efforts, which formed the foundation for this book. In 2010 we took keen interest in the city of Detroit, and efforts to reimagine the spaces and places therein. Clayton, a geogra-pher, was attentive to the global forces that had scarred the physical environ-ment and cityscape, as well as counter narratives that challenged those forces. Josh, a communication scholar, was fascinated with the lived experiences of people who utilized those counter-narratives, as well as the ways in which they co-constructed them—and experienced them—through media and performative practices. That initial project concerning Detroit illustrated the intersection of neoliberalism, austerity policies, digital media, activism, and communicative practices of resistance. The findings from that overarching project produced the following publications:

- Atkinson, J. D., & Rosati, C. (2012). DetroitYES! and the fabulous ruins virtual tour: The role of diffused intertextual production in the construction of alternative cityscapes. *Critical Studies in Media Communication*, 29, 45–64.
- Atkinson, J. D., Rosati, C., Berg, S., Meier, M., & White, B. (2013). Racial politics in an online community: Discursive closures and the potentials for narrative appropriation. *Journal of Communication Inquiry*, 37(2), 171–185.
- Atkinson, J. D., Rosati, C., Stana, A., & Watkins, S. (2012). The performance and maintenance of standpoint within an online community. *Communication, Culture & Critique*, 5, 618–635.

What is more, these studies initiated other research that explored rural communities, cities in Germany, telecommunication policies, and lead poisoning in Flint, Michigan. Those efforts were published in the following:

- Atkinson, J. D. (2016). Hiding in plain sight: Acoustic participatory camouflage at the DDR Museum in Berlin. *Javnost—the Public*, 23(3), 237–254.
- Atkinson, J. D. (2017). Transformation, fractures, & boundaries: The case of stadtpunkte in the Mannheimer cityscape. *Explorations in Media Ecology*, 16(2–3), 175–193.
- Rosati, C. (2018). *Development as freedom* after flint: A geographical approach to capabilities and antipoverty communication. *Journal of Multicultural Discourses*, 13(2), 139–159.

Ultimately, all of these studies come together in this book, wherein we illustrate the following: (1) the relationship between austerity and the rise of unruly spaces in society, (2) the impact of such unruly spaces on communities, and (3) communicative practices of ordinary people to challenge or change perceptions about those spaces. It is our hope that this book will initiate more discussion and research concerning austerity and the forms of spatial activism described here. What is more, we believe that specific communicative strategies for the democratization of unruly spaces—when utilized correctly—can empower citizens to take control of their own communities, and create change in the face of constant government and corporate abuse.

Notes

1. Thanks to Edgar Landgraf for the reminder about Bakhtin. Also, see McCarthy (2007) for a similar take on TV culture.
2. NY's Schneiderman, like many state attorneys general, also pushed back against the waves of foreclosures with lawsuits to build a war chest for consumer protection. Schneiderman's office announced a fund of millions of dollars from legal settlements. For instance, one "investigation found that Ameriquest engaged in predatory and illegal lending practices to sell and refinance mortgages, including misrepresenting and failing to disclose loan terms, charging excessive loan origination fees, and inflating appraisals to qualify borrowers for loans" (New York State Attorney General, 2012b). Also the NYAG secured "more than $130 million for struggling New Yorkers as part of a national settlement with the nation's top five mortgage servicers" and also filed "a major lawsuit against the nation's largest banks and Mortgage Electronic Registrations System, Inc. for deceptive and fraudulent foreclosure filings" (New York State Attorney General, 2012a).

References

Bartlett, B. (2007). "Starve the beast": Origins and development of a budgetary metaphor. *The Independent Review, 12*(1), 5–26.

Blyth, M. (2013, May/June). The austerity delusion: Why a bad idea won over the west. *Foreign Policy, 92*(3), 41–56. https://www.foreignaffairs.com/articles/2013-04-03/austerity-delusion

Blyth, M. (2015). *Austerity: The history of a dangerous Idea.* Oxford; New York: Oxford University Press.

Bonnett, A. (2014). *Unruly places: Lost spaces, secret cities, and other inscrutable geographies.* New York, NY: Houghton-Mifflin Harcourt.

Coverley, M. (2009). *Psychogeography.* Harpenden: Pocket Essentials.

Desmond, M. (2016). *Evicted: Poverty and profit in the American city.* New York, NY: Crown Publishing.

Gross, D. (2008, October 7). Subprime suspects: The right blames the credit crisis on poor minority homeowners: This is not merely offensive, but entirely wrong. *Slate.com.* Accessed February 6, 2019, from https://slate.com/business/2008/10/the-right-blames-the-credit-crisis-on-poor-minority-homeowners-this-is-not-merely-offensive-but-entirely-wrong.html

Harvey, D. (2013). *Rebel cities: From the right to the city to the urban revolution.* New York, NY: Verso.

Ikonomova, V. (2018). National conference to defeat austerity will fight the power in detroit this Saturday. *Metro Times.* Accessed February 13, 2019, from https://www.metrotimes.com/news-hits/archives/2018/03/23/fight-the-power-at-the-national-conference-to-defeat-austerity-in-detroit-this-saturday

Lefebvre, H. (2003). *The urban revolution.* Minneapolis, MN: University of Minnesota Press.

McCarthy, A. (2007). Reality television: A neoliberal theater of suffering. *Social Text, 25*(4, 93), 17–42.

Mitchell, D. (2003). *The right to the city: Social justice and the fight for public space.* New York, NY: Guilford Press.

Mitchell, D. (2018). Revolution and the critique of human geography: Prospects for the right to the city after 50 years. *Geografiska Annaler: Series B, Human Geography, 100*(1), 2–11.

Morgenson, G. (2011, April 8). New York issues Subpoenas to Foreclosure Firm. *The New York Times.* https://www.nytimes.com/2011/04/09/business/09foreclose.html

New York State Attorney General. (2012a, March 22). A.G. Schneiderman announces $4 million settlement with New York Foreclosure Law Firm Steven J. Baum P.C. and Pillar Processing LLC [press release]. Accessed February 5, 2019, from https://ag.ny.gov/press-release/ag-schneiderman-announces-4-million-settlement-new-york-foreclosure-law-firm-steven-j

New York State Attorney General. (2012b, April 25). A. G. Schneiderman announces $3 million awarded for Foreclosure Prevention Legal Services statewide [press release]. Accessed February 5, 2019, from https://ag.ny.gov/press-release/ag-schneiderman-announces-3-million-awarded-foreclosure-prevention-legal-services

Wark, M. (2013). *The spectacle of disintegration.* New York, NY: Verso.

PART I
INTRODUCTION

The following chapters introduce readers to key concepts in the book, and demonstrate those concepts in terms of real world, lived experiences. In Chapter 1, we introduce the concepts of space, as well as unruliness and communicative democratization of space. In Chapter 2, we provide concrete examples of these key concepts, and how they have impacted the lives of people in one rural community. Overall, Part I of this book accomplishes the following:

1. Explains key concept of space, and its philosophical foundations.
2. Details the two primary lines of research in communication and media studies concerning space: (a) landscape and cityscape, and (b) communicative cities.
3. Explains the concept of unruly space, and demonstrates the rough typology of unruly spaces that has been developed in past literature.
4. Presents the case for the democratization of unruly spaces, and why such action is necessary in contemporary society.
5. Offers a case study of a community that has been deeply affected by unruly spaces around them.
6. Describes that community's response, which demonstrates the potentials and difficulties for the democratization of unruly space.

· 1 ·

UNRULY SPACES, CITYSCAPE &
COMMUNICATIVE CITIES

Imagine entering a building in which the interior is constructed in such a way so as to appear "upside down." There are actually several examples of such sites at fairs, carnivals, and amusement parks. The floor is the ceiling, and the ceiling is the floor. Chairs and tables are high above your head, while you avoid tripping over light fixtures and chandeliers standing at your feet. In these instances, the differences between that space and a "normal" room create a sense of fun or entertainment as you pass through and interact with the environment. You understand the first site as outside of the ordinary, and marvel at the change in perspective offered by the distinctive organization of the physical environment. As you leave the upside-down environment of the building, you re-enter a rather ordinary world in which objects and people are where they are supposed to be. Up is once more above your head, and down is under your feet. Nothing seems to be out of the ordinary here, and so you move through the environment taking little note of the things around you; the physical environment is once again taken for granted. Nevertheless, both spaces are very much active sites that shape knowledge and identity (e.g., Dickinson, 1997; Ott, Aoki, & Dickinson, 2011).

Now imagine walking through a commercial district of a large city. All around you are shops with colorful signs in their windows and advertisements at their doors, each competing for your gaze. Indeed, the style of the architecture and landscaping all about call for you to stop and look around. You feel that there is much here, and you wish to linger and take in all of the sights, sounds, and smells. After a while however, you return to your journey and leave the commercial district behind; your path now takes you into a nearby neighborhood. The infrastructure here looks as well made as it had been in the commercial district. The street and sidewalks are all in good shape, and the signs are clearly posted and serviceable. However, the houses and buildings all around you are bare of any decoration or interesting features. The walls are flat and bland, while the landscaping is unremarkable in any way. It's not that the neighborhood feels dangerous or menacing; it seems like an empty void. It is as if all humanity and meaning had been sucked from the spaces all around. Or more precisely, it was built with no meaning or sense of humanity at all. You no longer feel the need to stop or linger in this space, but rather press onward and leave the neighborhood behind. As with the prior example: both may seem different, but they are each active sites that shape knowledge and guide the identities of people as they pass through.

Finally, imagine an abandoned building on the outskirts of your hometown; it is an old house or church that stood empty for years. The building has fallen into disrepair, and become choked with wild vegetation and evidence of animal habitation. You might have driven by it hundreds of times along a nearby highway, but never taken notice of that site. On this particular day, you feel compelled to stop your car and pull into the drive. You have a strong desire to go into the building—to move through the doorway and interact with that space. As you approach the front door, you notice that the steps leading up to the house are crumbling, and the door hangs off of its hinges. Upon moving through the doorway, you see that the ceiling has collapsed and rainwater now flows freely into the interior of the building. Plants and fungus grow through the floorboards, pushing into the walls and remaining furniture. Compared to the comfort of your car or the orderly pathway of the highway nearby, the house feels wild and untamed. The differences between house and the comfort of your car seem extremely stark. Yet, these spaces shape knowledge and identity, like the upside down house and the commercial district.

The examples above are all spaces that anyone may encounter in their everyday life. In particular, three of these spaces—the upside down house, bland neighborhood, and abandoned house—are spaces that would typically make people feel strange, disoriented, or nervous. However, two of those three spaces could actually be considered to be "unruly," whereas one is as organized as those spaces that we would consider to be "normal." Which are unruly, and which is normal? For the purposes of this book, we would consider the bland neighborhood and abandoned house to be unruly spaces, while the upside down amusement park house would be considered to be "organized" or "normal." In many ways, the entertaining interior of the upside down house and the organized pathways outside of the building are not so different. They were structured in ways that control the movement of people and goods passing through. Upside down houses like the one described above have been meticulously designed in such a way so that movement through the space elicits feelings of excitement and enjoyment. What is more, such spaces have often been designed in order to efficiently move people through them, so as to maximize profits as people pay for entrance into those spaces. The other two examples noted above are spaces in which there was little or no attention to the organization—or at least, there had been little attention paid to their organization in a very long time. These spaces, then, lose meanings that may have once been associated with them, and even become subject to the forces of nature around them; these spaces have come to be seen by people as wild, inhospitable, or unruly. For those people who pass through them, or interact with the physical environment, the spaces seem to be peculiar or deviant. Such perceptions may lead people to feel uncomfortable within those environments, which often results in people moving through, and away from, those spaces as quickly as possible. In general, people tend to prefer spaces that are organized, or "normal," rather than those that are unruly. Increasingly, however, people in modern society find that they pass through or live within (or near) spaces that they (or other people) deem to be unruly. These perceptions of spaces as unruly can have significant implications for the lives of those people who must live in, or live near, those physical environments.

To understand unruly spaces, one must first comprehend the concept of space. The notion of "space" constitutes material sites largely devoid of meaning wherein people perform and interact (e.g., Burgin, 1996; Seamon & Sowers, 2008).[1] Offices, homes, and the material elements around them would all serve as good examples of space. They are those physical sites that people pass through or occupy as they work, eat, or sleep. Sidewalks, coffee shops, and plazas would all stand as good examples of spaces that we might encounter in society. For the most part, there are two approaches to space that are

---

1 See Lefebvre (1992) and Massey (1994, 2005) for much more nuanced explorations of "space" as a concept beyond our more operational usage.

crucial to our arguments and claims concerning the democratization of unruly spaces: cityscape/landscape, and communicative cities. The first addresses the construction of meaning structures and their attachment to spaces in society. The second addresses the role that physical spaces play within modern cities. For the most part, we see these as intertwined.

Landscape & Cityscape

Integral to our discussions in this book are two related concepts: cityscape and landscape. Both constitute the socially constructed aspects of physical environments; they are the ways in which people perceive materiality. Indeed, both landscape and cityscape are formed through communicative practices at the local and national/global levels, and stand as a knowledge about physical spaces. Landscapes are collections of spaces connected together and imparted meaning by shared perceptions socially constructed through communicative practices and media representations. Such communication builds knowledge about spaces and imbues meaning to them, which influences the ways in which people perform and interact. Geographers Cosgrove (1988) and Mitchell (2000) both describe landscapes as socially constructed knowledges about material spaces, which informs actions and shapes identity when people pass through and interact within such space. As Cosgrove (1985) argued, "landscape," the shared view and way of seeing a portion of the terrain, "is an ideological concept" (p. 15). It describes something ordinary (Meinig, 1979), taken for granted (Cosgrove, 1988), and made to appear natural (Olwig, 2002). Simultaneously material and representational, landscape, as Cosgrove (1985) claims, is "a way in which certain classes of people have signified themselves and their world through their imagined relationship with nature, and through which they have underlined and communicated their own social role and that of others with respect to external nature" (p. 15). Landscape, in this sense is hegemonic, naturalizing relations of ruling between dominant and subordinate social groups but not without contest (Mitchell, 2000).

Cityscape projects a material-representational form of power into the built environments of urban space. Cities like New York and San Francisco are places that most people have encountered before they have physically visited them, as news accounts, fables, and popular media that depict those sites are circulated and reproduced across contemporary society. Such fables and depictions, when accumulated together, form an image that is infused into everyday life (Abercrombie & Longhurst, 1998; Debord, 1994), and stand as the building blocks for a readable text referred to as a cityscape that people across contemporary society recognize as "New York" or "San Francisco" (Barthes, 1991; Burgin, 1996; Lerup, 2000; Lynch, 1960; Soja, 1995). As an individual "reads" such cityscapes they develop knowledge about space and their own location within that space, which, in turn, influences their own identity (Burgin, 1996). Such shared views of city-space, planned and constructed by powerful social actors is, in Mitchell's (1994) terms, "an instrument of cultural power" (pp. 1–2), mediating and ordering not just views, but experiences of urban space within the city itself or from afar. Scholars within the field of communication have explored the concepts of cityscape and landscape through two primary lines of research: (1) the ways in which communication and images construct cityscapes or landscapes (e.g., Sadler & Haskins, 2005); (2) the construction and evocation of nostalgia and memory about spaces (e.g., Dickinson, 1997, 2006). Both lines of research have provided valuable insight into the construction of cityscape, as well as perceptions about built environments that make up cities.

In reference to the first line of research, communication scholars have examined the way in which images constrain the conceptualizations of landscapes and cityscapes. One important example of this line of research comes from Sadler and Haskins (2005), who explored the "postcard effect" built from topographical categories featured in television programs like *Seinfeld*, *Friends*, and *Felicity*. The concept of topographical categories was first developed by Lynch (1960) to make cityscapes "legible," and to provide a language for the discussion and analysis of them. Essentially, the topographical categories are five types of images associated with the city that people recognize and recollect: landmarks, districts, nodes, paths, and edges. Landmarks are objects or architecture that is unique to a city and "are the most frequently identifiable elements of the city because they can be used as references to other parts of the city" (Sadler & Haskins, 2005, p. 202). The landmark is the site that anchors all of the other images to one city, as with the Statue of Liberty in New York or the Golden Gate Bridge in San Francisco. Districts are also identifiable elements of the city used as a reference point, but are different from landmarks as they can be passed through and inhabited; Times Square would serve as an example of a district of New York. Nodes are the public spaces where people live, work, and play such as apartments, restaurants, and nightclubs. Paths are the infrastructure of the city that allows people to move from one point to another, such as streets and sidewalks. Edges are the boundaries that act as a break between different parts of the city like rivers, walls, or hedges. Sadler and Haskins claim that the images of New York landmarks and districts featured in external shots in television programs like *Friends* are used as anchors, while picturesque and glamorous nodes, paths, and edges (e.g., parks, upscale coffee shops and nightclubs) frame the city and eliminate the "grittiness" of the actual site. Such anchoring and framing produces a pleasurable hyperreal cityscape that exists only for the tourists' gaze. One can readily imagine a postcard of New York containing shifting images of the skyline, Greenwich Village, and coffee shops filled with hip smiling people with an inscription at the bottom that reads: "I ♥ NY"; a phrase often depicted on t-shirts and bumper stickers.

In reference to the second line of research, communication scholars have examined the production and invocation of powerful forms of nostalgia and memory in shaping perceptions about physical environments. For instance, Dickinson (1997, 2006, 2015) has examined the ways in which narratives and images in suburban communities in the United States create a sense of nostalgia that informs knowledge and identity. In his examination of Old Pasadena, Dickinson (1997) revealed that the combination of legend and architecture played an important role in the formation of nostalgia and memory, which guided the "shoppers browse." Specifically, the images associated with the architecture, like many of the narratives inscribed into historic markers placed throughout downtown Pasadena, stood as multiple legends that suggested a variety of nostalgic histories. The Mediterranean and Spanish Colonial styles called on nostalgia for the exotic that simultaneously emphasized southern Europe and settlement of the western frontier, while the organization of buildings mirrored a more traditional Main Street America of the 1950s that constituted nostalgia for a middle-class notion of home. Housed within the city and surrounding area were additional nostalgic sites, like Banana Republic and Victoria's Secret, which called for consumption-oriented performances by the individuals who are passing through. Such legends created a sense of importance, while also hiding from sight less glamorous memories of Pasadena's past (e.g., unsavory bars and adult bookstores) and problematic aspects of urban Los Angeles. The city, and the larger cityscape, stood as a site that called upon multiple nostalgic memories through legends and architecture, and allowed for the emergence of identities and performances from the decisions that people made within the site. In addition, Dickinson's

(2006) investigation of the film *Pleasantville* illustrates "risk" as an important component of the nostalgia associated with the suburban landscape. The movie was released in 1998, and told the story of two teenagers in late 20th Century suburban America who were pulled into a 1950s black and white television program reminiscent of *Leave it to Beaver*. The appearance of the two teenagers threw the orderly structure of the town out of balance, leading to several characters and places "colorizing" as they opened their minds to new possibilities. The town of Pleasantville itself was organized in a way that called on nostalgic memory of 1950s Main Street, and white middle-class notions of home. According to Dickinson, the colorizing of people and places in that black and white world, as well as stories about the world outside of Pleasantville told by the two protagonists, stood as dangers that were exciting yet controlled by the safe boundaries of traditional Main Street. The excitement allowed for the full range of human emotion, which added to the authenticity of the nostalgia experienced by the audience. Finally, in his book *Suburban Dreams*, Dickinson (2015) explains that imagery and narratives associated with suburban corners of the US informs residents' goals in life through rhetorical spatialities. Essentially, the physical environments in the suburbs are organized in such ways so as to position the residents who dwell there to "embody, enact, and urge values, beliefs, and actions" (p. 4). In particular, elements in the architecture stand as proofs or arguments for the dreams that should be achieved (typically consumption of material goods or authentic experiences), and the nightmares of which residents should be wary (typically racial Others).

Overall, these two lines of research focus on the ways in which communication stands as an important foundation for cityscape, which influences perceptions of physical spaces. Images, narratives, or characteristics in the physical environment build new knowledge or nostalgia, which influences identity as people move through, or interact with, particular spaces in a city or region. Television programs like *Friends* and *Felicity* shape audiences knowledge about New York City, which influences the ways in which they interact with spaces in the city if they travel to that destination. Conversely, the architecture in Pasadena, or in other suburbs, creates an engaging nostalgia that informs people passing by about the spaces all around; this nostalgia influences identity, and calls for certain behaviors or actions (like shopping or browsing). These lines of research effectively demonstrate the communication shapes perceptions of space, which in turn influences the ways in which people perform or engage within those spaces.

Communicative Cities

In addition to communication studies concerning images and perceptions of space and cityscape, there has also been significant media and communication research concerning the material environments of "communicative cities." The notion of the communicative city focuses on the built or material aspects of physical environments, and how they enhance or hinder communication. Such research has strong connections to the study of media ecology (e.g., McLuhan, 1988; McLuhan & Powers, 1992). Whereas the communication research concerning cityscape and space noted above focuses on perceptions and image, media ecology research examines the role of physical environments in communication—particularly within urban environments. Past research by geographers and media scholars such as Hall (1969), Jacobs (1963), and Mumford (1962) demonstrates that cities, and the spaces within them, are not static, and subject to change and rearrangement over time. In addition, there are fixed and semi-fixed features of a city that can also shape communication within, and throughout, the city. According to Gumpert and Drucker (2008) cities can be "communicative" through the presence and quality of different spaces within the material environment. All cities have features that allow for some degree of communication like buildings, parks and other open spaces, roads and transportation, and media technology. Essentially, cities that have features that allow for free movement and local media, as well as sites that allow for citizen interactions and political debate, foster vibrant communication. When these features exist together in high quality, they allow for the emergence of a communicative city.

Past research concerning communicative cities has focused primarily on those features associated with the media, as Gumpert and Drucker note that they characterize the city more than anything else. They claim that cities are often defined "by what media are available; media developments and media obsolesce" (p. 202). Such media features allow for citizens in and around the city to construct knowledge about the material environment, thus shaping the ways in which they move through and interact with the environment. The city itself, in this sense, imbues the many spaces with meaning; this is similar to the social construction and perceptions noted above. In this way, then, citizens are responsible for much of the meaning inscription that is carried out, which is accomplished with the media available to them within the physical environment of the city. Nevertheless, physical spaces, like parks or coffee shops, also play an important role in the construction of communicative cities. These are the sites in which citizens congregate, share ideas, and debate issues. These are different, yet no less important, than the "capabilities" discussed later in Chapter 3; those aspects of the physical environment give rise to hope and dignity for citizens within a community. Communicative cities prove to be integral to widespread democracy as they allow for the free flow of people and goods, which is necessary for the rise and debate of ideas across a society. Whenever the communicative qualities are disrupted, possibilities for interactions and engagement within cities may become limited—or even eliminated. Should such disruptions become prevalent throughout a nation or society, there can be dire consequences for democratic structures.

For the most part, we often find ourselves in modern society located within "communicative" spaces and places, which are the foundations for modern democracy and capitalism. It is particularly important to understand that the communicative spaces described by Gumpert and Drucker are very organized, controlled, and structured. Like the upside down house described at the beginning of this chapter, they are constructed in such a way to effectively facilitate the passage and assembly of bodies; they are also often organized in such a way to draw the gaze of people and create a sense of excitement. In most of the globalized world, our communities have increasingly become shaped and defined by these controlled, organized, communicative spaces. It is no surprise, then, that spaces not controlled or neglected often create a sense of dismay or uncertainty for people passing through or living therein. Communities in the midst of gentrification or surrounded by abandoned factories stand as sites that are deemed uncontrolled by people as they interact with those spaces. In the case of abandoned factories, wild plants or crumbling structure stand as obstacles to the passage through those spaces. In the case of the gentrified community, the changes in rules about movement and behavior can stand as similar obstacles to passage through and interaction with communities. For people within those spaces, they are deemed to be wild or "unruly."

Unruly Spaces

Socially constructed cityscapes and landscapes, as well as the qualities and characteristics of communicative cities, can be negatively influenced by the rise of unruly spaces. The concept of unruly spaces and places was developed by Bonnett (2014) in his book *Unruly Places* in order to facilitate a dialogue about those disorganized sites that people feel are peculiar, different, or scary. Essentially, these are sites that are not controlled or structured like those in

which we commonly find ourselves in the communicative spaces or mani-
cured cityscapes of contemporary society. These sites stand out to people as
they pass through; they seem strange and exotic. Their strangeness lays in the
fact that they seem to be wild and untamed, like jungles or lost ruins. They
are exotic in that people feel like explorers or interlopers as they pass through,
which is typically much different from the feelings that arise from interactions
and passage through more "normal" spaces in society.

In his discussions concerning this concept, Bonnett made suggestions for
makeshift categories of different unruly spaces that he encountered around
the world. These categories were largely unrefined with little definition, yet
hinted at a typology that could be used to describe and discuss the unruly spaces
that exist in the corners and fringes of society. There are lost spaces, in which
some parts of the history has been forgotten or purged altogether. Bonnett
uses the city of Leningrad (today St. Petersburg) to provide an example of
such lost spaces. In St. Petersburg, there are constant artifacts and relics of
the communist city still embedded into the physical environment. However,
the political shift away from communist regimes has left people in the city
with little knowledge or memory regarding the images or terminologies left
behind. Without knowing about these artifacts of the communist past, people
often ignore them and pass them by as they traverse the city. In many cases,
these lost spaces fall into disrepair, often because of neglect. Such disrepair
makes for a physical environment that seems wild or deviant, which creates
a sense that they should be avoided or passed through quickly. Another category hinted at by Bonnett are hidden geographies, which are often concealed
from sight in some way; in many cases they have been abandoned and subsequently concealed by nature as they have come to be overgrown. The vast
underground labyrinth of tunnels and constructed caves beneath Minneapolis
is one such space. These long forgotten access tunnels and remains of demolished buildings far underground are largely unknown to the citizens and travelers who walk about the city above. Nevertheless, this subterranean space,
hidden deep below the city, has become a tourist destination for many modern
urban explorers. Such explorers are people who seek out the excitement of
traversing spaces of which few people are aware, and fewer still have traversed.
Yet another category alluded to by Bonnet are so-called enclaves, in which
differing borders (physical and symbolic) weave across one another—often
creating much confusion as people navigate and negotiate those boundaries.
One such enclave is the dual villages of Baarle-Nassau and Baarle-Hertog that
sit within and on top of each other. Baarle-Nassau is Belgian, while Barrle

Hertog is Dutch; the borders between the two nations zigzag throughout the dual villages creating much confusion about who and what belongs where. Something permitted on one street maybe illegal on another.

There are still more categories encapsulated in Bonnett's book. He hints at the notion of spaces of exception, dead cities, and temporary islands as unruly spaces. These are spaces that have been deeply changed by massive demographic shifts, wars, catastrophes, or climate change. Each of these makeshift types, despite their lack of definition and refinement in his book, provide a launching point for the discussion of those spaces in contemporary society that are different from organized communicative spaces of which many people are accustomed, and leave people feeling out of sorts. Essentially, these sites can corrupt a cityscape by constructing a knowledge that gives rise to disdain or fear. Such a knowledge can lead people to hurry through particular cities or urban environments, or to avoid them altogether. What is more, the lack of organization or the presence of symbolic obstacles in these kinds of spaces hinders the free movement of people, ideas, and goods to which many have become accustomed in communicative cities of the globalized world. Whenever we pass into lost spaces or hidden geographies, we might perform very differently than we would in those more "normal" spaces. We might seek to get out as fast as we possible, or we might stop to bask in the uniqueness of the environment. In some instances, however, people try to tame or control what they view as unruly. In this book, we explore the communicative strategies that have been utilized by people to make-sense of—and democratize—unruly spaces that they encounter in their lives.

Following the introduction to this book, Part II addresses the relationship between austerity and unruly spaces in contemporary society. Specifically, we look at two cases: (1) the development of public policy and representations of "financial emergency" in Flint, Michigan; (2) the use by police authorities of telecommunications systems in order to regulate and/or undermine public protest in Egypt and in the San Francisco Bay area. Thinking of this in terms of communicative austerity, we look at the role of police, public policy, and economics in the ongoing struggles over cityscape and landscape. We look at how authorities and the public struggle over the available means of communication, in which police and governments control the power to shutdown networks. We also demonstrate how economic decline gives rise to changes in the use of resources within physical environments. In each of these cases, these struggles and changes are often associated with the emergence of unruly spaces within local communities.

In the first case, we examine the impact of hidden geographies on cities. In particular, we look at the cityscape and physical environment of Flint, Michigan, and the ways unruly hidden geographies there have influenced public policy. The use of financial necessity as a tool of erasure of the social life of places involves particular communicative strategies at both ends. One need not look further than the crises of healthcare, infrastructure, opiate addictions and deaths, child poverty, and—tying many of these together—lead poisoning in the water supply in the United States, which the humanitarian disaster of Flint particularly brought to wider attention. After switching water sources in Flint for cost purposes, the new more corrosive and improperly treated water caused mass lead poisoning, Legionnaire's disease, and ongoing irregularities in maternity and child development.

In addition, we look at the ways in which social control is often enacted over unruly spaces, like the spaces of exception in Oakland and Cairo. As protesters of the shooting death of a man by Bay Area Regional Transit police attempted to gather in Oakland, they found that cellular phone service underground was shut off in an effort to disrupt the protest via the use of mobile communications. The Electronic Frontier Foundation, an organization dedicated to digital freedom, noted on their website that BART officials were engaging in similar police tactics of suppression as the former president of Egypt, Hosni Mubarak. The issue here, as many commenters observed, is what appears to be a broad international set of struggles over the necessary infrastructure for political dissent, taking place in liberal capitalist democracies and capitalist dictatorships alike. This is often discussed in terms of the political rights of citizens, like the rights to free speech. We engage this issue in terms of unruliness, in terms of being left behind. Austerity is always necessarily accompanied by coercive force and police power. In the following section, we investigate the communicative strategies to bring the hidden and lost landscapes of police violence and austerity to broader public attention.

Communicative Democratization of Space

Now that we have started to imagine different unruly spaces that might be encountered in everyday life, let's imagine that we come to realize that spaces near our own homes or communities are similarly unruly or "wild." We might come to realize that there are hidden geographies nearby that we never really examined, or lost spaces that you never knew were important parts of a communal past that you share with others. The unruly nature of these spaces has also disrupted the communicative nature of your city or region. If nothing else, these unruly spaces often disrupt the communicative capacity for your community; the flow of people, resources, and ideas into the community and out to the broader world might be diminished or stopped altogether. This would, in all likelihood, change the ways in which you perceive your home, neighborhood, and community. Would you feel despair? Anguish? Anger? Would you pack up your belongings and move away? Would you try to rebuild this place, like it had been in the past? Or would you work to make it into different space altogether?

One response to such actions might be to protest against policies or power structures that have created the problems and unruliness around our homes. However, such actions often feel doomed to fail. Past research has addressed the role of space and place in dissent, protest, and social movement. Many of these past discussions about geographies of public dissent have grown out of research concerning militant particularism. Williams (1989) first developed the concept of militant particularism through fictional essays in his book *Resources of Hope*, wherein he explored socialism and political culture in Great Britain. Harvey (1996) took up the concept and developed it into a functional theory that illustrated the ways in which social change and social movements emerge from the bottom-up. Specifically, the concept of militant particularism highlights the important connection between social change and place; there are different scales for militant resistance against power structures in society. Williams and Harvey both claim that militant actions taken in one local place to change oppressive practices or create equality are made abstract by outsiders who are sympathetic to the activists' cause. The abstract militancy can then be transferred to other places, or even utilized as a framework for national or global level social change. Essentially, a change in scale takes place as outsiders observe the actions of local activists; social change moves from small-scale local resistance, to large-scale national or global resistance.

Harvey does not look kindly upon militant particularism, as he claims that aspects of the militancy often become lost in abstraction from the local level to the national level (Featherstone, 1998). In his own research concerning the closure of a factory in Cowley, England, Harvey (1996) notes that academics like him were responsible for the process of abstraction. The workers engaged in flexible forms of political struggle that were shaped over periods of time by the impacts of the closure on their families and community. The academics studying the struggle, conversely, were focused on the political structures and actions utilized by the workers at specific moments that they made their observations; they were interested in the ways these struggles could be incorporated in other places around England. In this way, then, the workers' struggles at the local-level were quite flexible and malleable; those struggles changed and shifted in response to threats to the community. The abstraction, conversely, was a fixed vision of actions and structures in the moments that they were observed by academics on the ground. Harvey came to realize that the workers' lives were lost in the abstraction of the militant actions in Cowley. The flexibility of the local level struggle was translated into a rigid, almost dogmatic, vision of resistance and political change for use in other places. Harvey's critiques are not without warrant. There are numerous examples of protests and activist events that fail to create significant social change, or challenge dominant power structures in society. For the most part, these failures are often caused by the rigidity that is created through the process of abstraction. Activists focus on global issues and policies, all the while losing sight of the local-level communities and residents. For these reasons, then, abstract or formulaic prescriptions for protest against the social forces creating unruliness around our homes would mostly fail; such abstractions would exclude the lived experiences that created such protest.

This is where we see the importance of communicative democratization of unruly spaces. In her classic work, *Landscapes of Power*, Zukin (1991) writes, "We are fascinated by Los Angeles and Miami because we think they show us the future" (p. 220). More than twenty years later, we encounter a future that appears much more austere, chaotic, and even catastrophic. The "imagineers" and "hotel-civilization" of the 20th Century represented, correctly to Zukin, a "power to lure the imagination" and its corollary—"the domestication of fantasy in visual consumption" (p. 221). This domestication of fantasy, both tamed and compliant with the 20th Century's privatization of social life, has matured its internal contradictions over these two decades and we now see something beyond the façades of theme parks and resorts: unlivable rents, mass shootings, deadly struggles over racialized police power, rising child poverty, and the wholesale poisoning of a former industrial powerhouse's water supply. But it is also in this context that the project of "domestication" and "democratization" lives on, and functions beyond militant particularism described by Harvey. With chaos comes a new demand to bring those localized spaces under control—either by elites in authority, or by the inhabitants who live in the midst of the unruliness. The impulse of domestication has found in this era, not just the amusement park but also the landscapes of crisis management and emergency as its preferred format. This trend transcends the police or the state; it has permeated civil society as well, with pioneers and explorers venturing into crumbling parts of cities. And, even urban development looks to humanize the sterility of the suburban aesthetic.

Increasingly, we find that people around the world work together with like-minded people in order to change knowledge and perceptions about those spaces around them. These efforts are aimed at taking control of those unruly spaces and making them feel more managed or organized for the people who live and travel through them. By constructing new knowledge, and creating new perceptions about these spaces, such activists can effectively alter people's identities as they move through and interact with those physical environments. Indeed, much of the past research concerning space and place over the past decade has addressed this very phenomenon. Many communication and media scholars have illustrated the ways in which citizens (broadly, city inhabitants), working through community organizations, or the public or private sectors, have effectively domesticated these unruly spaces around them; their efforts have changed the ways in which people move through, and interact with, those particular spaces that were once avoided. In this way, then, they have successfully altered or expanded their communities.

In our own research over the past several years, we have observed citizens coming together to engage in what we have come to call communicative democratization of unruly spaces. By this, we are interested in the use of various strategies of communication to construct different perceptions about physical environments for those people who live in or around them. Through these actions, these citizens change the way in which people move through and interact with spaces that others might have avoided or left behind. On the surface, this seems almost petty when compared to monumental social problems facing people today, like immigration and healthcare. However, in the case of sites like Flint, for instance—poisoned with lead-tainted public water—being left behind is not so simple. Many such spaces are avoided or left behind, but they are also marked by stigma, which carry material and dire consequences. There are certainly many physical environments in contemporary society that people come to perceive as dangerous or problematic. Such perceptions are typically born from the fact that these spaces are neglected, misunderstood, out of sight and/or mind, or not represented in discourse or media. They are often divested by "footloose capital" and downsized, abandoned by their tax base in white flight, given high risk insurance markers, and put under heavier police and executive authority by governments.

The dominant view of those places can often have a very deep impact on the lives of residents within those sites.

To a large extent, what we have witnessed playing out on the landscape has been a struggle over both the image and the material functioning of physical environments. Like the black and racially mixed working class neighborhoods of Detroit's Black Bottom or the southern Bronx, New York in the middle of the 20th Century, which were marked as slums and slated for demolition, the production of images is fundamental to, and constitutive of, the production of the city itself. As Williams (1977) explains, "mediation is a positive process in social reality, rather than a process added to it by way of projection, disguise, or interpretation" (pp. 98–99). In this sense, struggles over the landscape are part of the larger ideological struggles of class society, evolving in their tactics and consequences. Austerity has, for the last forty to forty-five years, been an important feature of that struggle in US cities, in which being left behind is both strategy and outcome of subjecting urban life to capitalist market forces.

Within this book, we explore different strategies for communicative democratization of unruly spaces by people in the city of Detroit, as well as urban environments in Germany. In each case, different strategies, such as transformational memory revival or diffused intertextual production, allowed for residents to challenge dominant, problematic perceptions about the spaces that have come to be understood as unruly; essentially, these people presented alternative visions of the space so as to change interactions with— and within—the physical environment. Each communicative strategy carried with it particular pros and cons; there were advantages to each, but each also entailed problems. In this way, then, we hope that this book will be valuable to not only scholars, but to practitioners of social change as well. The book also conveys important concepts that can build on literature concerning social activism and democracy. In addition, the communicative strategies we observed can serve as templates that may be used to humanize similar unruly spaces. This is no small thing, as the spaces in which people live can deeply affect their emotional and physical health.

Make no mistake, we emphasize communicative practices and perception within this book, but we fully understand that such perceptions are no substitute for materials necessary for healthy and productive lives. Hunger, disease, and unsafe living conditions are not perceptions; they are the results of very real material aspects to the physical environment. We are never stating herein that if people merely change the way that they view their inadequate housing or empty cupboards, that their lives will be better or richer. An empty stomach can only be remedied with food; unsafe housing can only be corrected through development and construction. However, changing the way in which environments are perceived can alter interactions with the physical elements of those sites, as well as other people within those environments. The communicative democratization of space by citizens within local communities can stand as a starting point for the interconnection of multiple communities, so that they might work together to actually transform the physical environment themselves. We feel that the communicative democratization of unruly spaces can stand as an activist endeavor, in which local communities and citizens can take control of their own physical environments. Through these actions city inhabitants can be empowered to shape their own communities themselves. This is particularly important because in the age of austerity, many communities and citizens cannot rely on responsible aid from governments or businesses. The following pages provide an overview of each of the environments that are covered throughout this book.

Strategies for the Communicative Democratization of Space

By constructing new knowledge and perceptions about these unruly spaces, citizens can effectively alter identities of people as they move through and interact with those physical environments. Indeed, much of the research concerning space and place over the past decade in the field of media and communication has addressed this very phenomenon. Our own research projects have effectively illustrated different ways in which people have used communication to make certain spaces seem less wild or inhospitable. For the most part, these strategies involved the use of media to construct mediascapes that stood as a backdrop against which citizens performed communicative democratization of space. According to Appadurai (1996), people construct mediascapes from images and narrative elements taken from the different media that they consume, and use them to construct imagined lives. Essentially, the engagement with mediated texts—either through consumption or co-production—construct for audiences backdrops that inform their identity and performances in everyday life. The strategies that we have discovered in our research involve the production of texts by citizens that allow for readers or users to create new knowledge, which serves as a backdrop for performances within unruly spaces.

In each case below, the use of media served as a form of participatory engagement, a concept that can be categorized as either sociological or political. According to Carpentier (2016) the first entails consumption of media contents and rituals that create a sense of community, while the latter involves participation in struggles over ideology or power. What is more, the political form of participatory engagement is associated with media or media practices that allow for equal access to users (Carpentier, 2011). Our collaborative and individual research studies on these topics, many of which have been published in communication and media journals, stand as the basis for the chapters that make up this book, and illustrate these strategies in greater detail. Below, we provide an overview of the primary strategies of communication that we have observed citizens use in their efforts to take control of unruly spaces around their communities.

Transformative Memory Revival

Part III of the book initiates the discussion concerning communicative strategies that have been used to democratize unruly spaces in modern cities. In particular, these chapters focus on the transformation of knowledge and perceptions about urban spaces in modern Germany. After the Second World War, over seventy five percent of the infrastructure and buildings in Germany had been destroyed by Allied bombings. The ensuing reconstruction lasted well into the 1960s. Indeed, there are those who claim that reconstruction continues to this day, as the initial reconstruction sought to simply alleviate homelessness. The emergent construction was inadequate to serve more advanced social functions, and left people feeling isolated; such isolation created social problems like drug use and criminal activity (e.g., Hawley, 2010; Leick, Schreiber, & Stoldt, 2010). Subsequent reconstruction was needed to replace this insufficient housing and construction throughout the '80s and '90s (Diefendorf, 1992; Keller, 2000). Much of the initial reconstruction involved the erection of blasé style architecture over sites that had once featured grand buildings built in the rococo or baroque styles. The choice of these kinds of architecture helped hide from sight the cherished past of the German Empire, as well as the atrocities of the Third Reich. What is more, the erection of memorials throughout the latter half of the 20th Century placed great emphasis on memories about the Nazis and their Holocaust. This emphasis hid many aspects of Germany's past, including the history and problems associated with the socialist state of the German Democratic Republic (Hawley, 2010). In this way, then, there are many sites throughout the cities of Germany that would adhere to Bonnett's rough definition of lost spaces. These are material sites that are tied to interesting moments of German history, which have come to be ignored and passed by, or through, with little thought or attention. What is more, the emphasis on blasé architecture during the years of reconstruction has created environments that many deem to be psychologically sterile and isolating (Leick et al., 2010). The bland edges and pathways around these lost spaces help to make them unruly, in that they create discomfort or unease for people who live in, and pass through, many German cities.

One particular research project examined historical markers that were embedded into the physical environment of Mannheim, an industrial city in southwestern Germany. These markers helped to create new knowledge and altered pathways through, and interactions with, specific parts of the city. This was a strategy for democratization of unruly lost spaces that we came to call transformative memory revival. The markers highlighted spaces that were now ignored among the blasé environment, or which ceased to exist during the Second World War. Essentially, members of the city government wanted to restore knowledge about the city's lost spaces in order to change the way that people viewed the physical environment. The hope was to bring tourism and business into the city, as well as create an environment in which citizens could take pride in their communities. A case study of the linguistic environment was conducted (see Papen, 2012) by walking about each one of the districts of the city in search of different historical markers that had been installed by the city government. Whenever a marker was discovered it was photographed, as well as the immediate area, and the location of the marker was plotted into a Google map for further examination and evaluation. City leaders in charge of planning urban development were also interviewed in order to build a sense of how the historical markers were selected and placed around the city. Analysis of the data illustrated where the historical markers were placed, and where they were not. For the most part, these historical markers provided information about lost spaces, which projected a sense of history and significance about those spaces into the physical environment. These markers were placed on or near: (1) community nodes (e.g., apartments, homes, schools, places of worship), (2) commercial nodes with high traffic (e.g., shopping centers, downtown areas with multiple businesses), or (3) public nodes with high traffic (e.g., the hospital, tram stations). In many of these cases, the historical markers were installed on or near otherwise bland looking structures or empty sites in the physical environment, which people normally hurried by with little thought or inspection. Given the installation of the markers into the material environment, however, people would stop to read the texts and thoughtfully study the area. Ultimately, the lost spaces were highlighted, which changed the ways in which people interacted within the blasé environment of reconstruction architecture. Many of the physical environments in the city that had been deemed unruly were made interesting and engaging.

Another research project that was conducted in Germany built on this particular strategy of communicative democratization. In this case, the research demonstrated the substrategy of transformative memory modification that was utilized within a privately owned museum in the center of Berlin. This museum highlighted lost spaces connected to the former state of East Germany that had come to be ignored because of the places throughout the country that emphasized the Nazi regime over the Cold War era. For the most part, memorials throughout the country have built a strong memory about the atrocities of the Nazis, which have profound influences on the shape of landscapes and cityscapes in Germany. Conversely, there are very few memorials to the problematic past of the Stasi and Politburo that ruled over East Germany until 1989. For the most part, those spaces throughout Germany stand as lost spaces similar to those described above. The museum was instrumental in structuring public memory concerning physical spaces and cities in the socialist German Democratic Republic (GDR). The exhibits and testimonials through the museum shifted the focus of memory from the Nazis to the socialist state of the GDR, which held important implications for renewed memory about lost spaces in cityscapes of eastern Germany.

In order to properly study the museum, as well as its role in the cityscape of Berlin, a qualitative content analysis of exhibits on display at the site was conducted (see Altheide & Schneider, 2013; Atkinson, 2017; Mayring, 2000; Schreier, 2012). In particular, an inductive form of analysis was conducted, in which the researcher examines artifacts and allows for categories to emerge from the reading. The museum consisted of two sections dedicated to telling the story of life in East Germany: Everyday Life and Politics. These stories helped to illuminate lost spaces in East Berlin and other cities, and provided knowledge about their role in Germany's past and present. Ultimately, the content analysis demonstrated that the exhibits and texts found throughout the museum aided in the modification of memory about urban spaces in East Germany. Although many aspects of this memory were problematic, there was now more of an emphasis on the connections between the Stasi and Politburo to physical sites in the city of Berlin (and other German cities). In this way, then, the city became less suspicious for people who survived Stasi atrocities; people felt free to discuss the past, and seek reconciliation. However, this public memory about the GDR and the socialist past of Europe reinforced political views about Western dominance and capitalism, and emphasized the importance of the United States in world affairs. Through sites like this museum, tourists built a knowledge in which the GDR citizenry had little connection to, or responsibility for, politics and actions taken by that former socialist state.

Diffused Intertextual Production

Part IV of the book explores a web community dedicated to the study of, and dialogue about, Detroit, Michigan. This research relied on Sadler and Haskins' topographical categories, as we examined discussion threads on a web forum that described those aspects of the physical environment within the city. For the most part, many parts of the city stood as a hidden geography, as partially described by Bonnett, which have been abandoned and fallen into ruin. Over the years, several of these sites have been swallowed up to some degree by the so-called urban prairie (e.g., brush and trees growing wildly within the city), and bypassed by traffic. For decades, media representations of this city have focused on those burned out edges of the hidden geography that can still be seen from a distance, creating knowledges about the physical environment as blighted and dangerous. This has constructed knowledges and identities that lead people to despise the physical environment of the city. What is more, people feel compelled to avoid Detroit, or to bypass it at all costs.

The online community that was the subject of the research was built around an online tour of the city, referred to as a virtual tour of the city ruins. This tour depicted the city as lost and fabulous ruins, similar to Athens or Rome. This intertextual framing (see Ott & Walter, 2000; Warnick, 2007) allowed for users of the website to see the city as something different from the typical mainstream media representations to which they were accustomed. What is more, the intertextual frame of the virtual tour was linked to an inter-active web forum where people could discuss the city; these discussions were typically framed by the experience of the virtual tour. Together, we engaged in a qualitative content analysis of both. In this study we conducted a deduc-tive form of analysis in which we searched for pre-existing categories within one hundred sixty two discussion threads posted on the forum. In particular, we searched for comments about Sadler and Haskins topographical categories within the discussions about the physical environment in the city. As postings were examined we looked at the topographical categories that were discussed, and how members of the online community described them. In addition, we conducted a secondary inductive content analysis to examine threads that involved some conversations or references to race or ethnicity. We searched for references to race or ethnicity in general, to the race or ethnicity of specific people, or to discussions about people of color that were deemed to be controversial (e.g., Al Sharpton, Kwame Kilpatrick). We also conducted postmodern interviews (see Atkinson, 2017; Gubrium & Holstein, 2003) and focus groups in order to ascertain the influence of the interactive media components on performances and rituals of community members as they engaged in the physical environment of Detroit. Overall, we were able to collect narratives and data from eighteen members of the community through our interviews and focus groups.[1]

We found that the members of the web community engaged in four different performative roles in their discussions online through the interactive forums: Historians, Storytellers, Indigenous Urban Planners, and Explorers. The Historians often posted old information and materials in discussions about topographical categories. For example, some Historians would post pages from old telephone books from the 1940s or 1950s, or old postcards that depicted buildings as they appeared long ago. The Storytellers would weave narratives that had been passed on to them by their parents or grandparents about the city as it was before its decline. The Indigenous Urban Planners would engage in debates about which physical sites should be preserved, and which should be swept away for new construction. Finally, the Explorers would go out into the physical environment and take pictures, bringing them back to the web community like artifacts; such artifacts would serve as the focus of deliberation, and open up new topics for historians and storytellers to discuss.

Overall, these findings demonstrate the communicative strategy of diffused intertextual production, which emerged from the simultaneous presence of an intertextual anchor and the interactive platforms. The knowledge gleaned from this strategy about the hidden geographies by the members of the online community served as the foundation for a participatory civic identity. Essentially, the intercreative act of contributing materials and commentary through online forums constructed a knowledge about the city as a site that was worthy of exploration and discussion, rather than derision and avoidance. Compared to other forms of democratization of space described in

Parts I and III, this strategy and emergent identity was the only to fit the notion of political participatory engagement described by Carpentier (2016). This is because diffused intertextual production developed from the access made available by the interactive platforms, as well as the focus on the struggle over meaning structures that come to represent the city. Such knowledge led users to search for more information, and engage further with other people that they met through the forums. What is more, we found that diffused intertextual production also gave rise to a standpoint performance, which entailed the actions of community members in the physical environment of the city, which was guided by the knowledge and identity cultivated through the interactive platform.

In addition, our research also highlighted a substrategy of diffused intertextual production that was enacted by some of the members of the community. We noted that some people in the community engaged in creative narrative appropriation, in which stories from one community were "poached" and utilized by others that were linked by the forums and the virtual tour. Essentially, the narrative appropriation allowed for bridges to develop between communities that were typically separated by the hidden geography of Detroit. Through our interviews and focus groups, we found that one person on the forums had utilized stories about urban gardens to build a farm in the middle of the city. The emergence of the urban gardens and farm allowed for white middle class members of the community to engage with working-class African American communities that they typically avoided because of their concerns about dangers associated with the hidden geography within that section of the city.

Summary

Overall, this book provides valuable ideas about the nature of space (unruly and otherwise) and performance in contemporary society. We find this to be particularly important as our world is increasingly filled with spaces that have become unruly; they are neglected or abandoned, their history is forgotten, and rules or meaning structures that govern spaces change over time. As the economies of the world shift, seas rise, and infrastructure continues to degrade, unruly spaces are increasingly becoming a major part of our local level communities, and the larger society around us. There are obvious material problems associated with the rise of unruly spaces in our society. They create problems for people seeking work, and make it harder for people in poverty to get access to food, healthcare, and education. Simple changes in perception will not fix these issues. Larger social programs and government policies are necessary to alleviate the problems and inequality that often stems from, or cause altogether, the rise of these unruly spaces.

Aside from the material problems, there is another significant problem associated with these unruly spaces: they disrupt the qualities necessary for communicative cities. For us, this is where communication, perceptions, and the democratization of unruly space become important. Communities may find themselves isolated because of unruly spaces like abandoned buildings or factories. How might they build bridges to other communities or the wider society? Cities may find that the flow of people and ideas are disrupted because of feelings of malaise created by the physical environment. How might those cities reverse those trends? We argue that these are occasions in which the communicative democratization of unruly spaces becomes invaluable. In these cases, citizens may take it upon themselves, or work together, to build new knowledges about those spaces that have become problematic. Through their efforts they can change the ways in which people perceive such spaces, and consequently alter their pathways through, and interactions with, those spaces.

In many ways, we see the communicative democratization of unruly spaces in contemporary society as a new strategy for activism as we move into the mid–21st Century. In a world in which governments have become increasingly focused on austerity and isolation, corners of our social world will come to be neglected, abandoned, or forgotten altogether; these environments will become the unruly spaces that can threaten the qualities of communicative cities, which are the foundation of modern democracy around the world. Indeed, there is significant evidence in the wake of nationalistic movements in recent years that these trends are accelerating and compounding. Rather than waiting on governments to step in and act, citizens and activist organizations can take it upon themselves to at least alter the perceptions that their communities have about many of these unruly spaces. In this way, then, those communities may at least connect to the larger civil society, and the voices of those people may be heard; those communities may at least be able to once more engage in the qualities and aspects of communicative cities.

Note

1. The members comprised of fifteen white people, and three African-American, which is considerably different from the demographics of the city of Detroit (82 % African-American,

10 % white). The demographic breakdown was also reflected in DetroitYES! community. Although there are no statistics that illustrate the racial demographics of the DetroitYES!, all of the members who we interviewed told us that the community was "overwhelmingly" white.

References

Abercrombie, N., & Longhurst, B. (1998). *Audiences: A sociological theory of performance and imagination*. Thousand Oaks, CA: Sage.

Altheide, D., & Schneider, C. (2013). *Qualitative media analysis*. Thousand Oaks, CA: Sage.

Appadurai, A. (1996). *Modernity at large: Cultural dimensions of globalization*. Minneapolis, MN: University of Minnesota Press.

Atkinson, J. D. (2017). *Journey into social activism: Qualitative approaches*. New York, NY: Fordham University Press.

Barthes, R. (1991). *The responsibility of forms: Critical essays on music, art, and representation*. Berkeley, CA: University of California Press.

Bonnett, A. (2014). *Unruly places: Lost spaces, secret cities, and other inscrutable geographies*. New York, NY: Houghton-Mifflin Harcourt.

Burgin, V. (1996). *In/different spaces: Place and memory in visual culture*. Berkeley, CA: University of California Press.

Carpentier, N. (2011). The "ordinary" on commercial radio and TV: A reception analysis of the subject position of ordinary people in the participatory programs *Recht van Antwoord* and *Zwart of Wit*. *Communication Review, 14*, 1–23.

Carpentier, N. (2016). Beyond the ladder of participation: An analytical toolkit for the critical analysis of participatory media processes. *Javnost—The Public, 23*, 70–88.

Cosgrove, D. (1985). *Social formation and symbolic landscape*. Totowa, NJ: Barnes & Noble Books

Cosgrove, D. (1988). Geography is everywhere: Culture and symbolism in human landscapes. In T. Oaks & P. Price (Eds.), *The cultural geography reader* (pp. 176–185). New York, NY: Routledge.

Debord, G. (1994). *The society of the spectacle*. New York, NY: Zone Books.

Dickinson, G. (1997). Memories for sale: Nostalgia and the construction of identity in Old Pasadena. *Quarterly Journal of Speech, 83*, 1–27.

Dickinson, G. (2006). The *Pleasantville* effect: Nostalgia and the visual framing of (white) suburbia. *Western Journal of Communication, 70*(3), 212–233.

Dickinson, G. (2015). *Suburban dreams: Imagining and building the good life*. Tuscaloosa, AL: University of Alabama Press.

Diefendorf, J. (1992). *In the wake of war: The reconstruction of German cities after World War II*. Oxford, UK: Oxford University Press.

Featherstone, D. (1998). Some versions of militant particularism: A review article of David Harvey's Justice Nature and the Geography of Difference. *Antipode, 30*, 19–25.

Gubrium, J., & Holstein, J. (2003). Postmodern sensibilities. In J. Gubrium & J. Holstein (Eds.), *Postmodern interviewing* (pp. 1–20). Thousand Oaks, CA: Sage.

Gumpert, G., & Drucker, S. (2008). Communicative cities. *International Communication Gazette, 70*, 195–208.

Hall, E. (1969). *The hidden dimension.* New York, NY: Anchor Books.

Harvey, D. (1996). *Justice, nature and the geography of difference.* Hoboken, NJ: Blackwell.

Hawley, C. (2010, August 20). Living with sin: Germany comes to terms with its ugliest Buildings. *Spiegel Online International.* Accessed on October 2, 2014, from http://www.spiegel.de/international/germany/living-with-sin-germany-comes-to-terms-with-its-ugli-est-buildings-a-712535.html

Jacobs, J. (1963). *The death and life of great American cities.* New York, NY: Vintage Books.

Keller V. (2000). *Streiflichter aus alt-Mannheim.* Erfurt, Germany: Sutton Verlag.

Lefebvre, H. (1992). *The Production of Space* (1 edition; D. Nicholson-Smith, Trans.). Oxford, OX, UK; Cambridge, Mass., USA: Wiley-Blackwell.

Leick, R., Schreiber, M., & Stoldt, H. (2010, August 10). Out of the ashes: A new look at Germany's postwar reconstruction. *Spiegel Online International.* Accessed October 2, 2014, from http://www.spiegel.de/international/germany/out-of-the-ashes-a-new-look-at-germa-ny-s-postwar-reconstruction-a-702856.html

Lerup, L. (2000). *After the city.* Cambridge, MA: MIT Press.

Lynch, K. (1960). *The image of the city.* Cambridge, MA: MIT Press.

Massey, D. B. (1994). *Space, place, and gender.* Minneapolis: University of Minnesota Press.

Massey, D. (2005). *For Space* (1 edition). London ; Thousand Oaks, Calif: SAGE Publications Ltd.

Mayring, P. (2000). Qualitative content analysis. *Forum: Qualitative social research* [Online Journal], *1*(2). Accessed October 1, 2002, from http://www.qualitative-research.net/fqs-texte/2-00/2-00mayring-e.htm

McLuhan, M. (1988). *Laws of media: The new science.* Toronto, ON: University of Toronto Press.

McLuhan, M., & Powers, B. (1992). *The global village: Transformations in world life and media in the 21st Century.* New York, NY: Oxford University Press.

Meinig, D. W. (1979). Symbolic landscapes: Some idealizations of American communities. In D. W. Meinig (Ed.), *The interpretation of ordinary landscapes: Geographical essays* (pp. 164–192). Oxford, NY: Oxford University Press.

Mitchell, D. (2000). *Cultural geography: A critical introduction.* New York, NY: Blackwell Press.

Mitchell, W. J. (1994). *Landscape and power.* Chicago, IL: University of Chicago Press.

Mumford, L. (1962). *The city in history.* San Diego, CA: Harcourt, Brace & World.

Olwig, K. (2002). *Landscape, nature, and the body politic: From Britain's renaissance to America's new world.* Madison, WI: University of Wisconsin Press.

Ott, B., Aoki, E., & Dickinson, G. (2011). Ways of (not) seeing guns: Presence and absence at the Cody Firearms Museum. *Communication and Critical/Cultural Studies, 8*(3), 215–239.

Ott, B., & Walter, C. (2000). Intertextuality: Interpretive practice and textual strategy. *Critical Studies in Media Communication, 17*(4), 429–446.

Papen, U. (2012). Commercial discourses, gentrification and citizens' protest: The linguistic landscape of Prenzlauer Berg, Berlin. *Journal of Sociolinguistics, 16*, 56–80.

Sadler, W. J., & Haskins, E. V. (2005). Metonymy and the metropolis: Television show settings and the image of New York City. *Journal of Communication Inquiry, 29*(3), 195–216.

Schreier, M. (2012). *Qualitative content analysis*. Thousand Oaks, CA: Sage.

Seamon, D., & Sowers, J. (2008). Place and placelessness, Edward Relph. In P. Hubbard, R. Kitchin & G. Valentine (Eds.), *Key texts in human geography* (pp. 43–51). London: Sage.

Soja, E. (1995). Postmodern urbanizations: The six restructurings of Los Angeles. In S. Watson & K. Gibson (Eds.), *Postmodern cities and spaces* (pp. 125–137). Oxford, UK: Blackwell.

Warnick, B. (2007). *Rhetoric online: Persuasion and politics on the World Wide Web*. New York, NY: Peter Lang.

Williams, R. (1977). *Marxism and literature*. New York, NY: Oxford University Press.

Williams, R. (1989). *Resources of hope: Culture, democracy and socialism*. New York, NY: Verso.

Zukin, S. (1991). *Landscapes of power: From Detroit to Disney World*. Berkeley, CA: University of California Press.

· 2 ·

THE ENCLAVE AT WILDCAT HOLLOW

In this chapter, we introduce a case study that provides concrete examples concerning the problems and perils of unruliness, and also demonstrates the difficulties that can arise as citizens attempt to democratize such spaces. In particular, we examine lived experiences of people who have witnessed the emergence of unruly spaces from political and economic austerity in society, and the problems and struggles that they faced. For the most part, this chapter focuses on a region that stands as an enclave under Bonnett's (2014) taxonomy of unruly spaces. Such unruliness stems from the deterioration of the rules that had shaped identity and performance within the community for nearly one hundred years. These shifts in rules were wrought by the inflow of rural gentrification, which held deep economic changes for the region. In many ways, the enclave functions in a similar way to spaces of exception described later in Chapter 4; both entail the erosion or removal of rules for the use of spaces.

In response to such changes, some of the families in the region banded together into a trust network in order to pool resources and resist the alterations to the landscape. We see this trust network as an attempt by the residents to democratize the unruly spaces that emerged in their community with the influx of newcomers and growing gentrification. We find that there are positive and negative aspects associated with the use of this communicative strategy. In some respects, the trust network allowed for traditional residents to find their voices and counter the social forces that held a negative influence over the landscape around them. Conversely, the trust network reoriented the traditional residents as a community of closure, which made the problems of enclave more profound; the network maintained separation from other communities and neighbors in the region. This separation, in turn, created significant obstacles to the formulation of solutions to the problems that had given rise to the rural gentrification in the first place.

In the following pages, we outline the concepts of topographical silence, which arose from rural gentrification of one region in the Midwest. This topographical silence stands as one problem associated with the political and economic austerity of the modern age, and fosters the emergence of unruly spaces. We then turn to a description of the emergent trust network in the community, and its reliance on conservative alternative media. This reliance on alternative media for information and worldviews stood as the foundation for the community of closure for the traditional residents in the region. Finally, we explain this trust network further in terms of the concept of disruptive concretization, which stands in contrast to militant particularism—but is just as problematic—described by scholars like Williams (1989) and Harvey (1996), and discussed in Chapter 1.

Wildcat Hollow

Despite the trends of urbanization within the United States, the Census Bureau posits that roughly twenty percent of the population still lives in rural areas as of 2010. What is more, many rural areas are being abandoned as residents reposition to urban sites in search for jobs, while people from cities increasingly move into those rural areas for the low taxes and cost of living. Hines (2010, 2011) refers to such changes in demographics as rural gentrification, which is characterized in part by profound impacts on the rural land itself. In particular, he explains that consumption of experiences and quest for authenticity typical of the post-industrial middle class changes the ways in which land is used, traversed, and perceived. In fact, research concerning rural gentrification illustrates how such consumption practices clash with uses of rural lands by traditional residents, and often leads to conflicts and indignations (e.g., Daniels, 1999; Hines, 2010, 2011; Hoey, 2005; Salamon, 2003).

Wildcat Hollow is a rural community located in the southern portion of the Midwestern United States, and sits within a valley at the confluence of a major river and a smaller creek.[1] Until the last decade, the area was primarily comprised of forests, open fields, and pastures. Over the past sixty years, travelers could traverse the region by way of three state highways, several county roads, and numerous unpaved gravel roads. Roughly ten miles to the east of the region is a small agricultural town of roughly three thousand people, while a larger town of six thousand lies fifteen miles to the north. Over twenty miles to the west is Queen City, which is home to a population of roughly 150,000 people (450,000 in the greater metro area). In this way, then, Wildcat Hollow is relatively remote, but not isolated from the rest of the world.

The region was settled in the early 1800s by pioneers moving westward in search of new opportunities and work. Those who stayed in Wildcat Hollow made a living by way of subsistence farming on small plots of land, which later gave rise to dairy farms at the turn of the 20th Century. The dairy farms grew significantly between the 1930s and 1980s, so that many often attended to herds of one hundred to four hundred head of cattle. These farms came to include milking barns, storage barns (for equipment, hay, etc.), silos for the storage of grain, and grain elevators. The growth of these farms raised the income of the residents and families of the region, and was the basis for the regional economy. However, the farms of Wildcat Hollow began to struggle in the 1990s due in-part to political-economic situations within the state and federal government, as farm subsidies began to diminish and milk prices plummeted. Neoliberal logics, outlined later in Chapters 3 and 4, were the driving force behind the de-regulation that diminished—and eventually eliminated—those subsidies that had supported the farms for decades. Droughts and floods took heavier tolls on those farms than in the past as there was less funding to subsidize lost income. These struggles were also due in-part to over-expansion of many of the families that operated the dairy farms. Farms that had once supported families of four or five in the past supported extended families of grandchildren and great-grandchildren. As the economic base for the region eroded and the farms failed to meet the needs of expanded families, many people began to leave for Queen City in search of part-time or full-time work. Those who found part-time work continued to toil on the family farms commuting back and forth, while those who found full-time work typically left altogether.

Not only did this economic erosion initiate an outward migration of people, but it also set the stage for rural gentrification of the region. As farms sold off land and homes were auctioned, a new type of settler began to move into the area. These were people typically coming from urban areas in Texas or

California, seeking lower costs of living and property taxes. These newcomers built their homes in Wildcat Hollow, and worked at jobs in Queen City twenty miles away. In many of these cases, the new residents sold modest homes their parents or grandparents purchased in the 1970s or 1980s in their previous states for large sums of money; that money, in turn, was used to fund the building of large estate-like homes. These new homes could be seen along the state highways through Wildcat Hollow, and were much larger than the farmhouses built throughout the 20th Century. These new homes were larger in terms of square footage and acreage surrounding them. Figure 2.1 illustrates one such home.

Such houses were not the only significant changes to the region, as the construction of new homes often meant clearing away old sites like shacks, barns, and other structures. In addition, much of the land changed significantly, as forests were cleared and fields transformed for large lawns around the newer homes. The addition of the new homes also required more power to the region, which led to the addition of new power lines atop numerous metallic

Figure 2.1. A new home in Wildcat Hollow.

towers. These new power lines and towers cross through recently cleared forests, as well the properties and yards of many traditional residents.

In this way, then, Wildcat Hollow stands as an enclave. One example of an unruly enclave provided by Bonnett was the dual villages of Baarle-Nassau and Baarle-Hertog that sit on the border between the Netherlands and Belgium. The national border zig-zags through the two villages, creating constant confusion about what belongs within which village and nation. The encroachment of the post-industrial middle class communities into the region creates a similar kind of confusion within Wildcat Hollow. Lands that had once been agricultural were now used for leisure. Gravel roads that had regularly been used for the conveyance of slow moving tractors and cattle, were scorned by new neighbors in the region. Essentially, the old rules for the use of the land and resources, as well as social rituals in the region, had changed in some parts of the landscape. However, it was unclear to both traditional residents and newcomers alike as to the location of the boundaries that dictated old and new uses for the land. Where did the traditional uses of land for agricultural purposes end, and the newcomer's pursuits of leisure begin? Such confusion about these boundaries made it difficult to move through the region, particularly for the traditional residents who needed to access fields and cattle. What is more, this confusion made the landscape uncertain, which hampered knowledge and the construction of identity. This is particularly true when one considers the emergence of topographical silence, which emerged from the rural gentrification and incursion of newcomers into the lands throughout the region.

In order to study space, landscape, and responses to rural gentrification in Wildcat Hollow I (Atkinson) engaged in a qualitative case study of the linguistic landscape, similar to one conducted by Papen (2012) in Prenzlauer Berg near Berlin. Such a case study included examination and photography of the material environment, as well as interviews with key people. In Papen's study, she examined political art and graffiti that was painted on buildings around the district of what had once been East Berlin. The research revealed that such art shaped the ways in which people viewed dilapidated buildings, and informed their interactions with the material environment. In order to conduct her research, Papen walked the streets of Prenzlauer Berg while she photographed and noted the political art she encountered. She also engaged in interviews with key activist artists in the city, who were able to explain to her processes of production, as well as meanings embedded within the art. In this case study, I travelled throughout Wildcat Hollow photographing pathways (e.g., roads), nodes (e.g., homes, farms, structures), and edges (e.g., fences, power lines) throughout the region. In addition, I interviewed fifteen of the traditional residents of the community who had lived there all of their lives. During the course of the interviews, I asked them about the region, how it had changed over the years, and how they dealt with those changes. The interviews also included questions about how people interacted, and with whom they typically interacted. Together, the photographs and interviews provided insight into the nature of space and social construction of landscape in Wildcat Hollow. Overall, this case study demonstrated two important concepts: (1) topographical silence in the region caused by rural gentrification, and (2) the emergence of a trust network and community of closure among the traditional residents. We explore both of these in the following pages.

Topographical Silence

The topographical silence in the region developed from the influx of newcomers taking advantage of the economic corrosion in the region. This topographical silence emerged from the changes to the land wrought by rural gentrification, which involved two inter-related issues. First, all of the traditional residents were acutely aware of alterations to material aspects of many of the spaces throughout the region. These alterations stood as contrasts between the old uses of the land, and the new. Specifically, new nodes and edges were erected, which stood in place of any dialogue with the newcomers who hardly (if ever) interacted with the traditional residents. The absence of the newcomers was largely due to their affiliation with fringe networks beyond Wildcat Hollow. Second, many important landmarks disappeared from the region; often, these landmarks were removed to make way for the new nodes and changes to edges. These landmarks had often stood as places of memory for cross-generational communication, wherein elders would take children and pass down knowledge of historical figures and events.

Contrasting Nodes & Edges

The photography of Wildcat Hollow, coupled with interviews of traditional residents, revealed that there had been substantial changes to the material topography in just the last ten years. The most dramatic change was to the nodes in the region, which was addressed earlier. One of the elders in the community described the dramatic changes to nodes, such as homes, over the course of the past decade:

> I tell you, the whole community . . . it's different from what it used to be. And it will be different ten years from now. You drive up and down these roads over here. There used to be two houses [on the land nearby]. I don't know how many houses [are] on it now, from here to the county line. And down toward [the river] now, those woods back in there have built up. I don't know these people. And there's some Russians that live in there. A family of Russians. I've never seen them. I wouldn't know if I see them. The whole community changes. The whole country. And it will change more.

Many of those new homes mentioned by the traditional residents were much larger than those they had built up and owned over the years. What is more, many of the traditional farmhouses had fallen into disrepair, and stood in contrast to the new estate-like homes. In many cases, the paint on those houses was faded and chipped, and in a few instances broken windows were boarded up. Some of the houses in the region were not in such a dilapidated state, but could barely be seen because of trees and brush that had grown up around them. In addition, it should be noted that many of the farms in the region had also fallen into disrepair, which added to the contrast between the newer nodes and those that had been part of the region for decades. In one case, the red paint on a large barn at the center of one of the bigger farms had faded and chipped, and loft doors were missing or removed. In addition, broken or obsolete machinery could be seen resting in front of the barn, while scrap metal had been discarded nearby. These differences were not only apparent in my photography, but were discussed in great detail by many of the traditional residents.

However, the size or state of these nodes was not the only alterations to the material environment, but also the edges around them. In all cases, newer residents had installed expensive gates and fences around their land. For instance, the home in Figure 2.1 discussed previously had expensive, white fencing on stone posts. Such fencing was significantly different from the barbed wire fences used to divide fields and farmland. Most of the traditional homes had no fencing, and those that did utilized the same farmland barbed wire used to contain cattle. In addition to the fences, newer homes also featured large expansive gates. One such gate can be seen in Figure 2.2.

The large, elaborate gate in the photograph entailed lighting so that people passing by at night could see it clearly. In addition, an intercom can be seen to the left side of the gate, which allowed visitors to contact the main

Figure 2.2. A gate at one of the new estate homes in Wildcat Hollow.

house from the road. This gate was not unique to Wildcat Hollow, as many of the newer residents installed similar gates at the entrance to their proper-ties. Again, these gates stood in contrast to those utilized on the properties of traditional residents, which were simple metal gates incorporated into barbed wire fencing. Such gates were typically rusted with age, and held onto wooden posts by simple chains. Again, these changes to the spaces of Wildcat Hollow were not only evident in my photography, but were also discussed at great length by all of the traditional residents.

The nature of the traditional nodes and edges in the region stood in stark contrast to those recently built. The traditional residents did not miss this dis-tinction. During the course of my interviews many traditional residents stated that they felt "pushed out" by the newcomers in their larger expensive houses. An interview with one of the elders in Wildcat Hollow helped to illustrate this issue:

> You take the community. I've worked on nearly every farm around here. Right here
> in this community, these little old farms have sold off. People have bought up plots

of land and built houses. You don't know who lives there now. And they don't talk to you. They wave. Maybe. You don't know who they are. It's terrible.

It is important to note, however, that the traditional residents told me that they had very little contact with the newcomers. This was due in large part to the fact that many of those newcomers held jobs and worked in Queen City; they spent their days commuting and working outside of the region. Such a lifestyle on the part of the newer residents is referred to as job sprawl, and constitutes another characteristic of rural gentrification (Glaeser & Tufts, 2001). Those newcomers were rarely present to engage in any direct communication with their traditional resident neighbors. Most of the traditional residents were aware of this fact, and talked about it throughout the interviews.

The differences between old and new nodes, as well as the imposing edges, created a sense of distance and dissimilarity. In the absence of any meaningful communication with the new residents, significant alterations of space made many traditional residents perceive that they were being pushed out or even disrespected. As one traditional resident put it, he felt "scared" by the changes that he had seen around his home in the past few years. Many traditional residents also noted that the presence of the new power lines and metal towers as edges to the entire region punctuated the alterations to the environment, and stood as constant reminders to them that there will be numerous newcomers moving into the region in the years ahead.

Missing Landmarks

Just as important to the contrasts in the physical space of Wildcat Hollow were the disappearance of many key landmarks. These landmarks had been important sites for conveying history over the years, as well as orienting children to the region. In some cases, the landmarks were torn down to make way for the new nodes and edges being erected throughout the region (e.g., homes, power lines). In other cases, newer residents purchased landmarks for private purposes. Overall, the landmarks can be considered to be social resources available to everyone and necessary for the establishment of landscape in Wildcat Hollow; pilgrimages to those spaces were long-running rituals for many families. The disappearance of these landmarks held important implications for the formation, or rather corrosion, of knowledge in the region.

To really convey the importance of these landmarks, their connection to the passage of knowledge should first be established. Throughout Wildcat

Hollow there were numerous sites that had been simple nodes or edges long ago; original white settlers in the region had typically built such nodes. As time passed, many nodes disappeared due to calamity or to make way for more practical uses of the land (e.g., removing abandoned, dilapidated homes to make way for fields for crops). Those older nodes that remained were often forgotten and ignored for years. However, as they were rediscovered or noticed by the traditional residents, they recognized them as connected to a bygone era. Such connections to the past led many traditional residents to see those former nodes and edges as important landmarks. As time went by elders would often take children and young adults to those landmarks and tell them stories about the people who lived and worked there, who built them, and the function of those spaces in the history of the region. In this way, then, the landmarks in Wildcat Hollow served as places of memory, in which past people and events are evoked in order to structure the production and reproduction of social memory (e.g., Casey, 1987; Cresswell, 2015).

> One of the primary ways in which memories are constituted is through the production of places ... The very materiality of a place means that memory is not abandoned to the vagaries of mental processes and is instead inscribed in the landscape—as public memory. (Cresswell, loc. 2800)

Essentially, these were sites where important communicative practices took place that shaped meaning and knowledge about spaces around the region; pilgrimages to these landmarks were integral to the social construction of landscape. This knowledge informed people how to interact with and move through the physical environment; such knowledge imbued the nodes, paths, and edges of the region with meaning.

For instance, there was one old "shack" in the region that had once upon a time been the home of one of the original white settlers, whom we refer to as Uriah Severesen. He had moved into Wildcat Hollow in the early 1800s, and built his home in a small meadow a short distance from the river; there he raised a family that included his wife and seven children. When the Civil War broke out, Severesen had family on both sides; one son fought for the Confederacy, while a grandson served the Union. Given that he had family on both sides of the conflict, he refused to ever choose a side, and regularly offered aid to his son and grandson when they travelled through the region; for this reason, Confederate Bushwhackers captured and killed Uriah Severesen in 1863. The Severesen home was considered to be rather unremarkable, and stood vacant and crumbling in that small meadow for decades. As time passed, it was one of only a few original settler homes that remained in the region, and was noted as a "special place" in Wildcat Hollow. In this way, the old Severesen home became a landmark to residents. Elders would take children and youths there to walk the grounds that Uriah Severesen had walked, and convey his story to them. For many of the traditional residents, the point to the Severesen story was that blood relations and kin were more important than larger political forces.

A multitude of such sites existed around the region that stood as landmarks for the traditional residents of Wildcat Hollow, and hence sites for the passage of knowledge. However, as the physical environment and spaces of the region were altered by the arrival of new residents, many of the landmarks disappeared. Some of the landmarks were simply cleared away to make room for new nodes and edges. One such case involved the disappearance of an old cemetery located along one of the state highways through the region; we refer to this as the Carter Cemetery. The Carter family established and used the cemetery in the mid–1800s; the last grave was dug there in 1906. The Carters left Wildcat Hollow in the early days of the 20th Century, but the headstones in the cemetery remained in a small clearing in the woods. When the state highway was built through the region, it was detoured around the small cemetery during construction. Given that it was visible from the highway, then, many people would stop and look at the headstones, and tell stories about the Carter family. However, one of the traditional residents explained that the headstones were removed when a doctor from Queen City bought the land. The doctor did not build anything on the old burial site, but removed all evidence of any burials from that space. For the most part, traditional residents around the region did not approve of the removal of the headstones, as it was deemed to be an important site in the community. In fact, someone in the community took it upon themselves to plant a small stone along the highway commemorating the cemetery, and noting the names of the Carter family that were buried there. No one interviewed claimed to know who had placed the stone there.

In addition to landmarks that were cleared away, there were also landmarks purchased by newcomers, who made such spaces "private" and off limits to others. One such landmark that we call the Cantrell Store was located along one of the state highways through the region. The store was established in the early 1900s, and had been the primary grocery market for residents in Wildcat Hollow for decades. The store was passed down in the Cantrell family for generations and never renovated or changed over the years; the store looked largely the same as it had at the turn of the 20th Century. As in the case of the Severesen home and Carter Cemetery above, traditional residents noted that elders would take children to the Cantrell Store to buy items and tell stories about the history of the site. The structure that was once the Cantrell Store still stands today, but it is a private residence. According to one traditional resident, a newcomer to the region bought the store. Rather than tear it down and build something different, however, the newcomer kept the store section intact and renovated the loft as a living space. In this way, the structure still held its historical façade within, but those elements were "privatized" and closed away from traditional residents.

The store was not the only landmark to be claimed by newer residents to the region. One of the traditional residents informed me that a wealthy new landowner from Queen City took the dilapidated and crumbling house of Uriah Severesen out of the region. According to this resident, the Severesen house had been on land that was owned by one of the long-standing families in the region. When the elder of that family passed away, ownership of the land and everything on it transferred to his oldest son. Shortly after the elder had passed, the wealthy man from Queen City asked the son if he could take possession of the Severesen house; apparently, he collected early American architecture. The son agreed, and the next day the wealthy newcomer arrived with a small crew of workers, and they dismantled the old structure piece-by-piece. According to traditional residents, the building is now "hidden away" on the newcomer's estate, no longer accessible to the Severesen descendants or families of Wildcat Hollow.

Topographical Silence

Ultimately, the simultaneous erection of contrasting nodes and edges, as well as the disappearance of important landmarks, demonstrated topographical silence. We see this as one of many problems that have emerged in the current era of austerity, alongside the networks of invisibility and deprivation of capabilities (see Chapter 3), and policing of communication infrastructure (see Chapter 4). This concept entails changes in the material environment, as well as the corrosion of knowledge that had shaped perceptions about spaces throughout the region. The new homes and leisure activities of the newcomers resulted in significant changes to the material spaces and social resources, of which traditional residents were acutely aware. Without seeing or directly communicating with the newcomers, the drastic changes wrought on the material environment stood as the only means for the traditional residents to understand their new neighbors. In addition, the disappearance of key landmarks where knowledge was traditionally passed down to younger generations led to a corrosion of knowledge about those material spaces in the community. The alterations and disappearance of landmarks created a silence around the material topography of Wildcat Hollow—at least for the traditional residents who had lived in the region all of their lives. For traditional residents, the material topography of the region was changing right before their eyes, while their children and grandchildren accrued very little historical knowledge integral to the foundation of the landscape.

Many of the elders in the community noted that the emergence of new material elements within the environment rendered the region unrecognizable. Houses that had stood for generations, where people regularly gathered and discussed events and issues, vanished seemingly overnight. In their stead were large houses, shut away from the region by large fences and imposing gates. They knew nothing about the newcomers to the region, except that they and their land were inaccessible. This was particularly problematic, as it stood in contrast to the landscape that had been cultivated from knowledge passed on for generations at important landmarks. The elders had learned about the nodes, edges, and pathways around Wildcat Hollow decades ago by visiting landmarks with their parents and grandparents. The stories passed down shaped knowledge about the spaces in the region, as well as movement through those material environments. For those elders, the landscape of Wildcat Hollow constituted spaces of family and work, where people shared in access to social and natural resources. Those elders often explained that the lessons learned from stories about people like Uriah Severesen and the Cantrell family taught them how family and neighbors should engage in work together, so as to cultivate important resources from the land that would allow them to maintain a sense of dignity and hope for the future. Whenever anyone in the region needed help for health reasons or farming, everyone knew that they should quickly come together so as to provide aid. If someone in the region needed to water their cattle during a drought, everyone understood that the individual could move their herd across neighbors' lands to rivers or streams—or the individual could build irrigation lines across those lands so as to access water.

In this way, then, the landscape was a way of viewing the collective spaces in the region as connected together and entangled; houses and farms did not stand in isolation from one another. The landscape was flat and non-hierarchical, as described by Marston, Jones and Woodward (2005), in that the material environment was open to all, so that people could help one another and access the multiple resources necessary for their work and lives. In fact, when elders spoke of the past, they often noted that this way of viewing the material topography led everyone to know one another intimately. For this reason, people knew that they might access one another's land for farming purposes whenever there was any need to do so. In fact, many of the important landmarks throughout the region were on private land owned by any one of the long-standing families, but were considered free to all; one need only open a rusted gate to travel into the meadow of Uriah Severesen's home.

Over the years, those elder residents moved through and interacted with the material environment across the region in much the same ways that their parents and grandparents had for decades. However, the recent alterations to the spaces in Wildcat Hollow disrupted the rituals and interactions around social resources and landmarks, and transformed the landscape that had been cultivated over the years; the region became an unruly enclave. Where once neighbors knew one another and traversed each other's land freely, imposing fences and gates now barred access to pathways through the region. Furthermore, silence replaced constant communication, and faceless nodes created the only real knowledge about new neighbors. This important discrepancy stands as part of the larger concept of topographical silence, in which the spaces no longer match the landscape socially constructed in the past. What is more, the perceived disrespect communicated by the silent nodes and edges made elder residents feel isolated and alone in a world they barely recognized.

The corrosion of knowledge is more relevant in terms of the younger traditional residents of Wildcat Hollow. In their case, the landmarks that helped the previous generations to pass on knowledge and socially construct landscape have disappeared during their lifetime. Only the oldest of them ever had the opportunity to visit the Severesen home or peruse items at the Cantrell Store. Many of these residents have only heard about historical figures like Severesen and the Caldwell family through conversations between elders. Two of the traditional residents who were in their mid-thirties both lamented the fact that they will never get to show their children the home of one of their ancestors, or take them to similar landmarks. Both of these residents realized that the disappearance of these spaces created a significant disconnect for the younger generation from their history. As one of those residents noted to me:

It bugs me, just because I'm getting older. We're about two generations removed from the kids not knowing anything about [Wildcat Hollow]. [Our family] used to live down around [town], but [the kids] couldn't tell you where. Right here where these five houses sit, this was a hay field. They won't remember any of that. And it's coming. And there's nothing anyone can do about it.

One of the younger traditional residents in his early twenties told me that he had little knowledge about people or places in Wildcat Hollow's past, and had no interest in those topics. Such disconnect of the younger generation from the history of the region and the knowledge passed down from elder generations constitutes knowledge corrosion, which will further alter the landscape in years to come. Essentially, the knowledge passed down over the course of generations will end with the youngest generation; the history of Wildcat Hollow will fade into silence. This will allow for wealthy, post-industrial middle class newcomers to rewrite the rules and rituals around use of the land.

The Trust Network & Community of Closure

The topographical silence that permeated the region led to the construction of a trust network by traditional families who had lived there for several generations. For the most part, this trust network was built so as to break the silence of the unruly enclave formed over the past decade of economic austerity. The construction of this trust network can be seen as an attempt at democratizing the enclave. However, we deem this democratization to be severely deficient, as it amplified the economic problems in the community. The nature of their trust network, and its reliance on performativity within the context of activist alternative media, transformed those families into a community of closure. Past research concerning alternative media has demonstrated the ways in which right-wing alternative media create communities of closure and isolation in contemporary society. For instance, Atton (2004) examined web materials and print publications of the British National Party (BNP), a racist organization that argued for racial purity and segregation in Great Britain. In his research, he found that the BNP texts constructed experiences of repression by Other's of color, which positioned readers as victims. In this way, then, the audience became suspicious of Other's of color, and enclosed themselves from outside communities; this is similar to the notion of "communities of closure" developed by Couldry (2000). More recently, Atkinson and Berg (2012) explored emergent themes within alternative media used by Tea Party activists, and found an over-arching theme about purity conveyed to the audience. They noted that activists utilized the theme to scrutinize politicians and separate true conservatives from the RINOs (Republicans In Name Only). What is more, Atkinson, Chapius, Cruz, Gilkeson, Kaunert, Kluch, and Kimathi (2017) have demonstrated how such themes have been made transferrable to general society through articles concerning popular culture typically found in contemporary alternative media. Themes like "purity" can be applied beyond politics, to things like movies and hairstyles.

These research projects have helped to illustrate the ways in which alternative media spur separation and the emergence of communities of closure. The interviews with the traditional residents in Wildcat Hollow also demonstrated these issues, as analysis of the interview data revealed three interconnected categorical roles that people played in the trust network: (1) Curators, (2) Intermediaries, and (3) Alternative Media Visionaries. These three roles were interconnected as each influenced one another, and the latter two often overlapped, as all of the Visionaries were also Intermediaries. Overall, these three roles in the network shaped perceptions of, and reactions to, the topographical silence caused by rural gentrification.

Essentially, a network of traditional families who had lived in Wildcat Hollow for multiple generations emerged as more newcomers moved into the region. According to Tilly (2005), trust networks are political entities formed by people so that they may pool material and social resources in response to pressures of public politics; such networks often resist changes that are forced upon members. In many respects, trust networks are the starting place for militant particularism, which is a form of resistance against socio-political forces described in the previous chapter. People in trust networks intensify their personal connections, share their resources, and aid and shield one another from the scrutiny of public politics. In this way, then, "trust networks consist of ramified interpersonal connections, consisting mainly of strong ties, within which people set valued, consequential, long-term resources and enterprises at risk to the malfeasance, mistakes, or failures of others" (p. 12). Those people who protect the network and act as "faithful participants" who are rewarded with "personal attention, help with personal difficulties, long-term reciprocity, and cushioning against possible disasters or disabilities" (p. 13). Those who are not faithful, or who fail to properly protect the network, are excluded and stigmatized; mechanisms within the network "magnify distinctions between people you can trust and people you should distrust" (p. 15).

The Wildcat Hollow trust network was comprised of a series of different families—or clans (to use the term utilized by many of the members of the community)—that functioned as interconnected nodes. Three of those clans acted as the hub of the network: Johnson, Smith, and Adams clans. These families were also in constant contact with other, peripheral clans: Sanders, Anderson, Jones, and Hinderson clans. All of these clans exchanged information, pooled labor and resources, and confided regularly. This form of network served all of these clans well during the years when agriculture was the economic base of the region, and that economic base served the population well enough. In recent years, however, the network took up the role of responding to the pressures placed on the community from rural gentrification (see Daniels, 1999; Hines, 2010, 2011; Salamon, 2003).

The category of Curators entailed those people who pooled resources and engaged in strong interpersonal relationships within their own clan in the network. They looked favorably upon other clans in the community, and gladly worked alongside them from time to time. However, most of their time and efforts were focused on their own family members and children. More importantly, these individuals tended to be the elders, and had long memories about events and spaces in Wildcat Hollow. These were the individuals who often had the greatest insight about the changes to physical the environment and social resources over the decades. In many cases, they told stories about the 1940s and earlier. One such individual could recount stories about the Civil War passed down to her from people who actually engaged in that conflict.

One topic Curators often discussed at length with other people in the trust network was the changes to the physical environment over the years. In addition, many of the curators also talked at length with people in their clans about past traditions and rituals that had largely faded away over time. For instance, one of the Curators in the Johnson clan often had discussions about funeral rituals that are no longer practiced:

> We dug the graves by hand. That actually used to be a little bit of a treat. This fellow died, and you have people saying that you need your grave dug by Wednesday. Well, Tuesday we'll meet up there, and there might be twenty people show up. We'd take turns. We'd actually dug with picks and shovels.

One of the elders in the Adams clan said that he lamented the disappearance of rituals around work; specifically, he would talk to people about the past practices of "hauling hay":

> [My] dad bought a 1944 Ford tractor. Him and [many of the other elders] done all of the farming around from here to [town]. They helped each other farm. Well neighbors

don't do that anymore. They got their own stuff, and to heck with you. We used to really farm. We've hauled hay for [everyone]. All of them. Baled hay. It's changed a lot over the year.

Essentially, these elders noted to people how the "cradle to grave" rituals of the community have largely disappeared, and lamented the fact that people no longer worked together as one unit. For the elders of the different clans, the old way of life had largely disappeared over the course of a few decades.

The category of Intermediary entailed those individuals who spent much of their time engaged in strong interpersonal relationships with people from other clans in the trust network. They pooled resources and spent time alongside those people just as often as they did with people in their own clans. Typically, these people shared stories and problems of their respective clans to one another, thus allowing for the passage of information throughout the network. In many ways, the Intermediaries constituted the threads that connected the different nodes in the trust network together.

One member of the Johnson clan serves as a good example of such an Intermediary. During the interview, he talked about how he would regularly meet with members of other clans to have "beer drinking sessions" and talk about work and farming:

We will get together here at [my] workshop or over at theirs. Get together socially with [Adams] at their house. Like for a beer drinking session or something like that. We talk about what we're all doing. How's it going job wise … We talk about a variety of things I guess. We'll talk agriculture. We talk current events … I'd say just farming, music, the past a lot. Like growing up and stuff. Things like that. We talk also about going to school together. How our lives turned out after graduating high school. Things we did between graduation and this point in our lives now.

Talking about the past—particularly their past together—helped to strengthen their interpersonal bonds beyond their respective clans. These bonds allowed for information to move from one clan to the next. Aside from such relationship-oriented talk, the Intermediaries also discussed farm work and problems that they faced at the local level in Wildcat Hollow and beyond. Such information was taken back to the clans, and dispersed through discussions at dinner and work.

The category of Alternative Media Visionaries entailed those individuals who frequently used right-leaning alternative media, like the radio programs produced by Rush Limbaugh and Glen Beck, and websites like RedState.com and blogs associated with groups like the Tea Party Patriots. Such texts were constructed as alternative media through the interpretive strategies utilized by these individuals. As noted by Rauch (2007), interpretive strategies are one way in which media can be made alternative by the audiences; they choose to see such texts as alternative to the mainstream. These Alternative Media Visionaries engaged in two important activities within the trust network: (1) they utilized the theme of purity associated with narrowmobilization to filter relations within the network, as well as between the network and outsiders, and (2) they connected specific political arguments and issues conveyed in those alternative media titles with situations that unfolded in Wildcat Hollow.

First, the Alternative Media Visionaries brought the abstract theme of "purity" expressed through conservative alternative media into the trust network, and made it concrete. The Visionaries were very aware of the worldview of "purity" conveyed in conservative alternative media like RedState.com, which was described in past research concerning alternative media audiences. According to Atkinson and Berg (2012), the theme of purity entailed a black and white worldview of enemies and heroes. Within this theme, heroic political figures (e.g., Ted Cruz) enacted ideals of Protestant Christianity and the Founding Fathers while enemies (e.g., Barack Obama, Nancy Pelosi) ignored such ideals. This stood as abstract, however, as the discussions in those texts were primarily philosophical. The only examples provided to audiences in those texts were solely at the national political level, and focused on debates over issues like healthcare or taxes. The Alternative Media Visionaries put these themes into action within their local community in Wildcat Hollow.

For the most part, the themes were put into action as the Alternative Media Visionaries scrutinized relationships in the region. It is important to note that in the context of their research, Atkinson and Berg described a similar process of scrutiny in terms of conservative Tea Party activists:

> Activists constantly compare politicians and other political actors to templates of purity that are outlined in their alternative media. If a political actor or group measures up, they are welcomed into the fold. If they do not, they are sent away or even attacked. (p. 531)

Essentially, Atkinson and Berg claim that conservative alternative media is utilized by activists to scrutinize political relationships and actions. In the case of Wildcat Hollow, this abstract theme was similarly used, but for the scrutiny of activities and connections between the different clans. In this way, then, the Visionaries watched over the connections between the Intermediaries, making sure individuals and interconnections adhered to the heroic ideals of purity. This notion of scrutiny did not come from the interviews with the Alternative Media Visionaries, but emerged from the interviews with other clan members (Curator and Intermediary alike); such individuals often described a significant concern about being stigmatized by the Alternative Media Visionaries. One of the Curators in the Smith clan, for instance, noted that there were certain people (whom she would not name) that often monitored relations between clans, and interactions between the clans and newcomers. Another Curator in the Johnson clan similarly noted such scrutiny by certain members of the network, also without "mentioning any names." He noted, "you have to watch what you say" around the community, as certain people become angry over "penny nanny little things."

One Intermediary from the Smith clan summarized these notions about the Alternative Media Visionaries, as he noted that there were some people in the region who were too reliant on conservative media for information. He explained that their reliance on such media made them much more distrustful of outsiders:

> [They] get sucked into [conservative media] and they start trusting people less and less. Until that maybe it's the reason that it's harder to get in with our neighbors now. Well, if I go talk to [my neighbors] and find out that [they're] way too liberal, well [particular people] might be offended . . . And all of the sudden you have turmoil in your little community.

Essentially, the Alternative Media Visionaries held deep suspicions about people who were outside of the trust network. They watched to make sure that outsiders did not become too close to people in the trust network—or vice a versa. In many ways, the trust network came to resemble the "communities of closure" described by Couldry (2000), which Atton (2004) claimed was often cultivated through right-wing alternative media.

In addition to filtration of relations, the Alternative Media Visionaries also connected specific political issues in alternative media content to the rural gentrification in Wildcat Hollow. For instance, one of the members of the Adams clan connected the influx of new residents to the region to descriptions of "dangerous" Syrian refugees featured on RedState.com and in Rush Limbaugh broadcasts. Essentially, he claimed that dangerous elements of the Middle East were moving into the United States and taking up positions from which they could wage war against Americans. He claimed that the newcomers were not necessarily terrorists, but he felt that everyone needed to be wary. Similarly, one of the brothers noted above in the Smith clan connected the hardships of the farms in the region to the influence of "radical" animal rights activists on society described in right-leaning alternative media. As he noted at one point:

> The more neighbors you get, the more you have to worry about what are their opinion of what you're doing, and how will they handle what they see? Will they take things out of context? Oh my gosh, those animals might be sorely treated, or there might be something here that we don't like … And I think that if there's a big change in my lifetime, it's how you have to treat everything with kid gloves because you're going to have so many people around here who are trained [by activists] to look for anything that doesn't seem kosher.

What is more, the connections that the Alternative Media Visionaries made between content and problems in the region shaped their resistance against rural gentrification. These performances sharpened the distinctions between the network and outsiders created through the filtration of relations. Some Alternative Media Visionaries liked to drive farm vehicles slowly along the roads through the region, forcing traffic to slow down and irritating newcomers. One particular member of the Adams clan frequently travelled around Wildcat Hollow wearing his gun belt and pistols. He also liked to target shoot late at night outside of his home, which was less than a quarter of a mile away from a series of large new homes in the region. That particular Visionary often claimed to other people in the network that he liked to shoot at night so "those people know who they're living next to, now." Two Alternative Media Visionaries also worked to get people in the trust network licensed to conceal and carry firearms; they helped prepare people for the permit test, and took them to appropriate testing sites. For these Visionaries, guns emphasized the trust network's connection to the past, and difference from the newcomers. The weapons would also serve as a means to protect themselves if "truly bad" newcomers (like Syrian refugees described in right-leaning alternative media) were to move into any of the new housing.

Overall, the interviews revealed three different emergent roles played by the members of the trust network. The Curators formed the long-term memory of the community, and could always explain to their fellow clan members how things have changed and how things used to be. The Intermediaries formed the bonds between the different clans in the network sharing information about present day problems, as well as the past. The Alternative Media Visionaries, finally, were audiences who read and used right-leaning alternative media; they connected specific problems stemming from rural gentrification to political issues at the national and global level described in alternative media. They often discussed these connections with Intermediaries, who took concerns back to the clans. What is more, the Visionaries used the theme of purity described in past research concerning conservative alternative media to scrutinize and filter relations within the trust network; they acted as the guardians of the network, separating the heroes who demonstrate conservative principles from suspicious newcomers. Ultimately, then, the performances of all of the members of the trust network were rigidly constrained by knowledge about history, and visions of purity. This process prevented new ideas from entering the community that could have created positive economic changes, and kept rationales for resistance hidden from newcomers and outsiders.

Disruptive Concretization

The interviews illustrated how abstract themes described by Atkinson and Berg in their past research were made concrete within a trust network facing serious economic problems, as well as the topographical silence caused by rural gentrification. We would not go so far as to say that these abstract themes alone were responsible for the isolation of the trust network from newcomers and outsiders; Tilly notes that such networks often insulate themselves from the outside world. However, there was a process at work that compounded the isolation of the Wildcat Hollow, which we call disruptive concretization. This concept functions similar to militant particularism described in past research, as it involves abstract concepts and scale; in this case, however, the process is reversed.

In contrast to militant particularism described in Chapter 1, disruptive concretization entails making abstract themes from the global or national level concrete at the local level; this concretization impedes interconnections between a network and the outside world. Despite the advances to roads, infrastructure, and communication technologies over the decades, the resistance of the Alternative Media Visionaries in Wildcat Hollow did not seem to spread to other nearby farming communities, or to be abstracted to another level. Although the region was remote, it was by no means secluded from the rest of the world; the trust network, however, was extremely isolated as there was suspicion of newcomers and other outsiders. At the heart of this isolation were those members of the network who were avid readers and users of right-wing alternative media that espoused the theme of purity associated with the narrowmobilization described by Atkinson and Berg (2012).

Disruptive concretization stands as an opposite of militant particularism described by Harvey (1996), Featherstone (1998, 2005), and others; in the case of militant particularism, specific local actions spread to other regions. D'Arcus (2003) and Ahmed (2012) have written about external ideologies or agencies blocking militant particularism (see Chapter 4). In the case of Wildcat Hollow, militant particularism was blocked by the self-isolation of the trust network. Indeed, the resistance enacted by Alternative Media Visionaries could not easily be witnessed by anyone outside of the region as their actions emphasized sharp distinctions between the members of the trust network and newcomers. Essentially, the theme associated with right-leaning alternative media became a backdrop against which key figures within the trust network performed resistance, such as publicly bearing arms and hindering traffic. As relations in Wildcat Hollow became filtered, and as the Visionaries engaged in performances that compounded differences with newcomers, the trust network was increasingly isolated; there were significant consequences of such isolation.

One way to help illustrate the important impact of disruptive concretization on the isolation of the trust network is by looking closely at many of the interviews with Intermediaries (those who were not also Alternative Media Visionaries). Interviews with these traditional residents revealed that they spent a great deal of their time outside of Wildcat Hollow. Most of these individuals had taken up jobs in Queen City because they knew that their respective farms could not support them; instead, they helped in evenings and on weekends with the farm work. In many cases, these individuals had made contact with people outside of the trust network, and those relationships had provided new ideas about how they might use their land in alternate ways; in some cases, new forms of farming could be initiated (e.g., terrace farming), while in others, the land could be leased and rents collected. However, these individuals felt reluctant to discuss these things within the trust network, as their new relationships and ideas might seem "impure" to the Alternative Media Visionaries. Such ideas, then, were abandoned, while their new connections beyond the trust network were hidden or downplayed while they were in Wildcat Hollow. This hiding and downplaying is not just consequential as it compounded economic problems in the region, but it also made resistance invisible. Whenever alternative media visionaries performed resistance against the social and economic forces driving the rural gentrification around them, there was no way for it to be abstracted and spread beyond the region. Outsiders were never able to observe the actions of resistance, let alone learn about rationales for those actions. The resentment for changes to Wildcat Hollow was only visible to people within the trust network; newcomers and outsiders were unaware of these problems.

Discussion

The previous pages provide more concrete examples of key concepts that were explained in Chapter 1, and demonstrate the human toll of those issues. In the case of Wildcat Hollow, there was a direct line that connected the following concepts together: rural gentrification, topographical silence, trust network, and disruptive concretization. Rural gentrification arose from the economic forces associated with neoliberalism and finance capital (discussed in greater detail in Part II). The rural gentrification observed in Wildcat Hollow is a significant problem associated with the age of austerity. Many communities, like Wildcat Hollow, have lost funding or an economic base, and have no way of replacing that capital. In those cases, such communities often fall into disrepair, losing economic value as home and land prices plummet. Such economic degradation makes these communities susceptible to gentrification from newcomers; a process that leaves the landscape or cityscape physically altered, which can corrode knowledge and memory for those traditional residents that remain. Such topographical silence makes these communities unruly spaces, like the enclave of Wildcat Hollow, as traditional residents become increasingly unsure about where and how they may interact with the physical environment. What is more, the unruliness of topographical silence compounds the economic realities of communities facing the combined problems of austerity and gentrification. The lack of knowledge and confusion makes it all the more difficult for the traditional residents to revitalize a region, or engage in economic development.

The formation of trust networks is one way in which such unruliness may be brought under control, and spaces made to be democratized by the people who live within and around them. In the case of Wildcat Hollow, the trust network became a way of creating and circulating knowledge about the past after many important landmarks had disappeared. Over the years, people had taken younger generations to important landmarks and passed along information about the land and the people who had lived there decades ago. This passage of information was integral to the formation of the landscape, as well as construction of identity that informed the ways in which people interacted with the physical environment. As that knowledge base corroded from rural gentrification of the region, there was need for it to be replaced. The trust network emerged and allowed for traditional residents to pass knowledge in new ways, which broke the topographical silence that they faced and created a sense of control and stability over the unruly spaces around them. This knowledge allowed for the different clans to come together and create a communal sense of space and identity.

This democratization was not without its problems, however, as the over-reliance on conservative alternative media as a backdrop for the performance of resistance against the forces of rural gentrification transformed the network into a community of closure. The use of conservative alternative media within the trust network stood as a form of sociological participatory engagement (Carpentier, 2016). Essentially, the heavy consumption of media helped Visionaries to feel empowered as they faced drastic changes to the community. What is more, it gave rise to specific rituals of surveillance, which transformed the families into a community of closure. The dominant theme of "purity" found throughout such texts in past research gave rise to performances of resistance that involved filtering good people from bad. Although there was increased dialogue and communication within the enclave, the performative actions of filtration made the clans isolated from other communities. Their efforts for resistance or change were invisible to neighboring communities, leaving them alone in their efforts. What is more, the closure from other communities left the traditional residents in the enclave looking to the past to solve modern economic problems. In this way, then, we view the construction of trust network in Wildcat Hollow as a particularly flawed example of the democratization of an unruly space. It could be that performances guided by different media environments would have given rise to a different kind of trust network; specifically, one that did not collapse into a community of closure. Only future research on different communities and trust networks can provide an answer to that question.

Ultimately, this chapter stands as a bridge to the rest of the book. The case of Wildcat Hollow provides more insight concerning key concepts raised in Chapter 1. In particular, Wildcat Hollow demonstrates key experiences of people and communities deeply affected by unruly spaces, while also providing an example of the potentials and pitfalls to the democratization of spaces by the citizenry. The following chapters in this book explore the global forces that have driven austerity and unruly spaces, as well as other (more successful) communicative strategies for democratizing such unruly spaces in contemporary society. In terms of the latter, we will demonstrate communicative strategies in Parts III and IV that open dialogue and allow for citizens to construct new knowledges about the spaces around them. These sites have their flaws as well, but represent to us the best instances of such democratization and can serve as examples for communities who struggle with the problems of austerity on a daily basis.

Note

1. The names of all people and places have been altered to secure the anonymity of participants.

References

Ahmed, W. (2012). From militant particularism to anti-neoliberalism? The anti-enron movement in India. *Antipode*, 44(4), 1059–1080.

Atkinson, J. D., & Berg, S. (2012). Narrowmobilization and tea party activism: A study of right-leaning alternative media. *Communication Studies*, 63(5), 519–535.

Atkinson, J. D., Chapuis, S., Cruz, G., Gilkeson, S., Kaunert, C., Kluch, Y., & Kimathi M. (2017). Feminist Jedi and a politically correct empire: Popular culture and transformative bridges in alternative media content. *Journal of Alternative and Community Media* [online journal], 2.

Atton, C. (2004). An *alternative internet*. Edinburgh, UK: Edinburgh University Press.

Bonnett, A. (2014). *Unruly places: Lost spaces, secret cities, and other inscrutable geographies.* New York, NY: Houghton-Mifflin Harcourt.

Carpentier, N. (2016). Beyond the ladder of participation: An analytical toolkit for the critical analysis of participatory media processes. *Javnost—The Public*, 23, 70–88.

Casey, E. (1987). *Remembering: A phenomenological study.* Bloomington, IN: Indiana University Press.

Couldry, N. (2000). *The place of media power: Pilgrims and witnesses of the media age.* London, UK: Routledge.

Cresswell, T. (2015). *Place* [E-reader version]. Malden, MA: Wiley-Blackwell Publishing.

Daniels, T. (1999). *When city and country collide.* Washington, DC: Island Press.

D'Arcus, B. (2003). Protest, scale, and publicity: The FBI and the H Rap Brown Act. *Antipode*, 35(4), 718–741.

Featherstone, D. (1998). Some versions of militant particularism: A review article of David Harvey's justice nature and the geography of difference. *Antipode*, 30, 19–25.

Featherstone, D. (2005). Towards the relational construction of militant particularisms: Or why the geographies of past struggles matter for resistance to neoliberal globalization. *Antipode*, 37(2), 250–271.

Glaeser, E., & Tufts, Y. M. (2001). *Job sprawl: Employment location in US metropolitan areas.* Washington, DC: Brookings Institution, Metropolitan Policy Program.

Harvey, D. (1996). *Justice, nature and the geography of difference.* Hoboken, NJ: Blackwell.

Hines, J. (2010). In pursuit of experience: The postindustrial gentrification of the rural American West. *Ethnography, 11*(2), 285–308.

Hines, J. (2011). The post-industrial regime of production/consumption and the rural gentrification of the new west archipelago. *Antipode, 44,* 74–97.

Hoey, B. (2005). From Pi to pie: Moral narratives of noneconomic migration and starting over in the postindustrial Midwest. *Journal of Contemporary Ethnography, 34*(5), 586–624.

Marston, S. A., Jones, J. P., &Woodward, K. (2005). Human geography without scale. *Transactions of the Institute of British Geographers, 30*(4), 416–432.

Papen, U. (2012). Commercial discourses, gentrification and citizens' protest: The linguistic landscape of Prenzlauer Berg, Berlin. *Journal of Sociolinguistics, 16,* 56–80.

Rauch, J. (2007). Activists as interpretive communities: Rituals of consumption and interaction in an alternative media audience. *Media, Culture & Society, 29*(6), 994–1013.

Salamon, S. (2003). *Newcomers to old towns.* Chicago, IL: University of Chicago Press.

Tilly, C. (2005). *Trust and rule.* Cambridge, UK: Cambridge University Press.

Williams, R. (1989). *Resources of hope: Culture, democracy and socialism.* New York, NY: Verso.

PART II
GLOBAL FORCES—AUSTERITY & UNRULY SPACES

The following chapters expand the concept of unruly space by connecting such material environments to policies, problems, and perils associated with modern capitalism and neoliberalism. Specifically, these two chapters explore the different global forces that create unruly spaces in contemporary society, or compound the problems that such spaces pose to communities and regions around the world. Chapter 3 explains some of the key origins of austerity associated with contemporary political and economic policies adopted by many nations and cities over the last few decades. The chapter also illustrates the ways in which unruly spaces impact the material, built environment. Specifically, this chapter explores how such austerity has made spaces in the city of Flint, Michigan invisible—or hidden geographies—and subsequently compounded the deadly problems associated with them. In Chapter 4, we examine the ways ruling elites typically deal with unruly spaces, which often leads to new forms of unruliness. Such was the case in Cairo and the San Francisco Bay area, as police and authoritarian forces disregarded laws and rules about telecommunications to cut off protesters who resisted the global forces of neoliberalism. Overall, Part II of the book accomplished the following:

1. Explains key origins of austerity in contemporary neoliberalism, as well as its connections to politics of resentment.
2. Demonstrates the role of resentment and finance capital in unruliness.
3. Provides evidence for the impact of such unruliness on the instrumental freedoms, or capabilities, of urban spaces.
4. Illustrates typical strategies of control utilized by authorities to control unruliness, and how such strategies expand unruliness.

· 3 ·

THE HIDDEN GEOGRAPHIES OF FLINT

The case of unruly spaces in contemporary society described in the previous chapters is not something to be taken lightly, or brushed off as insignificant. It is true that Bonnett (2014) presents some of his unruly spaces and places as curiosities, or spaces that elicit simple emotional responses and little more. However, many unruly spaces have detrimental impacts on human beings and the landscapes around them, as demonstrated in the case of Wildcat Hollow. In many cases, the rise of unruly spaces can be traced to some of the most ugly and horrifying aspects of humanity: racism, exploitation, and violence. The problem that scholars have raised is that such unruliness is typically met with calls for austerity, often to punish those who helplessly live in the midst of such chaos. As more cities and nations embrace policies of austerity and such physical spaces increase in number, unruly spaces often expand to encompass and engulf more communities. This is not simply an issue of perception or inconvenience. The widespread emergence of unruly spaces across contemporary society holds negative implications for neighborhoods, health, education, and democracy. Part II of this book expands scholarly understanding of unruly spaces, and demonstrates the global forces that create many of them. In the following chapter, we explore the ways in which unruliness developed in the physical environment of Flint, Michigan, and how policies of austerity compounded emergent problems. For the most part, this would constitute an examination of the physical aspects of the material environment, including the communicative qualities described by Gumpert and Drucker (2008). We begin with a discussion of the politics of resentment—or, organizing a public (and partisan) sense of grievance and ill will—and explore its connection to the rise of hidden geographies in the city.

Resentment

A memo arrived at the desk of Michigan's governor, Rick Snyder in late–2011. Its preamble, while contemptible to many at the time, would only reveal its deadly and horrific human costs several years later, as it set in motion the mass poisoning of Flint, a city of over 100,000:

> On October 5th, 13th, 17th, 21st, and November 7th 2011, Flint Financial Review Team members met and reviewed information relevant to the financial condition of the City. Based upon those reviews, the Review Team concludes, in accordance with Section 13(4)(d) of Public Act 4 of 2011, the Local Government and School District Fiscal Accountability Act, that a local government financial emergency exists within the City of Flint, and that no satisfactory plan exists to resolve that emergency. Therefore, the Review Team recommends the appointment of an emergency manager. (Flint Financial Review Team, 2011)

The so-called "Fiscal Accountability Act" had already precipitated a state-wide struggle over public pensions, UN-violating policy of water shutoffs, and home repossessions in Detroit. But, it was the humanitarian tragedy of Flint that made national sentiment finally turn on the prospects of "emergency financial management" in the economically abandoned parts of the country. Until then, Michigan had been watched closely as a model for other states and their local governments. The text of this act details the wide range of the state's "receivership":

> Public Act 4, an Act to safeguard and assure the fiscal accountability of units of local government, including school districts; [...] to provide for review, management, planning, and control of the financial operation of units of local government and the provision of services by units of local government, including school districts; [...] to permit a declaration of the existence of a local government financial emergency and to prescribe the powers and duties of the governor, other state departments, boards, agencies, officials, and employees, and officials and employees of units of local government, including school districts; to provide for placing units of local government, including school districts, into receivership. (Rep Pscholka, 2011)

As a result of this document, Ed Kurtz, Flint's Emergency Manager at the time, decided and put into motion a plan between June 2012 and April 2013 to switch the source of the city's water. Moving from Detroit Water and Sewage Department (DWSD) to Karegnondi Water Authority (KWA), Kurtz and company would save a reported $200 million over twenty-five years. To accomplish this, Flint would need to build its own pipeline access to KWA and in the interim turned to the Flint River, whose water the city began drinking on April 25, 2014. By May, residents began complaining about the smell and color of their new water. By August, E. coli and total coliform bacteria prompted several warnings to residents to boil their water. By 2016, reporting of widespread lead poisoning in Flint circulated in the national and international press. More than 20,000 people, many children, faced a lifetime of special medical care, debilitating health conditions, and developmental disorders.

Flint and its water crisis are usefully thought of in terms of "unruly spaces" (Bonnett, 2014), and the senses of unease that surround them, because of their defiance of predictable categorization in two ways. First, Flint represents a kind of humanitarian crisis that so-called developed places, wealthy nations, and "first worlds" are unprepared to imagine. Such crisis does not happen "here." Second, the alleged humanitarian crimes committed against Flint residents confound the prevailing neoliberal notion that economic balance sheets—living within one's economic means—are concerns superior to the quality of life one should live.

Within these pages, we explore how neoliberalism's double impulse towards overt austerity and covert resentment unfold across what we describe as the hidden geographies of Flint's water infrastructure and material conditions of possibility for leading a meaningful life. These conditions of possibility are the literal groundwork for what development scholars like Nobel Prize-winning economist, Amartya Sen (2000), often call "capabilities," or "instrumental freedoms" (like, access to education, water, food security, democracy). Crucially, this geography of infrastructure is not, in our view, "hidden" just because it is underground. But, rather, the geographies, networks, and spaces that compose capabilities and, more abstractly, the notion of necessary "instrumental freedoms" themselves became overrun and submerged beneath the image of Flint (and other Michigan cities) as being financially derelict. We draw on a critical reading of Sen's "capabilities approach" to poverty in the so-called developing world and advocate its application to impoverished places in developed nations to understand, in this case, key forms of invisibility imposed as a component of neoliberal austerity policies. In doing this, we explore geographies of resentment and "imaginary revenge," in the context of the Flint crisis, which based on the logic of "financial emergency" allowed for the production of toxic forms of invisibility.[1]

Flint, Invisibility, & Geographies of Resentment

Incorporated in 1855, Flint boomed as an overland stop on the route between Detroit and Saginaw. Already a center of 19th Century carriage production, by the early 20th century "Vehicle City" quickly also became a hub of the growing auto industry, home to Buick, AC Sparkplugs, Chevrolet manufacturing (though its headquarters were in Detroit), and many more who came and went. Flint's booming industry drew international immigrants but also a migration of black and white Southerners. As an industrial center, it had an active and at times radical labor movement. But, like parts of the South, it had an organized Ku Klux Klan and undertook specific policies to racially segregate the city neighborhoods, its policy-making bodies, and its labor unions.

By the mid–20th Century, Flint undertook a set of urban renewal policies designed in the model of many US cities. The institutionalized segregation produced by the New Deal, Home Owners' Loan Corporation's standard mortgage redlining practices—among common racial steering and blockbusting in real estate—created a twisted foundation for the "renewal" of the 60s and 70s. As Highsmith (2009) notes, such practices and policies "hardened the area's residential color line" (p. 349). A key to this renewal was the St. John Street neighborhood in the north side, a ninety percent African American community between the Flint River and the tracks owned by the Chesapeake & Ohio Railway. That project, Highsmith explains, "produced a government-sponsored, policy-driven pattern of Jim Crow that helped to make metropolitan Flint one of the most racially segregated and economically polarized regions in the United States" (p. 349). St. John Street redevelopment, conceived by a variety of groups and government agencies including Flint's Urban Renewal and Housing Department and the Department of Community Development, "cleared three hundred acres of commercial and residential land in the St. John neighborhood, relocating nearly all of its three thousand black residents into segregated replacement housing" (p. 349). The intention was to make room for "General Motors (GM) factory expansions, an urban freeway, and an industrial park" and failed to improve the city's economic fortunes—and likely worsened them. Highsmith provides more detail:

> By the early 1980s, despite the expenditure of nearly $150 million and the creation of countless plans and proposals by planners, business executives, and local activists, the St. John project had yielded a city that few visited, that fewer considered a likely place in which to invest, and that perennially led the nation in unemployment. (p. 349)

The collapse of the Flint economy, like many American cities, paired residential suburbanization with the increased suburbanization and automation of industry. From the 1970s to the early–1990s, Flint lost twenty seven percent of its population. As whites moved to the suburbs, the municipality itself became segregated and increasingly economically isolated. By 1990, about eighty percent of Genesee County blacks lived in Flint, and eighty percent of whites lived outside of the city limits. The white population decreased from ninety five percent in 1940 to less than fifty percent in 1990. In 1989, GM famously closed multiple factories in the area. The city's overall population, which peaked at 200,000 in the 1960s, was in free-fall and poverty grew along with unemployment.

Flint had the highest unemployment rate in the country (thirty percent) in the early–1980s. In 2013, the city's population had dropped below 100,000 with nearly half of its population living below the poverty line. As Clark (2018) recently remarks in her book, *The Poisoned City*, "Neglect, it turns out, is not a passive force in American cities, but an aggressive one" (¶ 22).[2] More pointedly, as Beasley—former executive director of the Michigan Committee on Civil Rights and tireless activist/public servant—chided Flint's director of urban renewal programs in 1973: "The City of Flint is deeply implicated in its ghettoes, City of Flint institutions created them; City institutions maintain them" (quoted in Highsmith, 2009, p. 349). As household poverty grew in Flint, so did its municipal poverty.

Like many US cities, as its tax-base hollowed, so too did Flint's inability to maintain many of its municipal services without debt. Eventually, unable to keep pace with the upkeep of its water infrastructure, the city found itself paying some of the highest water rates of all the cities connected to the Detroit regional water system. By 2010, Flint's inability—along with many other Michigan cities—to pay its bills as part of this long historical economic process fueled a set of hardline tactics by newly elected Michigan Republicans, who came to power during the Tea Party backlash against the

Obama administration. The perspective of this political backlash was to use financial policy as a means of social discipline.

Detroit was the largest test case of this, to which the same political perspectives across the country were paying close attention. On the subject of Detroit's potential bankruptcy, pundits like Joe Scarborough on MSNBC in 2013 blamed public employee pensions and local politicians' lack of political backbone to impose the necessary cuts to those so-called "legacy costs." This comment resonated with the debates lingering from the 2010 midterm elections and were elevated to the national stage in the 2012 presidential campaign, in which Republican candidate Mitt Romney talked about "makers" versus "takers" in America. Like Ronald Reagan's 1976 invocation of the "Welfare Queen," Romney depicted an immoral part of the country, content to freeload off those hardworking citizens. With public comments like this, he reconsolidated a long history of discourse about the "good" deserving Americans, and the "good" deserving places. Conservative pundit Mary Matalin (2012) echoed this trope on a CNN program, claiming, "there are makers and takers. There are producers and parasites." The political venom aimed at these financial "parasites" is the foundation of this growing political climate of resentment, seeking justice against the underserving "takers" oppressing the hardworking, good Americans.

The state's Emergency Financial Manager became the political arm of this ideology—beyond suspending the democratic process for financial "exception"—and had the power to essentially create corrective social policy through financial austerity: for example, cutting pensions under the auspices that they are too expensive.[3] The "revenge" that this social policy sought was "imaginary" in the sense that it neither rectified the situation of its self-styled "victims" (i.e., Romney's "good" Americans), nor did it correspond to the actual complexity of problems facing Flint or other struggling cities. Commenting on the Detroit bankruptcy, Wallace Turbeville (2013)—former Goldman Sachs vice president turned Demos senior fellow—noted that the environment within which something appears too expensive is entirely socially constructed. Pensions, according to Turbeville and others were both a small part of and generally irrelevant to Detroit's financial problems. Rather, Wall Street "rate swaps" on city debt and declining state funding were larger elements of the city's cash flow problems. Rate swaps restructured city debts and put the municipality under greater authority by large investment banks. On this Wall Street debt, Turbeville explains:

The deals included provisions that would allow the banks to terminate the swaps under specified conditions and collect termination payments, which would entitle the banks to immediate payment of all projected future value of the swaps to the bank counterparties. (p. 5)[4]

The circumstances around Flint's financial receivership were closely parallel and used the creation of the state's emergency powers to solidify and naturalize a set of financial conditions that were multivalent and socially built. It would seem, then, that financial receivership created social policy on the basis of such a "natural" condition.

We see this in terms similar to how Mahmud (2012) describes neoliberalist policy as "suturing debt to discipline." As Mahmud explains:

The subprime mortgage saga and the entrapment of the working classes and racial minorities into circuits of credit, then, resulted from the financial sector's search for depth and liquidity, as debt became the primary instrument to sustain aggregate demand. Redesigned legal regimes and public agencies were critical to this transformation. (p. 479)

The ability to discipline the everyday lives of ordinary individuals was strategically linked to new imperatives of the state in managing financial responsibility. This has its most concrete link in the threats to cancel pensions of public retirees and, most importantly to us, in the shifting of water sources to restructure the municipal budget.[5]

While the conditions of exception are clear here, we want to highlight how these forms of emergency autocracy (see Chapter 4) operated in the context of a set of hidden geographies, physical spaces concealed from sight, and social relations obfuscated by the particular ideological constructions of place based on resentment. Bonnett (2014) uses "hidden geographies" to describe how travelers may pass them by with little notice or knowledge of their existence. The Labyrinth described in Chapter 1, for example, lying largely unknown deep below the surface of Minneapolis, serves as one example of this sort of place. Another example Bonnett provides of hidden geographies is the North Cemetery in Manila, unseen by most travelers. In the populated capital city of the Philippines, rent and prices have become so expensive that it is quite impossible for most working-class families to live anywhere near their jobs. Many of those families have taken up residence in the graveyard in the northern portion of the large city, building homes among the tombs and graves for free. An entire community has sprung up out of sight and concealed from the rest of the citizenry in Manila. These spaces, when discovered or encountered by outsiders, will frequently create a sense of uncertainty, unease, or fear. Such feelings often arise because of the degradation to the material aspects of the space from neglect, time, and nature. In cases like the North Cemetery—where people occupy and live within these spaces—degradation or negative perceptions of outsiders can have dramatic impacts on the people who live in those spaces.

Geographers' interest in landscape has always included a sense of the "hidden" elements of place. Or, concomitantly, that the production of place always entails a process of hiding. Mitchell (1996) describes landscape as ideology, for instance, in that it hides the contradictions of its production. For instance, the image of the abundance of California landscape is built by actively hiding the poverty of migrant laborers and their everyday lives. Or the image of feckless and irresponsible municipal government and the hard, unchangeable financial realities they lack the backbone to face, hides the complex social processes of "financial emergency." But how do we understand those things that are typically invisible, like infrastructure? In Flint, the invisible networks of what Lefebvre calls the "urban process"—and many of which are labeled communicative qualities by Gumpert and Drucker—push us to understand the ideological nature of what is hidden. In turn we are left to ponder as to how hiding is crucial to a political environment based on resentment and cruelty, and ultimately to the forms of humanitarian catastrophe that such cruelty attracts.

Describing famines, which are often thought of as the most innocuous humanitarian disasters, Sen (2000) explains:

> The political economy of famine causation and prevention involves institutions and organizations, but it depends, in addition, on perceptions and understandings that accompany the exercise of power and authority. It depends particularly on the alienation of the rulers from those ruled. (p. 173)

The mass poisonings in Flint were not caused by a so-called "act of God," drought, or natural contamination of water, but rather the result of key governmental choices. Those making important decisions were not equipped with the appropriate information, concern, or empathy to govern the city's water system in a just way. As if describing Flint directly, he continues, "Even when the immediate causation of a famine is different from this, the social or political distance between the governors and the governed can play a crucial role in the nonprevention of the famine" (p. 173). Despite the combination of factors of old pipes and the Flint River's corrosive water quality, this was not a "natural" disaster; lead poisoning was instead analogous to how Sen describes the Irish Potato Famine, a tragedy inflicted on its people—an unnatural, political disaster. However, this alienation or distance he describes is not just lack of contact or information; it is also, especially in these parallel cases, a toxic worldview. Sen quotes Joel Mokyr, who notes, "Ireland was considered by Britain as an alien and even hostile nation" (Sen, 2000, p.173). In the case of Flint, this poisonous government was also the embodiment and articulation of a convoluted ideology of national hostility and racism that has deep roots to the invisibility constructed from the growing politics of resentment in 2010 (though having much older roots).

What Sen describes as "alienation" is the ideological underpinning of the production of the forms of invisibility and kinds of hidden geographies we are interested in here. While overt bigotry may seem invisible here as well—and it is—we are particularly interested in how the forms of instrumental freedoms, underpinned by water infrastructure became hidden by neoliberal austerity and its production of Flint as a place defined primarily by financial emergency. But racism is not always hidden in the Flint case. Many had speculated that racism lay at the heart of state bureaucracies poisoning a poor city whose population was fifty-four percent African American—that it would never have happened in a White suburban town. When a secret recording of Phil Stair's (of Flint's Genessee County Land Bank) explanation of the crisis's underlying cause was leaked to the press, (at least) an element of this worldview could be seen in the real world. He explained to a Flint activist:

> Detroit was charging all its customers [e.g. Flint and other cities] for the cost; they weren't collecting from their residents. They weren't shutting the water off, they were letting bills go forever, but they were charging everybody else, they covered them. Well, Flint has the same problems as Detroit, fucking ni**ers don't pay their bills, believe me, I deal with them. I don't want to call them ni**ers, shit, I have, shit, I just went to Myrtle Beach, 24 guys, and I was the only white guy. I got friends, I mean, there's trash and there's people that do this. . . . They just don't pay their bills. Well, Detroit didn't collect on their bills, so they charged everybody else, but Flint, Flint had to pay their bill to Detroit. (Abbey-Lambertz, 2017, np)[6]

Stair's remarks push us to see the brutality hidden in regimes of financial accountability. Alienation or distance, of course, are abstract euphemisms in this context for dehumanization, a narrative of who belongs within a community of concern and who is deserving of exclusion, the criteria, spoken or not, of sentencing groups to what is known as "social death" (see Patterson, 1982). However, we would be blind to not notice the elision in these comments of race and financial responsibility. Crucially, this toxic "distance" would not be possible without another corrosive form of alienation: the separation and distance between the varied economic components of a larger social process. That is, without the alienation of the commodity form, the "distanciation" of the various components in the circulation of capital, Stair's ideological reductionism would not be possible (see Cleaver, 2000; Harvey, 1984; Marx, 1992). The imposition of market logics in Detroit is presumed to exist in a post-racial universe but is indeed saturated to the core with racial ideology. As Kinney (2016) incisively remarks, "the racialization of place is not a symptom of capital but is produced by and in relation to capital" (p. x).

From the outset, the poisoning of Flint was determined by money, as decisions made over money, the presumed mismanagement of money, future savings of money, and the presumed cost of misbehavior to others. If, as Sen (2000) suggests, Flint's poisoning was the result of a "distance of the governors from the governed" (p. 170), and this distance allowed dehumanization to flourish, and money crucially facilitated this distance and formed an alienated framework for governing the health of the city. The question was never, how healthy are the people in Michigan cities, but how healthy are their budgets. What is central is how racial resentment and financial logics are mutually constitutive.

Here, the problem is not just prioritizing means over ends but mistaking means as ends-in-themselves. While Sen shows this with great empirical and theoretical power, he misses the crucial crux of the issue: a vital force behind "unfreedom," cruelly illustrated in the Flint case, is capitalism itself and its attendant forms of fiscal individuation and responsibility for social problems. One can contextualize Flint in a longer history of race and capitalism. For instance, the critical study of race, gender, and imperialism over the last one hundred or more years has demanded the recognition of how capital is built on and simultaneously demands the production of key forms of difference linked to economic value (e.g., Davis, 1983; Marable, 1999, 2007; Melamed, 2011; Roediger, 2007). As Wilderson (2005) explores, the burgeoning capitalist world system was built in the context of a White supremacist system of social and "natural" scientific classification, identifying who is—and is not—"human." Social death was the consequence of being classified as not human, and "idleness"—the unwillingness to work—was rationale enough to exclude particular groups from the human family. This exclusion is not synonymous with "invisibility" here, but is rather a particular kind of visibility that hides all other considerations and commitments. It was this revocation of social rights that formed the moral and legal foundation of American slavery.

Marx (1992) engages in a similar critique of the mythology of "primitive accumulation," in which society's "lazy rascals" were not, in some prehistoric period, industrious and, therefore, did not accumulate (and, thus, deserve) the wealth of their rich contemporaries. His detailed historical research reveals, to the contrary, that inequality is built through the combination of myth and violent (legal) dispossession and enclosure. Further, Marx's scathing critique of Malthus's dangerous equation of animal and human "surplus populations" shows that the politics of surplus or "burdensome" people is endemic to the capitalist system itself (the "absolute general law of capitalist accumulation"), in that it produces great deprivation and suffering as it also produces great wealth and opulence (Marx, 1992). The Eugenics movement transformed this Malthusian ideology into a pseudoscience, used to justify involuntary steril-ization programs (and inspired the Final Solution) based on a financial-ge-netic rationale. Describing what she calls "racial capitalism," Melamed (2011) explains:

> ... the trick of racialization [is] a process that constitutes differential relations of human value and "valuelessness" according to specific material circumstances and geopolitical conditions while appearing to be (and being) a rationally inevitable nor-mative system that merely sorts human beings into categories of difference. In other words, racialization displaces its differential value making into world-ordering sys-tems of difference, concealing its performative work with its constantive work. (p. 2)[7]

Capitalism requires inequality, race displaces the economics of value onto a discourse of social inclusion and exclusion, of deservingness and unde-servingness, and of life and death. Through its objective measures of fiscal accountability, Michigan's assessment of "financial emergency" in its cities revealed a false and dangerous equation of social value with wealth. In doing so, this elision expressed one of the most fundamental principles of the capi-talist market: exchange-value over all others. Buried deep in the discourse of the so-called "invisible hand" and market adjustments is, in the case of Flint, a kernel of the Eugenicists' dream—each supports themselves, while those who cannot deserve exclusion/death. Conveying an advocacy of this view as explained in a 1931 issue of *People Magazine*: "If the idealistic argument for seeking race improvement doesn't appeal, Dr. [James] Bossard thinks there is a practical motive just as convincing: The socially inadequate cost the rest of us $5,000,000,000 a year" (Bossard, 1931, p. 10). Paralleling the policy discourse (public and private) regarding Michigan's cities, Bossard forecasts, "some shrewd observer has remarked that social problems will be dealt with 'when, and if' the man on the street feels the pinch of the defective classes on his pocketbook" (p. 47).

The economic logic of dehumanization, of social death and its constituent invisibility, was wielded by and justified for its political proponents, causing a humanitarian crisis in Flint. In Emergency Manager, Gerald Ambrose's exit letter to Governor Snyder, he details his successes:

> The deficits in the General Fund and Water Fund have been addressed. The Water Fund is now solvent, although not at the level indicated as adequate; and the remaining $7 million General Fund deficit will be eliminated by June 30, 2015, with a loan authorized by the Emergency Loan Board. Citywide cash flow is now more than $67 million. (Ambrose, 2015, p. 2)

The managers, following their charge, took the social crisis in Flint and pushed it "downward," democratized it, individuated it, and subjected its population to the crisis directly. But, Sen's approach to such "unnatural disasters" poses a moralistic problem of leadership, sympathy on the part of "governors," but misses the real problem of fiscal responsibility—that finance carries juridical force, and as such, the balancing of accounts becomes a crucial part of the ecosystem of this unnatural nature. No longer subject to the whims of nature (natural poverty), social life is now subject to the whims of finance and capital, subservience to the products of its own production: capitalist poverty (see Rosati, 2012).

Over the last decade or more there has been a downward pressure of accountability for development projects from creditors to the State, and to individuals (see Beck, 1992; Giddens, 1999; Roy, 2010). This must also be seen as a democratization of poverty, the movement of responsibility for poverty (as cause or cure) to individuals, without recourse to the state (Rosati, 2012). Further, coping with social construction of poverty, a capitalist society is increasingly drawn into the market forms of consumer choice and profit seeking. In this sense, Flint reveals the state as an active agent of the subjection of individual social life to the tyranny of the market by abdicating its role of upholding alternatives to exchange-value in the social order, drawn in no small part by the urban geographies of places like Flint: who lives in its cities, what economic activities happen there, and all the fictions around real estate valuations. Financial accountability hides from public view those alternative constructions of social value, rights to social well-being, and formulations of justice.

Hidden Geographies of Capabilities & Deprivation

We see a geographical approach to capabilities as an opposing impulse to the toxic forms of invisibility produced by politics of resentment and actualized in neoliberal austerity. One of the paradigm-shifting aspects of Sen's approach is his dismissal of previously celebrated proxies to freedom, predominantly gross national product (GNP) and income. Sen explains:

> The gap between ... an exclusive concentration on economic wealth and a broader focus on the lives we can lead ... is a major issue in conceptualizing development. ... [I]ncome and wealth are desirable for their own sake, but because, typically, they are admirable general-purpose means for having more freedom to lead the kind of lives we have reason to value. [...] An adequate conception of development must go much beyond the accumulation of wealth and the growth of gross national product and other income-related variables. Without ignoring the importance of economic growth, we must look well beyond it. (2000, p. 14)

In the best case, Sen urges us to seek choices that can be made in the present world, but to do so by looking past "means" to freedom and focusing instead directly on "ends," substantive freedoms themselves. However, the logistics of this approach are contentious and require fleshing out in the context of the democratization of capitalist poverty, so as to engage in a more rigorous theory and method of antipoverty practices. Nussbaum (2003), for instance, explains:

> The basic idea of my version of the capabilities approach, in *Women and Human Development*, is that we begin with a conception of the dignity of the human being, and of a life that is worthy of that dignity—a life that has available in it "truly human functioning," in the sense described by Marx in his 1844 *Economic and Philosophical Manuscripts*. With this basic idea as a starting point, I then attempt to justify a list of ten capabilities as central requirements of a life with dignity ... But in some form all are part of a minimum account of social justice: a society that does not guarantee these to all its citizens, at some appropriate threshold level, falls short of being a fully just society, whatever its level of opulence. Moreover, the capabilities are held to be important for each and every person: each person is treated as an end, and none as a mere adjunct or means to the ends of others. (p. 40)

For Nussbaum, the specific freedoms must be clear and upheld universally. Harvey (2009) extends this discussion, explaining that the meaningful description of such forms of freedom require an understanding of their geographical process and underpinnings:

> Clearly, the starting point of this is some sense of what the individual must be liberated from (and Marx's comment that human freedom begins when the realm of material necessity and physical dependency is left behind is a suggestive beginning). But, this liberated process can never take place outside of space and time, outside of place-making, and without engagement with the dialectics of socio-natural relations. (p. 260)

Sen's focus on states and localities in isolation presents poverty as a problem internal to an absolute geography of independent places and misses the deep relationality of a globalized world system. Further, Sen's analysis lacks an analysis of the instrumental, material, environmental conditions, which society builds to produce capabilities and freedoms. The theoretical limits of this, however, create a lack of geographical dynamism and specificity that sets the capabilities approach up for failure in many ways.

As Harvey's urging above indicates, the capabilities approach demands an understanding of urbanization and urban systems, much like what Lefebvre proposed forty years ago, as an expanding system of social production through the production of geographies of everyday life. In this sense, the urban fabric forms an evolving global network, encompasses agricultural production and the countryside, and forms the conditions of self-production in contemporary society (Harvey, 2009; Smith, 1992). In *The Urban Revolution*, Lefebvre (2003) suggests, "we must define the 'urban' not as an accomplished reality [. . .] but [. . .] as a horizon, an illuminating virtuality. It is the possible, defined by a direction, that moves toward [complete urbanization] as the culmination of its journey" (pp. 16–17). The urbanization of social life has, he explains, "ceased to be a municipal problem and has become national and global," which given the proper political project can liberate society from "repressive and banal urbanism or [. . .] the limitations of national development programs" (p. 148). The moment when "the search for solutions and modalities unique to urban society are foremost," Lefebvre argues, "[t]he urban problematic becomes a global phenomenon" (pp. 5, 15).

In this sense, Bonnett's notion of hidden geographies treats the relationship between place and invisibility in problematically isolated ways. Instead, the notion of hidden geographies requires "a proper social theory of space, which can apprehend social space as built, fought for, seized, invested in, maintained, lost, mourned, renovated or altered irrevocably" (Chari & Gidwani, 2005, p. 268). Linking Flint's "financial emergency" to international development programs in the so-called "third world," Michigan's neoliberal austerity resembles the traditional long-term programs for "behavioral and social change" advocated by mainstream agencies (e.g. UNICEF) as both blame the behavior of the poor (as "lazy rascals") for their poverty. If neoliberal austerity and the politics of resentment seek to individuate poverty, geographies of capabilities seek to visualize the hidden ways in which social life is built on and through a complex interconnection of spaces and places within an urban fabric.[8] To think of behavior alone is to treat space and geography in a problematically fixed and static way. But, further, to try to conform capabilities to an abstract and isolated "financial accountability" imposes a toxic invisibility. This resentment-based production of place and hidden under-utilization of the material elements of urban life (e.g. water infrastructure) precludes an engagement with what Lefebvre (and many after him) called the "right to the city," and how to make concrete "the right not to be excluded from centrality and its movement" (Lefebvre, 2003, p. 150). "Freedom" in this context demands a geographical understanding not just of isolated financial obligations but of the larger urban system of capacities and a principled commitment to a right of all to (or at least a public and rigorous debate about who should) be included in that global urban process. In other words, an understanding of the urban nature of capabilities is crucial to the denaturalization of capabilities.

Lefebvre's argument, which is similar to the capabilities approach in many ways, is this: We depend on the urban system, it makes us, and therefore we should have a right to be central to its movement, its products, and its transformation, which is our own transformation (Attoh, 2011; Harvey, 2013; Mitchell, 2003). Understanding the urban process allows us to consider capabilities in terms of how "resources are managed across space and time . . . [which are] transfers of economic wealth (surplus) from one place to another" (Schoenberger & Walker, 2017, p. 936). Further, it helps us understand the concrete existing urban forms as active agents in our social self-production.

> Cities are more than passive spatial containers for people and firms undertaking market transactions and realizing economies of agglomeration. Cities are physical objects ("built environments") and living systems ("urban ecologies") that have causal powers in their own right. Urban environments/ecologies can pose challenges to city dwellers that demand solutions in order that the usability and viability of urban systems be maintained. (Schoenberger & Walker, 2017, p. 936)

In this sense, any discussion of a politics of capabilities must also be a politics of the production of urban forms. That is to say, capabilities are composed of spatial interdependencies.

Flint's drinking water, as a poignant if obvious example, depends on Detroit's infrastructure and flows of resources between places. In this sense, access to capabilities is geographically distributed, shared, and the lifeline of multiple populations. The extensive development of water infrastructure in Detroit serves capabilities in Flint. This unseen interconnection was made visible in the regions water politics. These aspects of city environments and urban growth require an understanding beyond simple exchange and the agglomeration of markets and market practices (Schoenberger & Walker, 2017). Flint's water infrastructure is a "socio-nature" that reveals a politics of productive capacity and forces consideration of what capabilities are available to the people who depend on that capacity. Within this socio-nature, productive capacities are covered over and rendered invisible by the ideological imperatives of austerity and the real state-imposed force of financial accountability. Who deserves what "ends" is disciplined by one specific set of "means"—financial liquidity. The focus on financial accounting, in this sense, demands that we consider what is externalized (as costs or burdens), wasted, undeveloped, and developed in debilitating directions. Austerity practices and logics, therefore also hide and make invisible neoliberal geographies of waste, which do not bear an economic stamp.

Flint relies on international water sources (Detroit River and Lake Huron) attached to a regional system serving multiple (126 in seven counties) municipalities. The urban ecology by which human capabilities are produced and developed is composed of a complex flow of resources. When the city switched its supply from Lake Huron to the Flint River for financial reasons, it critically changed that ecology. This set of socio-natural flows was complicated when Flint's water management discontinued corrosion-control treatments required by EPA's Lead and Copper Rule. As Bellinger (2016) explains, "[t]o make matters worse, the addition of ferric chloride to reduce the formation of trihalomethanes from organic matter increased the corrosivity of the [. . .] water, reaching consumers [. . .] 19 times as corrosive as [. . .] Lake Huron" (pp. 1101–1102). As corrosivity increased, so did its ability to dissolve lead and other metals, eventually leading to a catastrophe. "In six of nine city wards, the water in twenty to thirty percent of the homes had a lead concentration above 15µg per liter, a concentration that triggers remedial action under the Lead and Copper Rule" (p. 1102). Ten percent of homes were above

15µg per liter, some had 158ppb, and at one house there was 397ppb. When Virginia Tech University researchers came to do an independent test in that house, they did thirty readings and came back with 200ppb as the lowest end and some above 5,000ppb, where the EPA marks water as "toxic waste" (Ingraham, 2016).

Campbell, Greenberg, Mankikar, and Ross (2016) explain how exposure to lead can cause long-term impairment of different capabilities in children, including "decrements in intelligence, development, behavior, attention, and other neurological functions." Quoting Landrigan and Bellinger, they convey a more specific picture:

> Lead is a devastating poison. It damages children's brains, erodes intelligence, diminishes creativity and the ability to weigh consequences and make good decisions, impairs language skills, shortens attention span, and predisposes to hyperactive and aggressive behavior. Lead exposure in early childhood is linked to later increased risk for dyslexia and school failure. (Campbell et al., 2016, pp. 952–953)

Capabilities in this sense are not precisely things, but part of the urban process dependent upon the actual physical nature of the urban environment that compose it, the constitutive flows, and interdependencies constitutive of its operation.

Scales of Invisibility & Austerity

Translocal flows of resources and constitutive dependencies across space demand an understanding of how to define and differentiate the kinds of places through which producing and depriving capabilities occurs in the urban process: it is in part through these definitions that the shape of development is determined. In the early 1990s, Smith (1992) asked, "Where are the political debates over the scale at which neighborhoods are constructed, the boundaries of the urban, what makes a region, the scale of the nation-state—or indeed, what makes the global scale" (p. 61)? Traditionally treated as neutral, "geographical scale" describes the material-imaginary politics of differentiating kinds of places and spaces and regulating the territorial relationships they have to each other (Brenner, 2000; Howitt, 1998; Marston, 2000; Smith, 1992). Referring to the study of geographic data, Marston (2000) cites Lan and Quatrochi's three connotations of scale: (1) cartographical scale, or the relationship between distances on a map and the physical distances they represent; (2) geographical scale, the spatial magnitude of a study or phenomenon;

and (3) operational scale, the level at which processes function. Likewise, she explains scale as influencing the level of resolution or grade of measurement within geographical studies. In contrast, Marston also summarizes a social constructionist understanding that "scale is not necessarily a preordained hierarchical framework for ordering the world … It is instead a contingent outcome of the tensions that exist between structural forces and the practices of human agents" (p. 220).[9] But, scale is also a way of describing the relations between places and spaces. Howitt (1998) uses the case of aluminum production to explain that a bauxite mine at Weipa, Australia, though not changing as a material phenomenon, plays very different roles as an element of local, regional, national, international and global scales.

Yet, Marston, Jones, and Woodward (2005) suggest that after years of misuse as a top-down determinant of social life (e.g., global capitalism causes local neoliberalism), scholars should forsake the concept of scale altogether, replacing it instead with a commitment to flat, and non-hierarchical geographies. Marston's critique and non-hierarchical commitments are shared in the present work. However, one must also consider what is lost when the scale of social relationships is ignored. Leitner and Miller (2007) suggest that one such casualty of abandoning geographical scale is the loss of attention to nested relationships between spaces, which create "differential opportunities and constraints for practices of individual and collective agents" (p. 119). In this regard, scale is crucial to understanding the complex of power relations built onto and across the social landscape. The struggle over racial integration in the US, and Michigan particularly, helps illustrate how social struggles produce and are produced by the social construction of scale. As suburbanization created what officials called a "white noose" around Detroit, the suburb of Warren refused to comply with federal anti-discrimination mandates, and eventually, in 1970, voted to drop a funded urban renewal program instead of complying with racial integration requirements (Darden & Thomas, 2013). For instance, while this was a struggle at one level over borders, it was likewise a struggle over what types of spaces would produce certain capabilities for some (i.e., Whites) and deprive others (i.e., Blacks). As Leitner and Miller (2007) point to the social-material institutional arrangements of the state as an important instance: "Responsibilities and capacities of different state levels, as well as relationships among these levels, are reconstituted on an on-going basis. Indeed, the scalar restructuring of state responsibilities and capacities has been one of the hallmarks of neoliberal globalization" (p. 120). In this sense, activism inside and outside mainstream politics, like those reactionary political forces that brought venture capitalist Rick Snyder to the Governor's office in Michigan two years after Barak Obama's historic presidential victory, revealed how the mobilization and occupation of key spaces of power relations by interests from the White suburbs and rural areas produced severe forms of deprivation and injury in urban communities of color (Leitner & Miller, 2007, p. 122). Financial accountability legitimated the politics of resentment and managed to cover over what should have been prevailing concerns for public safety, individual well-being, and social dignity.

Scale is a way of describing how we think of the spatial nature of social processes. The subjection of water to emergency management represents a change in the scale of controlling that piece of the urban system. And, to a large extent, it represented White revanchism scaled "up," thinking of it as a statewide matter, and no longer municipal. Scale is, on one hand, a matter of understanding and defining the socio-ecology of specific capabilities. It is also, on the other hand, a matter of different geographically defined struggles over shared group interests and the power to actualize those interests across space and time. Decision-making processes imply geographical scale; who (in what places) has the power to determine quality of life in other places, under what authority, with what geographical conceptualization of the common good? The Flint water tragedy can be seen in parallel to sectarian violence, or state-level politics that have tended to be home to violence against minorities and the poor (e.g., Jim Crow laws in contradistinction to *Brown vs. the Board of Education*, 1954).

The "Financial Accountability Act" referred to earlier with respect to Flint, is another example of this, extending a century or more of conflict over the racial distribution of social resources through the spatial relations of democratic institutions and their mediation of expansive circuits of capital. Some of the earliest epidemiology dealt with water and cholera in 19th century London, using maps to analyze and communicate the location of infected wells and assess the scope of the response to the health problem (Newsom, 2006; Schoenberger & Walker, 2017). And, the difference between London and Flint is instructive: whereas providing healthy access to water in London was important because an empire of industrial production and distribution depended on it, America's Rust Belt—the deindustrializing Northern and Midwestern regions—in which Flint is located, is a very different situation. The cities in this region no longer necessarily produce material wealth to be distributed to the world outside, but are rather seen in some cases as a financial drain on the surrounding areas.

Understandings of the public good have changed, as have whom those goods are meant to serve. Flint may represent indifference to some of these earliest lessons of urban planning/development (one geographical problem) or it represents a kind of ignorance of geographical knowledge amongst its governing regimes (a different geographical problem). In either case, however, we see the reduction of geographical knowledge of the deserving public and the public good into merely monetary flows, revenues, and fiscal matters. What followed from emergency management was a long-sought regional shift in power over the metropolitan water system as a new "Great Lakes Water Authority" is implemented and imposed over the region as part of the emergency plan. This is a shift in scale and in the interest groups represented at the management table, cutting the number of Detroit City representatives in half and including none from Flint. Here the issues of population size, vulnerability to water crisis, and other capabilities deprivation might be seen to overlap with how the scale of water governance is determined. Sen (2000) suggests:

> ... development requires the removal of major sources of unfreedom: poverty as well as tyranny, poor economic opportunities as well systematic social deprivation, neglect of public facilities as well as intolerance or overactivity of repressive states. Despite unprecedented increases in overall opulence, the contemporary world denies elementary freedoms to vast numbers—perhaps even the majority—of people. (p. 3)

In capitalism, the money form of value and wage-labor dominate exchange and access to capabilities. In addition, while Keynesian and socialistic approaches to public goods minimized their reliance on the profit motive (while still mediated by money and debt), the prevailing neoliberal regimes of the last forty years have made a project of subjecting all capabilities and aspects of the urban process to profit, investment, growth and other aspects of capitalist poverty. Sen contends this is not a good thing, that "today's prejudices (in favor of the pure market mechanism) certainly need to be carefully investigated, and, I would argue, partially rejected" (p. 112). Here we must assume that capital, as the "pure market mechanism," must be (at least partially) rejected. Yet, the abstract "purity" of any market mechanism is a fallacy, always part of the struggle over prevailing social norms and regulation (see Jessop & Sum, 2006).

Flint demonstrates how capital as capabilities' mediator confines and deprives the urban process's relational capacities. Both governments and private actors find themselves subjected to scarcities that may not necessarily correspond to resources that the conditions of monetary exchange mediate (i.e., price). Emergency Manager Ambrose (2015) explains to Governor Snyder:

Addressing these issues and putting Flint back onto a path to sustain financial solvency has been difficult for taxpayers, employees, retirees, and those utilizing city services. Taxes and fees have been raised, including a voter approved six mill special levy for police and fire; a special assessment for street lighting; waste collection was changed to a fee for service from a millage rate; and increases in utility rates to among the highest in the state. Services have been reduced to marginal levels (including public safety), as the workforce and employee compensation has shrunk by more than 20 %. And, retirees have seen their cost of retiree health care increase. As a result, much progress has been made ... (pp. 1–2)

The bulk of the resources listed by Ambrose are human (labor), but there is no money to pay workers. For the water system, there was certainly no shortage of water but somehow price demanded a toxic switch of water flows. As Sen's terms imply, water is a capability to which all must have free access, but capital will still mediate the production of the means to those ends. Someone—literally—will have to pay those debts, interest, and other costs. In the case of Flint, it was either taxpayers outside of Flint or its residents who must pay.

The conflict over Michigan's cities' fiscal accountability revolved around the seemingly high price of regional suburban water systems that depended upon Detroit's. Findings from the research collective called We the People of Detroit details a price comparison of several suburban water rates—including Detroit's wholesale rates—as a portion of each municipality's markup. The research collective then shows the percent markup by many municipalities, anywhere from a one hundred percent increase in Canton to one thousand percent Ferndale (We the People of Detroit, n.d.).[10] Their analysis shows that Flint's markup is roughly five hundred percent. Sen (2000) explains:

Just as it is important to emphasize the need for democracy, it is also crucial to safeguard the conditions and circumstances that ensure the range and reach of the democratic process ... there is also the need to examine the ways and means of making it function well, to realize its potentials. (p. 158)

Yet, Flint—having functioned through the democratic process—leaves us wondering how to safeguard democracy when finance and financial emergency are such a powerful arbiter of politics. The economic order has revealed tremendous compatibility with autocracy, just as it also contradictorily implies equality and free association. For Sen's capabilities approach, protection from preventable tragedies like famines is both itself an enhancement of freedoms and "is significantly helped by the use of instrumental freedoms, such as the opportunity of open discussion, public scrutiny, electoral politics, and

uncensored media" (p. 188). However, these instrumental freedoms—protests, public forums, etc.—did very little to protect Flint.

One problem with an urban system mediated by capital is that it will
always imply, within itself, a skewed productivity, one based on price and
individual payment, rather than on a right to the urban process without that
mediation. Price will always subject access to resources and capabilities to its
own alienated needs, not the needs of society, not individual capabilities, and
not instrumental freedoms. However, it is in this tension between what the
urban system could be and what price, wage-labor, and capital prevent it from
being that we find hope. Perhaps as Lefebvre (2003) may imply: "Urban reality modifies the relations of production without being sufficient to transform
them. It becomes a productive force, like science. Space and the politics of
space 'express' social relationships but react against them" (p. 15). In Flint,
the spatial politics of austerity, created two hidden geographies: first, it hid
the toxic infrastructure of water infrastructure beneath the question of cost;
second, it hid the abundant capacity of the urban system, and with it notions
of care and instrumental freedom within the social community, beneath a
politics of resentment.

Discussion

In Michigan, the dominant view of city inhabitants as "lazy rascals," evi-
denced by their economic poverty, had dire consequences and formed the
basis for the democratic process itself. The fact that interest rate swaps and
other institutional expenses were considerably larger did not stem the forces
of austerity and resentment. In *On the Genealogy of Morals*, Nietzsche (2006)
makes a surprising connection between cruelty and economies of exchange
expressed in the history of punishment:

> ... the creditor could inflict all kinds of dishonour and torture on the body of the
> debtor, for example, cutting as much flesh off as seemed appropriate for the debt: [...]
> there were everywhere, early on, estimates which went into horrifyingly minute and
> fastidious detail, legally drawn up estimates for individual limbs and parts of the body.
> (Nietzsche, 2006, pp. 40–41)

In Flint, the pound of flesh taken was in the form of poisoned children, whose
deprivation will last a lifetime. Financial accountability provided a framework
of resentment to create those toxic conditions. More importantly, financial
accountability created (and creates) a mechanism for hiding an additional

contradiction: the imposition of austerity on Flint residents was never going to settle any account for those who see the city as a place of "parasites." It would not lower angry voters' taxes. It would not resolve Wall Street's power over the city's debt; in the end, it would actually cost the state more. The subsequent wave of lawsuits and criminal charges against the state officials responsible for the alleged poisoning of Flint demonstrates what was at the heart of the project of austerity in the first place: an entire material way of life and system of places based in resentment, aggrievement, the collection of debts, and invisibility of all other values. On resentment, Nietzsche argues that punishment provides no actual equivalence for wrongdoing. Instead:

> The equivalence is provided by the fact that instead of an advantage directly making up for the wrong (so, instead of compensation in money, land or possessions of any kind), a sort of *pleasure* is given to the creditor as repayment and compensation,—the pleasure of having the right to exercise power over the powerless without a thought, the pleasure "*de faire le mal pour le plaisir de le faire*,"[47] the enjoyment of violating: an enjoyment that is prized all the higher, the lower and baser the position of the creditor in the social scale, and which can easily seem a delicious titbit to him, even a foretaste of higher rank. Through punishment of the debtor, the creditor takes part in the *rights of the masters*: at last he, too, shares the elevated feeling of being in a position to despise and maltreat someone as an "inferior"—or at least, when the actual power of punishment, of exacting punishment, is already transferred to the "authorities," of *seeing* the debtor despised and maltreated. So, then, compensation is made up of a warrant for and entitlement to cruelty. (pp. 40–41)

This "enjoyment of violating" is the hidden core of the deindustrialized network of places in Michigan and the global urban system more broadly. The highly visible legal case against the public officials responsible hides the broader context of a politics of resentment, which has been implicit in the neoliberal turn since the 1960s.

The lawsuits and national-scale oversight all came too late to prevent tragedy. The moral content of capitalist market logic overrode any other alternative in the existing political process. Nietzsche makes all of the above points in order to suggest another system for social life:

> It is not impossible to imagine society *so conscious of its power* that it could allow itself the noblest luxury available to it,—that of letting its malefactors go *unpunished*. "What do I care about my parasites," it could say, "let them live and flourish: I am strong enough for all that!" . . . Justice, which began by saying "Everything can be paid off, everything must be paid off," ends by turning a blind eye and letting off those unable to pay,—it ends, like every good thing on earth, by *sublimating itself*.

The self- sublimation of justice: we know what a nice name it gives itself—*mercy*. (pp. 46–47)

Money and criminal charges will not restore the capacities of Flint's poisoned children, nor will moral sentiment. Only an unmediated commitment to the conditions of survival, dignity, and equality of capabilities could have averted a tragedy of this particular kind. So, what could a market be? What forms of exchange, implicit in our current urban system, could be developed to create something more socially effervescent, more free, and less tied to social death than the capitalist mode of production? Perhaps Sen wants us to read between the lines. Freedom, in a capitalist urban system, is impossible and one must look for alternative frameworks for the connections between "economic power" and "substantive freedoms"? The urban system has proposed a future, perhaps, that Sen has exposed in its contradictions.

To take these questions seriously, investigations of "hidden geographies" must negate its sacred idols and ask critical questions about capital and exchange, but further about dignity, hope, and freedom we have all too often been unable to ask, and demand them across spatial limits. But, further, the case of Flint should push us to see the Moloch idol of capital, wage labor, and social death before us—of our own making and demanding the sacrifice of our children—amid the very model of financial accountability and demand more of our theory and practice of antipoverty, not because of Flint's uniqueness but because of the pervasiveness and interconnection of cases like it.

Notes

1. This chapter is largely based on research concerning the contemporary relevance of Sen's *Development as Freedom*, published in *Journal of Multicultural Discourses* (Rosati, 2018). Reprinted by permission of the publisher (Taylor & Francis, http://www.tandfonline.com)
2. From the website for the book, at https://us.macmillan.com/excerpt?isbn=9781250125149
3. See Chapter 4 for more on "exception" in what we see as an interconnected context.
4. He continues: "Such conditions included a credit rating downgrade of the city to a level below 'investment grade,' appointment of an emergency manager to run the city and failure of the city to make timely payments. Projected future value balloons in low, short-term rate conditions. This is because the difference between the fixed swap payments made by the city and the floating swap payments projected to be paid by the banks increases. Because all of these events have occurred, the banks are now demanding upwards of $250–350 million in swap termination payments." (Turbeville, 2013, p. 5)
5. See "The Eviction Lab" by Matthew Desmond (*Evicted: Poverty and Profit in the American City*, 2017) in collaboration with Princeton University (https://evictionlab.org/).

6. We have elected to edit this racial epithet.
7. Performative words incite action, constantive words describe situations.
8. https://www.unicef.org/cbsc/index_42328.html
9. In her reading of the discourse, Marston (2000) additionally distills three tenets of how scale production is conceived: (1) Scale is a way of framing conceptions of reality, which is constructed through and constructs the geographical organization of social interactions; (2) There are tangible outcomes and material consequences of these frames; and (3) Scale framings are frequently contradictory and contested, which may lead to deconstructions and reconstructions.
10. In a presentation, We The People of Detroit explained that sometimes water prices conceal other municipal costs for which the political will does not exist to raise taxes.

References

Abbey-Lambertz, K. (2017, June 5). Official resigns after blaming Flint water crisis on "n****rs who don't pay their bills." *Huffington Post*. Accessed November 17, 2018 from https://www.huffingtonpost.com/entry/flint-water-crisis-racism-unpaid-bills_us_59357729e4b0ca5db291d43b

Ambrose, G. (2015, April 28). Emergency manager exit letter. City of Flint, Office of the Emergency Manager. Assessed November 17, 2018 from https://www.cityofflint.com/wp-content/uploads/Emergency-Manager-Exit-Letter.pdf

Attoh, K. A. (2011). What kind of right is the right to the city? *Progress in Human Geography*, 35(5), 669–685.

Beck, U. (1992). *Risk Society: Towards a New Modernity*. Thousand Oaks, Calif: SAGE.

Bellinger, D. C. (2016). Lead contamination in Flint—An abject failure to protect public health. *New England Journal of Medicine*, 374(12), 1101–1103.

Bonnett, A. (2014). *Unruly places: Lost spaces, secret cities, and other inscrutable geographies*. New York, NY: Houghton-Mifflin Harcourt.

Bossard, J. (1931, April). What we pay: Cost of the socially inadequate. *People Magazine*. Accessed November 17, 2018 from http://www.eugenicsarchive.org/html/eugenics/static/images/1596.html

Brenner, N. (2000). The urban question: Reflections on Henri Lefebvre, urban theory and the politics of scale. *International Journal of Urban and Regional Research*, 24(2), 361–378.

Campbell, C., Greenberg, R., Mankikar, D., & Ross, R. D. (2016). A case study of environmental injustice: The failure in Flint. *International Journal of Environmental Research and Public Health*, 13(10), 951–961.

Chari, S., & Gidwani, V. (2005). Introduction: Grounds for a spatial ethnography of labor. *Ethnography*, 6(3), 267–281.

Clark, A. (2018). *The poisoned city: Flint's water and the American urban tragedy*. New York, NY: Metropolitan Books.

Cleaver, H. (2000). *Reading capital politically*. Edinburgh, UK: AK Press.

Darden, J. T., & Thomas, R. W. (2013). *Detroit: Race riots, racial conflicts, and efforts to bridge the racial divide*. East Lansing, MI: Michigan State University Press.

Davis, A. (1983). *Women, race, & class*. New York, NY: Vintage.

Desmond, M. (2016). *Evicted: Poverty and profit in the American city*. New York, NY: Crown Publishing.

Giddens, A. (1999). Risk and responsibility. *The Modern Law Review, 62*(1), 1–10.

Gumpert, G., & Drucker, S. (2008). Communicative cities. *International Communication Gazette, 70*(3–4), 195–208.

Harvey, D. (1984). *The limits to capital*. Oxford, UK: Blackwell.

Harvey, D. (2009). *Cosmopolitanism and the geographies of freedom*. New York, NY: Columbia University Press.

Harvey, D. (2013). *Rebel cities: From the right to the city to the urban revolution*. New York, NY: Verso.

Highsmith, A. R. (2009). Demolition means progress: Urban renewal, local politics, and state-sanctioned ghetto formation in Flint, Michigan. *Journal of Urban History, 35*(3), 348–368.

Howitt, R. (1998). Scale as relation: musical metaphors of geographical scale. *Area, 30*(1), 49–58.

Ingraham, C. (2016, January 15). This is how toxic Flint's water really is. *Washington Post*. Accessed November 17, 2018 from https://www.washingtonpost.com/news/wonk/wp/2016/01/15/this-is-how-toxic-flints-water-really-is/

Jessop, B., & Sum, N. L. (2006). *Beyond the regulation approach: Putting capitalist economies in their place*. Northampton, MA: Edward Elgar.

Kinney, R. J. (2016). *Beautiful wasteland: The Rise of Detroit as America's postindustrial frontier*. Minneapolis, MN: University of Minnesota Press.

Lefebvre, H. (2003). *The urban revolution*. Minneapolis, MN: University of Minnesota Press.

Leitner, H., & Miller, B. (2007). Scale and the limitations of ontological debate: A commentary on Marston, Jones and Woodward. *Transactions of the Institute of British Geographers, 32*(1), 116–125.

Mahmud, T. (2012). Debt and discipline. *American Quarterly, 64*(3), 469–494.

Marable, M. (1999). *How capitalism underdeveloped black America: Problems in race, political economy, and society*. Cambridge, MA: South End Press.

Marable, M. (2007). *Race, reform, and rebellion: The second reconstruction and beyond in black America, 1945–2006* (3rd ed.). Jackson, MS: University Press of Mississippi.

Marston, S. A. (2000). The social construction of scale. *Progress in Human Geography, 24*(2), 219–242.

Marston, S. A., Jones, J. P., & Woodward, K. (2005). Human geography without scale. *Transactions of the Institute of British Geographers, 30*(4), 416–432.

Marx, K. (1992). *Capital: Volume 1: A critique of political economy*. (E. Mandel, Ed., B. Fowkes, Trans.) (Reprint edition). London; New York, NY: Penguin Classics.

Matalin, M. (2012, September 18). More Romney video released: *The Situation Room*. CNN. Accessed February 1, 2019 from http://transcripts.cnn.com/TRANSCRIPTS/1209/18/sitroom.01.html

Melamed, J. (2011). *Represent and destroy: Rationalizing violence in the new racial capitalism*. Minneapolis, MN: University Of Minnesota Press.

Mitchell, D. (1996). *Lie of the land*. Minneapolis, MN: University of Minnesota Press.

Mitchell, D. (2003). *The right to the city: Social justice and the fight for public space*. New York, NY: Guilford Press.

Newsom, S. W. B. (2006). Pioneers in infection control: John Snow, Henry Whitehead, the Broad Street pump, and the beginnings of geographical epidemiology. *The Journal of Hospital Infection*, 64(3), 210–216.

Nietzsche, F. (2006). *On the genealogy of morality*. Cambridge, UK: Cambridge University Press.

Nussbaum, M. (2003). Capabilities as fundamental entitlements: Sen and social justice. *Feminist Economics*, 9(2–3), 33–59.

Patterson, O. (1982). *Slavery and social death: A comparative study*. Cambridge, MA: Harvard University Press.

Rep. Pscholka. Act No. 4, Pub. L. No. Enrolled House Bill No. 4214 (2011). Accessed November, 18, 2018 from https://www.legislature.mi.gov/documents/2011-2012/publi-cact/htm/2011-PA-0004.htm

Roediger, D. (2007). *The wages of whiteness: Race and the making of the American working class*. New York, NY: Verso.

Rosati, C. (2012). Media and the democratisation of privation: Towards new communicative geographies of anti-poverty. In S. R. Melkote (Ed.), *Development communication in directed social change: A reappraisal of theories & approaches*. Singapore: Asian Media Information and Communication Centre.

Rosati, C. (2018). *Development as freedom* after Flint: A geographical approach to capabilities and antipoverty communication. *Journal of Multicultural Discourses*, 13(2), 139–159.

Roy, A. (2010). *Poverty Capital: Microfinance and the Making of Development* (1 edition). New York: Routledge.

Schoenberger, E., & Walker, R. A. (2017). Beyond exchange and agglomeration: Resource flows and city environments as wellsprings of urban growth. *Journal of Economic Geography*, 17(5), 935–958.

Sen, A. (2000). *Development as freedom*. New York, NY: Anchor.

Smith, N. (1992). Contours of a spatialized politics: Homeless vehicles and the production of geographical scale. *Social Text*, 33, 54–81.

Turbeville, W. (2013). *The Detroit bankruptcy*. New York, NY: Demos.

We the People of Detroit. (n.d.). Mapping the water crisis. *www.WethePeopleofDetroit.com*. Accessed November 18, 2018 from http://wethepeopleofdetroit.com/communityresearch/water/#pricing

Wilderson III, F. (2005). Gramsci's black Marx: Whither the slave in civil society? *We Write*, 2(1), 1–17.

· 4 ·

BART, CAIRO, & SPACES OF EXCEPTION

Unruly spaces can have significant influence on the physical environment of cities or other sites in contemporary society. In many cases, unruliness can alter communicative qualities of cities, or the capabilities for hope or dignity described by Sen (2000). Such was demonstrated in the previous chapter, as a hidden geography in Flint deteriorated because of austerity measures that emerged from historical resentment, which created horrible problems for multiple communities in the region. What is worse, the unruliness of this hidden geography became the rationale for the introduction of additional austerity measures, which only compounded the problems facing residents. However, these physical issues are not the only problems that arise from unruliness and austerity. Oftentimes, austerity entails the enactment of control over communication processes—or communication qualities—within a city. In many ways, the control enacted by authority figures cuts citizens off from important communicative qualities described by Gumpert and Drucker (2008), and also further erodes perceptions about those physical sites that have been deemed to be unruly. Essentially, policies or actions to control communication in and around unruly sites impact the physical environment (as in Chapter 3), as well as the communication technologies necessary for democracy and construction of cityscape.

D'Arcus (2003) and Ahmed (2012) illustrate such austerity measures through their additional insight concerning the concept of militant particularism described in Part I. In their research projects, they note endeavors or processes that block the emergence of militant particularism and maintain the status quo. That is to say, government agencies or ideologies often keep militant actions contained to one site, so that they do not spread to other regions. D'Arcus provided valuable insight about this in his historical research concerning the Wounded Knee occupation by Native American activists in 1973. He noted that the Federal Anti-Riot Act of 1968 targeted people who used public spaces (e.g., highways) or facilities (e.g., mail, television, radio) to cause "public disturbances." By keeping activists away from public spaces and sites where mediated images of their militant actions could be recorded, the US government successfully kept actions like the Wounded Knee occupation from being abstracted to a large-scale global level and utilized in other places around the nation. In addition, Ahmed examined the anti-Enron protests in India in the early 1990s. In that case, Ahmed notes that "scale-jumping" through abstraction was complicated by ideologies and practices at the national and global levels. The neoliberal logic of corporate globalization that empowered companies like Enron permeated many sectors of state and national governments in India, as well as governments abroad and trade organizations around the world. As localized protests about economic concerns were enacted in communities threatened by Enron, they became abstracted to larger levels. However, the neoliberal elites in different parts of India and the world interpreted this abstract vision in different ways, so that the focus shifted from poverty to environmentalism and ethnicity. Essentially, elite logics and meanings shifted the focus of the rigid abstract vision in ways that often served the interests of those elites, and not the local community who started the protests.

In this way, then, D'Arcus and Ahmed demonstrate that efforts to change or resist the neoliberal policies responsible for many of the unruly spaces in contemporary society are typically doomed to fail. The following chapter illustrates two cases in which governmental power is used not only stop political dissent, speech, and protest, but give rise to what Bonnett (2014) describes as unruly spaces of exception. In these cases, the actions taken by authorities stood as a response to citizens protesting and resisting austerity measures, which had created a perceived crisis of unruliness for authorities in Cairo and the San Francisco Bay Area in the United States. In both cases, the authorities, creating more unruliness, used the rationale of emergency to shut down telecommunications and contract the ability of protesters to communicate.

Neoliberalism & Unruliness

Violence and resentment currently ooze from the pores of aging millennial globalist utopias and flat-world dreams. Exception and emergency now electrify the principles of constitutional democracy and republicanism. Even in the US, threats to journalists, suppression of free speech, and policing political dissidents seem now increasingly commonplace (in the White House alone). Over the last forty years, the economic practices of neoliberalism and equating the protection of private property rights with democracy and freedom have yielded a sordid paradox: while private property was meant to bring greater freedom (against tyranny) to the world, its protection has made way for greater authoritarianism and autocracy. While neoliberalist capitalism has destroyed many of the previous boundaries around national economies and cultures, those practices and processes have also built (and been built on) the groundwork for new forms of violence and discipline. According to Harvey (2007):

> Neoliberalism is in the first instance a theory of political economic practices that proposes that human well-being can best be advanced by liberating individual entrepreneurial freedoms and skills within an institutional framework characterized by strong private property rights, free markets, and free trade. The role of the state is to create and preserve an institutional framework appropriate to such practices. The state has to guarantee, for example, the quality and integrity of money. It must also set up those military, defense, police, and legal structures and functions required to secure private property rights and to guarantee, by force if need be, the proper functioning of markets. Furthermore, if markets do not exist (in areas such as land, water, education, health care, social security, or environmental pollution) then they must be created, by state action if necessary. But beyond these tasks the state should not venture. (p. 2)

Of course, one cannot speak of neoliberalism without reference to "belt-tightening" against the excesses of Keynesian or Socialist public goods.

Since the 1970s, privatization—by consent or by coup d'état—has likewise been used to resist threats of communism and resource nationalization, continually haunting the interdependencies between the global north and post-colonial world (Mitchell & Rosati, 2006). Yet, in the last two decades, globalist "privatization" amid economic growth has given way to nationalist austerity within economic crisis. With this austerity, the utopian ideologies of the free market have been crushed when put to the test under growing inequality, debt, war, and refugee crises. In response, globalism has turned to nationalist retrenchment, white supremacism, and a commitment to the auto-cratic powers of property holders. As Marx (1992) commented of a previous political-economic transition: "By declaring the people his private property, the king merely proclaims that the private owner is king" (p. 257). Under the utopia of a global village, neoliberalism has resurrected an insurgent world-philosophy of kings and paupers, of legitimate anti-democracy.

To be "unruly" in this political-economic context is to resist the autocracy of private property rights and make alternative claims to democracy in public spaces. But, in order to protect the prevailing public produced by neoliberal urban policy, executive authority often imposes conditions of exception against this unruliness. In the following pages, we explore the policing of contempo-rary protest through struggles to control telecommunications infrastructure. We look at the cases of Cairo, Egypt and the San Francisco Bay Area, USA to understand the interconnectedness of governmental force to preserve order in those places based in property rights and exception or emergency. We explore how these threats were constructed as worthy of exceptional action and a policy of preemption. Ultimately, we conclude by examining the aftermaths of these struggles and what they show us about potential connection between communication infrastructure, spaces of exception, and the right to the city.

Let's begin with a dramatic coincidence. On Thursday, January 28th, 2011—at the height of the "Arab Spring"—Egyptian telecommunications shut down just after midnight, causing data traffic in and out of the coun-try to drop by ninety percent. The sudden silence left the rest of the world dumbfounded, wondering what had become of communication technologies that had once appeared so robust and so liberating. One of Egypt's largest cell-phone providers (28 million subscribers), London-based Vodafone, reported from its website that mobile providers operating in select areas in Egypt were instructed to suspend services (Richtel, 2011). This is perhaps one of the most memorable events of the celebrated Arab Spring rebellions in Egypt, when the besieged dictatorship attempted to shut down the Internet and mobile phones in order to contain the expressions of outrage and discontentment unfold-ing in Tahrir Square and beyond. The former dictatorial regime was being overrun by a seemingly contagious rebellion. The ability to communicate an imagination of rebellion, in this case, occurred over physical infrastructures in and across the urbanized landscape. While in one instance, the communication of dissent appears virtual, its urban materiality is revealed in the power to control the infrastructure of that communication. Collective imagination of rebellion and the ability to effectively communicate such imaginings is revealed as a struggle over urban infrastructure and spaces of the city. For the US supported autocrat, Hosni Mubarak, this rebellion was a palpable emergency, which demanded an exceptional, autocratic response. In the US, the popular press was elated by the proof that social media could bring freedom to the oppressed, recoiled at the shutdown of communications, and condemned Mubarak for such actions as an exemplar of his repressive regime.

Yet, a similar scenario, relatively less marked by condemnation in popular news media, played itself out later that year in Oakland, California. As protesters of the shooting death of an African American passenger, 22-year-old Oscar Grant, by Bay Area Regional Transit (BART) police attempted to gather in Oakland, they found that cellular phone service underground was shutoff in an effort to disrupt the protest via the use of mobile communications. The digital rights group Electronic Frontier Foundation exclaimed on their website that "BART officials are showing themselves to be of a mind with the former president of Egypt, Hosni Mubarak" (Galperin, 2011, para. 5). At issue, as many commenters observed, was what appeared to be a broad international set of struggles over the necessary infrastructure for political dissent, taking place in liberal capitalist democracies and capitalist autocracies alike.

As we shall see, austerity, a policy practice synonymous with neoliberalism and Shock Therapy Economics (see Harvey, 2007; Klein, 2007; Mitchell & Rosati, 2006) is the handmaiden of emergency and legal exception. In the contemporary context, austerity must therefore also refer to the restriction of protest and non-property-based claims to democracy. We approach this type of political austerity through the shifting geographical history of free speech law and its intersection with new technologies. This will allow us to frame an infrastructural approach to free speech, the legal struggle over public safety, and exceptional governmental responses to public threats.

Oakland & Cairo

The San Francisco Bay Area and Cairo have very different histories. The first emerged as a finance, shipping-transportation, and manufacturing power out of a mid–19th century gold rush, and more recently as a hub of the computer and telecommunications industry. The other is an ancient city; modernized after Ottoman control, and later a protectorate of the British Empire in the early 20th Century, which finally became a hub of Arab and North African manufacturing and telecommunications in the 1990s. Yet, there are some compelling commonalities as well. In the mid–20th century, Egypt organized significant resistance to British-French-US and Soviet influence through the Non-Aligned Movement and "third world" nationalism, nationalizing the Suez Canal in 1956. In the Bay Area, activists that focused on free speech, developing nations, black and brown power were part of a dissident anti-imperialist, anti-white supremacist force within the new social movement networks of the mid–20th century. By the 1990s, both cities expanded as hubs of telecommunications and high-tech infrastructure. In 2011, both Cairo and Oakland became the centers of revolt, which became the staging ground for struggles over the nature of democratic expression and state security for the coming future.

In January, 2011, as 50,000 occupied Tahrir Square in Cairo's center, the city became a new flashpoint for the transnational "Arab Spring" uprisings that initiated in late–2010. This uprising was an activist endeavor against the autocratic regimes of Tunisia, Egypt, and Syria. These protests were also against the imposed austerity of international neoliberalism more broadly, which had culminated in the world financial crisis, and degraded physical environments and social capabilities of cities like Flint described in Chapter 3. Autocracy, corruption, poverty, youth unemployment, and economic crisis formed the bases of the popular uprisings spreading across the Arab world. This North African and Middle Eastern insurrection was greeted empathetically in the Bay Area, coping with overwhelming costs of living, crippling student debt, aggressive gentrification by the technology industry, and insufferable police violence.

In the Bay Area, the massive urban-tech machine had produced a region dedicated to growth but had made life for many untenable, bringing evictions and gentrification that left swaths of residents unwelcome in their own town. As Rushkoff (2017) describes, the Bay Area was caught up in a "winner-takes-all race for dominance" in which the various tech behemoths must "grow or die" (pp. 3–4). Protests beginning in early July 2011 in downtown San Francisco, set the stage for some of the most violent clashes of the efforts to "Occupy Oakland."

We see both Cairo and Oakland as spaces of exception; at least, during the timeframes that include public dissent. In many ways, exception is a potentiality for any place. This chapter looks at these two cities as test cases of sorts for new implementations of exception as part of the dominant project of neoliberalism, particularly in policing protest and public dissent. According to Bonnett (2014), spaces of exception are sites wherein typical rules established by the government or other authority figures are deferredxor dissolved. One such example provided by Bonnett to illustrate these unruly spaces was Camp Zeist, a Dutch military facility that was made into a Scottish territory in 1999, so that it could be used for the trial of two men accused of bombing Pan Am Flight 103 over Lockerbie, Scotland. The UN Security Council had demanded that the accused bombers stand trial in the country within which the terrorist attack had been carried out, but the Libyan government feared that the two men would not get a fair trial in the United Kingdom. As a compromise, the UK and Scotland agreed to take possession of the small military facility in the neutral Netherlands, and the Libyan government would send the two accused men to face trial. For three years, the normal rules of Camp Zeist were suspended, and Scottish rules and laws took precedent. In other cases, spaces of exception arise from social changes or activism that largely lead to the suspension or disregard of rules or laws. One such example was the stretches of Colombia controlled by the Fuerzas Armadas Revolucionarias de Colombia (FARC). The revolutionary FARC developed in the rural areas of Colombia from the struggles for land reform and anti-neoimperialism, and largely ignored the rules and laws concerning land-rites established by the government in the 1960s. In response, the US supported right-wing paramilitaries—funded by drug trafficking, Coca Cola, and other corporations—reveal how human rights violations and armed struggle are often part of the blurry boundaries between political norms and exception in the maintenance of "open" markets and protecting private property.

For our purposes here, exception is most usually invoked to engage an emergency that represents an existential threat to the prevailing legal order (Agamben, 2005). Indeed, exception is often invoked in order to control unruliness that authorities deem to be growing from certain governmental struggles or contradictions. In most cases, rules and norms of republican order and legislative democracy are suspended to afford unilateral executive power in order to cope with the demands of the emergency. Democracy is suspended, in order to save it (Agamben, 2005). Often even for an autocratic regime, the pretense of legal legitimacy still exists in ongoing emergency declarations. And, this does not mean, as Mubarak illustrates, that autocrats do not face emergency. What strikes us, as well as civil liberties activists in 2011, is the parallel reasons for protest and the homology of government responses between both the democratic and autocratic contexts.

The cities of Cairo and Oakland serve as spaces of exception on two fronts. In the first case, the state suspends norms of human rights and governmental process to protect the prevailing political-economic conditions and respond to public protest as an emergency: namely, shutting down telecommunications to preempt and undermine protest. In the second case, the political economic status quo, neoliberal austerity, poverty, corruption, and alienation—which the state protects against popular rebellion—represents an ongoing emergency to the people, against which protest and insurrection represent an appropriate if not necessary response.

The relatively elegant act of shutting down telecommunications revealed a crucial aspect of a co-evolving set of strategies for policing protest and dissent in the US and abroad through two constitutive processes: first, through violent responses because of the threat that protest purportedly poses to the public, and second, by controlling exposure and the circulation of knowledge and information about that protest because of the danger that the information itself may pose. In the Bay Area, BART officials conveyed something disturbing to First Amendment advocates—they claimed that the protests posed a public danger and needed to be preempted with an exceptional, and in this case, illegal action. Excellent and important work has been done on the geographies of free speech (e.g., Carpentier, 2008; Mitchell, 2016; Mitchell & Staeheli, 2005). But, Mitchell (2016) and others, focusing on the legal canon of free speech and public forum precedent, often miss telecommunications policy as a legal mechanism for producing public spaces. Common carrier rules in telephony, which are stipulated in "Title II" of the US Telecommunications Act of 1934, require among other things that the utility serve the general public without discrimination. In the case of BART's violation of telecommunications law we see one key to what we might call a kind of infrastructural approach to public space and free speech.

Yet, within this legal rationale, an infrastructural approach also demands more attention to the shape and biases (to use Harold Innis's term) of the built environment itself. The ongoing struggle over Internet Service Providers' common carrier status (i.e. "net neutrality") is one side of this infrastructural dimension of the geographies of political speech (e.g. a free and open Internet). But it is only so because of the effects the Internet's built structure have in amplifying, intensifying, and extending communication within and between cities, regions, and nations. Telecommunications law in general—and the growing debates about access to the marketplace of ideas via the Internet—implicitly engage both the material/infrastructural and ideological dimensions of public communication. As such, this increasingly provides an additional tool for critical legal geographers and public space advocates against the growing limitations of public protest, free speech, and political dissent in the US and Europe.

Austerity, Dissent & Geographies of Exception

Geographies of protest and dissent have become increasingly austere over the last thirty years. In neoliberal autocracies, like China and Egypt, dissidents are imprisoned, media and journalists are censored, and policing public outrage is militarized with growing intensity. Likewise, it is no surprise, and well documented, that public spaces for free speech and political demonstration in the US have been gradually eroded by legal precedent over the last century. It is just as well-documented that the development of neoliberal urbanism has also led to the privatization of previously public spaces and to the substitution of private or quasi-private spaces (like shopping malls and subway stations) for fully public ones, like the famed People's Park (Mitchell, 1995, 2003). Mitchell and Staeheli (2005) explain that legal precedent "over the past 60 years has constructed a particular landscape of dissent in the United States." They continue:

> While the landscape is highly developed in the US, it is not unique to it. Nor are the tools that have been used to construct it, including laws and bureaucratic rules, legal cases and changing police practices. The tools are used not to silence dissent outright, but rather to regulate it in such a way that dissent can be fully incorporated into, and become part of, the liberal democratic state. (p. 797)

This is, of course, different in many ways from a more autocratic government. But, the effects of the development of public speech and protest regulation in the US have been analogous, they restrain speech and especially protest by limiting its geography, where it takes place, and therefore the potential for public disruption. Mitchell and Staeheli explain that particularly, "the protest permit system in America has evolved as a means to actively shape, if not directly control, political dissent" (p. 797). Financial austerity imposes the will of the market against public demands for better quality of life. We see more than a simple coincidence between the convergence of financial and political austerity. Both represent an autocratic policing of public life and see discontent with that condition as an emergency. Spaces of exception betray the anti-democracy of neoliberal austerity and respond in kind to public dissent.

Overall, the arguments about geographies of protest and public political dissent tend to focus primarily on First Amendment issues, the laws regulating behavior in public, and the rights of property owners. But, there is another compelling angle for the struggle for less limited speech and protest, which has to do with looking not just at the surfaces of public and private spaces but also the telecommunications infrastructures that also compose them. There is a separate set of laws that regulate the use of telecommunications infrastructure, which, as we shall see, in some important ways entail stronger language to prevent censorship and preemptive silencing of public speech. In the context of contemporary protest, it is impossible to separate electronic media from public space, not just in the publicity of protest but its coordination and actualization as well. As built environments have become more mediated by social networks, mobile communications, and mapping applications (to name a few), ensuring a right to the infrastructure that enables protest is inseparable from the actual spatial practice of political dissent. The rules on access to those infrastructures have a related but different history from laws that regulate protest and speech in public.

Disrupting Dissent in Oakland, CA

The important foundation of the illegal shutdown of telephone systems by BART starts with the Communications Act of 1934. In that legislation, protections exist that prevent any interference with access to Commercial Mobile Radio Service (CMRS). One such protection entails the maintenance of 911 services, especially in the event of an emergency. The government deemed that such services should be maintained at all time, as telecommunications infrastructures serve as a public space responsive to public needs; any interference risks harm to the public. While a fortuitous loophole for protesters, the protection extends beyond simply ensuring access to emergency service. In addition, constitutional due process protections are also fortified in the rules governing public utilities. Due process protections are crucial to spaces of emergency and the exercise of exceptional police powers, as they are a (however small) bulwark against the tendency towards preemptive policing in protest and public demonstrations. Legal precedent is relatively firm in its fortification of this protection as it relates to the use of the telephone (Feld, 2011). In *Pike v. Southern Bell* (June 23, 1955), the Commissioner of Public Safety of Birmingham, Alabama, Eugene "Bull" Conor, tried to order the telephone company to disconnect the phone line of a suspected criminal, which the police thought was being used to facilitate a crime. The crimes, the Supreme Court of Alabama pronounced, were that he "operated a negro beer joint" and operated a lottery. As the decision continued:

> The "pendency" of a criminal case cannot be used as a predicate for punitive action under the American system. The present tendency and drift towards the Police State gives all free Americans pause. The unconstitutional and extra-judicial enlargement of coercive governmental power is a frightening and cancerous growth on our body politic. Once we assumed as axiomatic that a citizen was presumed innocent until proved guilty. The tendency of governments to shift the burden of proof to citizens to prove their innocence is indefensible and intolerable.[1]

The *People v. Brophy* (1992) takes this protection even further, denying any preemptive or "preventative" action in the disconnection of a member of the public from the telephone simply on allegation alone, even if it was by Earl Warren, California's Attorney General at the time. *Brophy* (1992) expounds:

> Public utilities and common carriers are not the censors of public or private morals, nor are they authorized or required to investigate or regulate the public or private conduct of those who seek service at their hands .... The telephone company has no more right to refuse its facilities to persons because of a belief that such persons will use such service to transmit information that may enable recipients thereof to violate the law than a railroad company would have to refuse to carry persons on its trains because those in charge of the train believed that the purpose of the persons so transported in going to a certain point was to commit an offense ...[2]

Indeed, not only did the office of Attorney General act illegally based on these preemptive disconnection prohibitions, but his office did not even have the police powers to carry out such an action. That authority was only granted to the California Public Utilities Commission (Feld, 2011). As the petition to the FCC by the activist group Public Knowledge for BART's illegal shutdown explains:

> When such denial occurs, the telephone company and the supposed authority order-ing the shutdown act in breach of the statutorily imposed duty to provide service and despite common carriage obligations. These principles are underpinned today by the common carrier obligations of Sections 201, 202, and 214 [of the Communications Act]. (Feld, 2011, p.10)

These protections, which do not help in the limiting of activities in public space, do present a paradoxical freedom to plan demonstrations, which cannot be censored by police, particularly not on a preemptive basis. But to understand this move towards emergency exceptions to the law to prevent protest, we have to consider the context within which "emergency" becomes meaningful to those who wield police powers.

"BART's top priority is to ensure the safety of its passengers," begins the August 20, 2011 letter to customers of the rail service. The letter continues:

> Prior to a planned protest on August 11, 2011, BART obtained credible information that led us to conclude that the safety of the BART system would be compromised. Out of an overriding concern for our passengers' safety, BART made the decision to temporarily interrupt cell phone service on portions of its system. We are aware that the interruption had the effect of temporarily preventing cellular communications for many BART passengers and their families; and we regret any inconvenience caused by the interruption. We want to take this opportunity to share some of the information that led to this decision.[3]

The letter suggests—at the height of public frustrations with the irrationality of the global economy—that a preeminent concern for public safety was threats to shopping, real estate growth, and general gentrification in the Bay Area. This was particularly true as the BART police had shot and killed Charles Hill in the San Francisco Civic Center Station roughly a month prior. Identified as a 45-year old "transient," Hill was reportedly "drunk and wearing a tie-dyed T-shirt and military-style fatigue pants."[4] He reportedly pulled a knife and was shot on the platform. A protest, in honor of Hill was planned for July 11, 2011. BART explains:

> On July 11, a group gathered at the BART Civic Center Station in San Francisco to protest the fact that, on July 3, a BART Police Officer shot and killed Charles Hill at that station. During that protest, one person climbed on top of a train and many other individuals blocked train doorways and held train doors open.

Even as BART explains the reasons for public protest in the Civic Center Station, they lay the groundwork for defining the July protest as illegal and dangerous. The public statement continues:

> During the course of the event, which occurred during the peak of rush hour, individuals used BART trains to move between stations, and caused the shutdown or partial shutdown of other stations. These actions violated the law by creating a serious threat to the safe operation of the BART system, disrupting the service of 96 BART

trains (approximately twothirds of the trains operating during the rush hour), causing the closing of stations, and putting at risk the safety of thousands of passengers and BART employees.

In this statement, BART presents the July protest as a public hazard, putting both passengers and employees at risk. This previous protest, not associated with a particular actor but as a generic practice, is held up as part of the rationale for exceptional action in August. A previous illegal protest became the justification for preemption of future protest.

The effectiveness of protest lies, of course, in activists' ability to disrupt business as usual in everyday life. In this sense, the geography of protest, as Mitchell and others have shown, is crucial to the practical effectiveness of First Amendment rights of free speech and protest. In the right location, activists can make contradictions experienced by one social group visible and felt by the broader public. But, the increasing control of acceptable protest locations, undermine the powers otherwise afforded by the First Amendment. BART explains:

> When trains are not able to move or pick up passengers, the platforms can quickly become overcrowded. This is very dangerous due to the increased possibility that people will fall from the platforms onto the trackway. The trackway is five feet below the platform edge and contains the electrified 3rd rail. Also, when one train stops, all trains behind it must stop. In some cases, trains must stop in tunnels, which delays the arrival of emergency medical help for passengers in need of assistance. Additionally, selfevacuation by passengers in underground tunnels is another potential dangerous outcome of interference with BART service.

BART's gambit was to allow the protest to be defanged or otherwise be treated as a threat to the public welfare.

Publicly, BART maintained its commitment to the First Amendment—they claimed that permissible protest space was allotted outside of the subway stations, not on the platforms—while they simultaneously gathered intelligence on the planned August 11 protest to determine how best to contain it:

> Early in the week of August 8, the BART Police Department received credible information that individuals were planning a surprise demonstration against BART police shootings at specific BART station platforms on August 11. On August 10, BART Police obtained further information regarding the individuals' plans for colorcoded teams to conduct lawless activity on the platforms. The additional information disclosed detailed organizational coordination among multiple "affinity groups" in addition to the organization that had sponsored the July 11 disruption. The August 10

intelligence revealed that the individuals would be giving and receiving instructions
to coordinate their activities via cell phone after their arrival on the train platforms
at more than one station.

BART's public explanation includes details of protesters' plans. They describe
how protesters were using cellphones strategically, as well as texting police
locations in order to calculate response times. This information from gathered "intelligence" on the planned protest "led BART to conclude that the
planned action constituted a serious and imminent threat to the safety of
BART passengers and personnel and the safe operation of the BART system,
at a level that could far exceed the protest of July 11." And, as a result of those
conclusions, BART explains that they "decided to interrupt cell phone service at targeted portions of its system for up to 4 hours, beginning at 4:00 p.m.,
the time that the individuals were scheduled to assemble. BART notified the
affected cellular service providers shortly before it implemented the temporary interruption. Service was turned back on at 7 p.m., earlier than planned,
when safety concerns abated." (BART.gov, 2011) This emergency disruption
and danger to business as usual prompted the police to use telecommunications infrastructure to undermine the ability to coordinate the location of
public protest. Such struggles over permissible public conduct, where and how
First Amendment rights will be actualized, are increasingly inseparable from
telecommunications infrastructures and rules governing them.

    This was not the first shooting by BART police. Two years prior, on New
Year's 2009, a BART officer pulled an unarmed 22-year-old black man, Oscar
Grant, off a train at Fruitvale Station, and in the process of his arrest shot and
killed him. These shootings by transit police and the increasing strong-arm
tactics of gentrification became part of the spark of a protracted battle for
the Bay Area by the Occupy Wall Street groups, and in turn became the impetus of further tactics of preemption and surveillance. We will discuss these
issues further in this chapter's conclusion. In the meantime, we turn to Tahrir
Square, Cairo to see a parallel space of exception.

Disrupting Dissent in Cairo

In Egypt, exception was the norm for over 50 years. Starting in 1967 with
the Arab-Israeli War, emergency was lifted briefly in 1980 and then re-im-
posed after the assassination of President Sadat in October of 1981 (Zwitter
2013). Despite its long and seemingly permanent state of emergency, Egypt's
disruption of political dissent represents something of a disturbing homology

with BART's in 2011. While augmenting Internet service has become, in fact, relatively common by governments facing political protests, the almost complete shutdown in Egypt was reported as "unprecedented," due in part to the online connectivity of its citizens. The unprecedented nature of this closure is based on two fundamentally urban scenarios described by Glanz and Markoff (2011). The first is that, while there have been heavy telecommunications infrastructure investments in Egypt over the years, fiberoptic pipelines out of the country are actually quite few. One of the urban hubs through which this shutdown was managed was a "telco-hotel" (infrastructural hub) in Cairo at 26 Ramses St., less than three miles from Tahrir Square where most of the protests were concentrated. This building is a network exchange for the fiber optic links of the five predominant communication corporations. The state-owned company Telecom Egypt possesses most of the nation's fiber optic infrastructure and leases lines to service providers. In this way, the company is able to leverage the infrastructure as a form of urbanized political control. The second scenario described by Glanz and Markoff has to do with the relationship between Egypt's infrastructure and the location of information on which the nation's communication relies. Much of the country's email information resides in data centers in the US, owned privately by Google and other international media companies. But this made little difference, as Glanz and Markoff (2011) maintain that the ability to communicate with domain name servers housed internationally was confounded. As Wael Amin, a Cairo-based software development company president and activist explains: "In Egypt the actual physical and logical connections to the rest of the world are few, and they are licensed by the government and they are tightly controlled" (Glanz & Markoff, 2011). It was also this tight infrastructural control that allowed the Mubarak regime to hack mobile phone provider networks and send pro-government texts that read: "Egypt's youth. Beware rumors and listen to the voice of reason. Egypt is above all so preserve it" (Ackerman, 2011).

In several ways, then, the scale of protest and political dissent was augmented or limited. In a different context, Boykoff (2007) describes how the actions of governments to limit the expansion and scaling-up of social movements and political dissent create a kind of "spatial compression." Something similar can be seen here in the physical limiting of the means of communication. In a similar sense, spatial compression can be used to describe what geographer Mitchell has shown famously in the development of free-speech zones, bubble laws in public space, homeless laws, and so forth, which have led to a shrinking of spaces where public engagement is possible. For the most part, these changes in public spaces have helped neoliberal elites to block the spread of militant actions and rebellion outward from local communities, which has been described by D'Arcus (2003) and Ahmed (2012). In many ways, media have also stepped in to supplement the contraction of public space in the form of public forums, Youtube, Facebook, other modes of public exchange outside of traditional public spaces, which have become more securitized, privatized, and restricted to the benefit of private property interests. While Mitchell suggests that electronic media can play a role in political organizing and urban democratic struggle, he remains skeptical about the effectiveness of those virtual spaces in the struggles for justice in the city. Indeed, Mitchell correctly comments that "virtual protest is no protest at all" and that "space is *made* public … through its taking" (2003, p.245). But, in the context of Egypt and the Bay Area, this argument neglects a set of connected politics around infrastructure and communication technologies. Rather, taking public space—what Mitchell refers to as "going *again* to Hyde Park"—not simply relies more and more on the infrastructures of and images circulated telecommunications but also involves taking those spaces as well (see Castells 2015). Mitchell's point, of course, is made in a political context that seems to forcefully favor Twitter, Facebook, Instagram, 8chan, and so on over Tahrir Square (or Hyde Park). But, Egypt and the Bay Area—without mentioning the growing global nationalisms—show us that communication technologies are no less part of that drama. It is not an either/or politics—public space is suffused with electronic communications and infrastructures which are also subject to exception, emergency powers, and spatial control.

In the opposite direction, Castells's assertion that "[t]here is no question that the original spaces of resistance were formed on the Internet" (2015, p.57) is also inadequate, since mobile media augmented a social struggle against conditions and terms that were old and deep in Egypt. The uprisings of 2011 were not simple outrage at an oppressive government or, worse, some sort of spontaneous liberation induced by mobile media. The notion that Egypt was either a "twitter revolution" or a simple uprising against an evil dictatorship is betrayed by an even closer look at the recent history of protest and economic struggles there. Labor strikes abounded in Egypt from the mid–1980s and early–1990s; from twenty-five to eighty labor actions per year (Beinin, 2009). This number increased during the late–1990s and 2000s to an average of one hundred eighteen per year. Workers' collective actions only further accelerated after 2004 and the appointment of Nazif as Mubarak's

Prime Minister, more than doubling to two hundred sixty-five in that year alone. As Beinin (2009) reveals:

> In defiance of scholarly work proclaiming the death of class as an analytical category, from 1998 to 2008 some 2 million Egyptian workers participated in 2,623 factory occupations, strikes, demonstrations, or other collective actions. At the time of writing, the movement is maintaining its momentum: in the first five months of 2009, there were well over 200 collective actions across the country. This constitutes the largest and most sustained social movement in Egypt since the campaign to oust the British occupiers following the end of World War II. (p. 449)

In this regard, the technological strategies that the world witnessed in 2011 by both protesters and the state are simply that: strategies utilized in existing circumstances and within existing struggles. And as such, the spaces of (counter) exception created by the democratic rebellions against the permanent state of emergency, in the process, drew telecommunications technologies into the struggle for justice in the city.

The Egyptian revolution illuminated the character of Mubarak's state of exception and the nature of its repressive methods. The regime was no abstract autocracy and the revolution did not demand "democratization" in the abstract. Instead, the rebellion was a response to the conditions of working-class life in Egypt, brought by long changes to Egypt's relationship within the world capitalist economy since, perhaps, Sadat's "Open Door" policy to foreign capital in 1974 (Beinin, 2009). In 2004, Nazif's job was to extend the open doors of Egypt's economy. Or, rather, to increase its responsiveness to demands put in place in 1991 by "Economic Reform and Structural Adjustment Program" agreements with the IMF and World Bank. These demands in 1991, as they did elsewhere in the world, entailed among other measures the privatization of elements of the public sector. This led to cuts in employment and to the erosion of gains in the quality of life achieved after the 1952 Egyptian Revolution (against British economic and political occupation) and during the period of Arab Socialism under Nasser (Beinin, 2009).

On one hand, what Egypt can reveal to us is that media politics are part and parcel of the broader globally connected struggles of working people over the quality of their lives, the determination of their time, and the priorities that the technologies of social production will serve. But, on the other hand, we must see how the infrastructures of communication—including physical public spaces like Tahrir Square—form the basis for articulating a (counter) exceptional space, imagining life beyond the autocratic power of capital and private property that its state of emergency both served and reproduced. In Egypt, this power, which Mubarak enacted and responded to, has been primarily expressed in the form of pressure for economic growth, financial accountability, and the expansion of global capital. Mubarak demonstrated crassly what Marx (1992) called the "absolute universal law of capitalist accumulation" (p. 794), how the accumulation of wealth in one place must always be the accumulation of deprivation and poverty in another. For Egypt, much of its contemporary turmoil comes from the contradictions of transnational capitalism (if not from one regime of accumulation, then from another). Not goods themselves but their relationship to the expansion of capital, to finance, GDP, balances of payments, and access to foreign currency, were and continue to be central determinants of the conditions of economic and political life in Egypt. Mitchell's (1999) work on this is worth quoting at length:

> Neo-liberalism was supposed to open Egypt to trade with the global market. In fact it did the opposite. The country's openness index, which measures the value of exports and imports of goods and non-factor services as a proportion of GDP, collapsed from 88 per cent in 1985 to 47 per cent in 1996/97. In the same period, its share of world exports also dropped by more than half. The value of non-oil exports actually shrank in 1995/96, then shrank again in 1996/97, leaving the country dependent on petroleum products for 52 per cent of export income. By the end of 1998 the situation was still worse, as the collapse of world petroleum prices forced Egypt briefly to halt its oil exports. In 1998–99 the US government quietly set about rebuilding the OPEC oil cartel, holding secret negotiations with Iran, Saudi Arabia, and Venezuela in which it traded political concessions for promises to cut production. The negotiations were a success, doubling the price of oil again within six months. But this unpublicised state management of world trade was too slow to solve Egypt's new balance of payments crisis and repeated shortages of foreign currency. (p. 457)

As banking and finance collapsed in the 1990s, so did the conditions of life for the bulk of Egyptians. Economic growth and the accumulation of wealth, for some, inevitably and necessarily led to the deprivation of others. But, further, this represents a lack of control over conditions of one's life, which is characterized not by the simple appearance of higher or lower wages, but the absolute subservience of social life to the structural necessity of profit and the expansion of capital. Such was also business as usual for the Mubarak regime.

During the communications blackout, Egyptians used their phones as amateur photographers and videographers to document what was happening and form the basis of their own exception to business as usual. The mobile technologies available to protesters and dissidents present us with certain tools for creating spaces of democratic exception to autocratic state power. But, they can be used as repressive, violent, and autocratic tools of the state of emergency in the most obvious case because lack of democratic control over their means of production can enable politically motivated blackouts and propaganda. These infrastructures became a mechanism of Egypt's pred-atory neoliberal capitalism, the private production of wealth, and as such, increasing the costs of life and thus the increased obligation to participate in worker's subservience to the expansion of their own impoverishment. Indeed, the expansion of wealth within and without Egypt required a commensurate expansion of poverty, articulated politically as a state of emergency.

Technologies obviously yield neither salvation nor damnation by them-selves. As Williams (1975) reminds us in his groundbreaking study of tele-vision, we must always guard against forms of technological determinism, which are increasingly influential in popular and scholarly discourse: e.g., "the [Internet] has changed the world" (p. 1). What Williams presses us to do, even as materialists, is examine not simply or only technological limits or "causes" or even who controls those determining spaces and technologies. We must also understand and critically engage the conditions of necessity[5] that define and determine their social uses, even as they are themselves limited and pres-sured by the material characteristics of technologies and built environments (Harvey, 2008).[6]

Media are even more involved in the "remaking of ourselves" than ever, and this takes place in inescapably urban ways (Harvey, 2008, p. 23). The notion of "the city" here is complicated. It tends to invoke simply tall build-ings and incorporated municipal boundaries. However, as French sociologist, Lefebvre reminds us that urban processes extend far beyond these limits. Harvey explains: "The right to the city had to mean the right to command the whole urban process, which was increasingly dominating the countryside through phenomena ranging from agribusiness to second homes and rural tourism" (p. 28). Media are fundamental elements of this urban process. Hardt and Negri (2011) describe the ways that media are part of the extension of what they call the metropolis, across the whole of the globe: "Today, however, the circuits of communication and social cooperation are becoming general-ized across the planet. Rural life is no longer characterized by isolation and incommunicability. There are, of course, different intensities of the common, but the lines of division have increasingly less relation to urban or rural envi-ronments" (p. 253). As part of the urban process, media function not just in the administration of nature, or as tools for resource managers and agricultural scientists, but they function in a crucial additional way. Media are part of the administration of human nature, of our own scientific study and management, and not for altruistic benevolence but for the survival of capitalism or the survival of a system of dispossession and exploitation. Following Mitchell's contention about *taking* space, any concern for justice in the city must in some crucial sense revolve around claiming a "right" to media, to the extensive and intensive deployment of technologies that transmit our voices and our imaginations.[7] Such claims to the city, to the urban process and its infrastructure, resist the spatial compression of democratic movements as we can see so clearly in the case of Egypt.

Not only did Egyptians use their phone cameras in the revolutionary struggle. There were also different mobilizations of other telecommunications networks to circumvent the Internet blackout. Landline telephone networks, for instance, allowed activists to reach out to the rest of the world. Through these lines, activists could reach "telephone numbers abroad that would automatically forward the messages to computer networks provided by volunteers, such as those of TOR (The Onion Router network)" (Castells 2015, p.65). In turn, these messages could be sent back to Egypt in a number of different ways, like accessing Internet proxies, using access points donated by French companies, or speak-to-tweet programs designed by Google and Twitter engineers that transferred messages left on a landline-based answering machine into tweets (Castells 2015). Likewise, Castells describes "[a]n international hacker organization, Telecomix, [that] developed a program that automatically retrieved messages by phone from Egypt and forwarded them to every fax machine in the country" (2015, p65). In this tactic, universities served as hubs that would then distribute messages to activist occupations. To *keep* Tahrir Square, Peter Fein (the public face of Telecomix) explained in 2011 how the hackers provided activists with "[i]nstructions on how to set up a wireless mesh network . . . a way of creating a communication network, often using mobile phones' Bluetooth technology . . . [or] . . . two-way radio mics. One of the things we started working on is a how-to, a set of instructions, to build two-way radios, walkie-talkies . . . with hardware that people already have and the best thing we came up with is if you take a normal clock radio, smash it apart and cross a couple of wires and you can get them to communicate with each other. They have a two-kilometre range . . ." (Madlena 2011, n.p.). Taking Tahrir Square, "making it anew as a *public* space," also required making anew the infrastructures, technological tools, and built morphologies of communication networks, taking *them*, making them constituent elements of public space.

This expanded expression of the "right to the city" in response to Egypt's repressive exception returns us to the Mubarak regime's message to "Egypt's youth" that "Egypt is above all" and must be "preserved." In this hacking of telecommunications, the regime used its force to "request" that protesters subordinate their demand for civil and human rights to the preservation of a decades-old state of emergency. On one hand, this revealed the (gross) inadequacy of the suspension of law to protect the national community from chaos. On the other hand, it showed that the lawlessness and chaos of the autocracy, justified by emergency, were threatened by an opposing force: mass rejection, an exception to the exception. The democratic struggle in Egypt exposes that the order, which emergency was meant to maintain, was simply the autocratic control of force. The struggle exposes the illegitimacy of state violence at the heart of its very legal foundation with a call to imagine a new order that cannot yet be brought into existence.[8] The improvised transformations of communications technologies were crucial in that reversal.

Discussion

As August in the Bay Area eventually turned to October, the grievances of the previous months' protests made a longer-term claim to the Oakland landscape. Frank Ogawa Plaza, a park facing Oakland City Hall, became the stage on which the Occupy Wall Street activists would take their stand against neoliberal austerity as "Occupy Oakland." As part of their place-based politics, they renamed the park, "Oscar Grant Plaza" to draw the violence of the daily operations of neoliberalism into the open, front and center before the seat of city government. Centralizing this state sanctioned violence, Occupy Oakland held up a mirror to the conditions of exception imposed by neoliberal austerity, echoing the famous aphorism by Benjamin (2006):

> The tradition of the oppressed teaches us that the "state of emergency" in which we live is not the exception but the rule. We must attain to a conception of history that accords with this insight. Then we will clearly see that it is our task to bring about a real state of emergency. (p. 392)

Connecting themselves to the growing Occupy protests in other US towns and cities, and around the world, they were there to fight against police brutality, poverty, economic autocracy, and growing inequality in access to social resources.

Likewise, the social media hashtag #muBARTak drew together the homology of neoliberal conditions of violence, austerity, and exception in both dictatorships and democracies. This hashtag likewise drew into question the assumed difference between the two types of regimes. We should not be surprise by this convergence, as austerity presumes autocracy, emergency, and exception in the first instance. Finishing his aphorism, Benjamin seems to address #muBARTak directly, only sixty years earlier (and describing the rise of Fascism):

> The current amazement that the things we are experiencing are "still" possible in the twentieth century is *not* philosophical. This amazement is not the beginning of knowledge—unless it is the knowledge that the view of history which gives rise to it is untenable. (p. 392)

Occupy Oakland exposed in plain view what BART had insinuated: that the spatial struggles over neoliberal austerity revolve around claims to emergency. However, police powers and the philosophy of preemption had more in mind.

Occupy Oakland had posed massive disruptions to business as usual in the east bay, particularly in its general strike (November 2, 2011) and shutdown of the international shipping Port of Oakland (December 12, 2011). And, two years later, Oakland had begun developing a massive urban surveillance network dubbed, the Domain Awareness Center. Harkness (2016) quotes Brian Hofer, Oakland-based lawyer and chair of the "Oakland Privacy" citizen's coalition:

> The Domain Awareness Center, or the DAC, was a port infrastructure improvement project. [. . .] At some point the project expanded to become a joint project of the city and the port that would include facial-recognition software, automatic license-plate readers, ShotSpotter, 700 surveillance cameras throughout Oakland unified school district, Oakland housing authority, 300 TB of data storage, along with other benign things like vessel tracking, tsunami warning, earthquake warning. (quoted in Harkness, 2016)

The infrastructural politics of public space and political speech have, since the Mubarak and BART shutdowns progressed beyond the control of a kill switch. The Domain Awareness Center, though defeated after months of public protest, aimed to cement on the terrain a landscape of exception. "It had originally been sold as a port infrastructure project, then it was sold to us as this thing for first responders to help with efficiency," Hofer explained. "The problem being," he continued, "the only time our previous version of this, the Emergency Operations Center, had been activated was in response to protests. So we had some suspicions" (quoted in Harkness, 2016, para. 5). While the tactics of preemption attempted by the BART police ultimately proved an illegal exception, the same logic sought a permanent presence in this infrastructure dedicated to even more intense protection of the flows of property and growth. As such, it points toward a new set of spatial struggles against "unruliness," particularly as they are found in protest and political dissent in public. Further, as the "unruly" resist, reject, and withdraw from the norms of the prevailing legal order, they posit an exception of their own. They reveal a growing tension in the production of urban environments and imaginaries around the nature of political life, drawing into question the legitimacy of state violence. In doing so, they challenge the foundations of legitimate law.

Egypt's situation deteriorated after the 2011 rebellion amid what Allinson (2019) describes as "counter-revolutionary" forces preventing the nation's democratic rejection of its state of emergency.[9] Facebook has been the subject of scrutiny around this counter-revolution (e.g., *The Facebook Dilemma* 2018), as well as its algorithm is implicated in sewing public division and discrediting activists through the distribution of "fake news" as early as 2011. Targeting activists, journalists, and public dissent in Egypt continues and escalates as part of its commitment to fighting terrorism in the region. The NGO Human Rights Watch suggests, "President Abdel Fattah al-Sisi's government continues to oversee Egypt's worst human rights crisis in decades and has escalated the use of counterterrorism laws to prosecute peaceful dissidents" (Human Rights Watch, n.d.). And yet the US, Germany, and Russia provide massive funding ($2.268 billion by 2015) to the regime as part of a strategic balance of ends and means. The weapons and tools bought with that support were partly "directed against the local ISIS insurgency in the Sinai, but also locked the Sisi regime into EU plans to 'police the region and secure Europe's southern border', and into regional counter-revolutionary interventions with UAE and Saudi forces in Yemen and Libya" (Allinson 2019: 343). Further, in the US emergency and the outlawing of dissent have become key components to pathways around foundational democratic processes like legislative funding appropriations (e.g., Trump's emergency wall gambit, see Gregg & Sonne, 2019) and public protest (e.g., Louisiana's law making some oil and gas pipeline protests felonies, see Brown, 2019).

As these trends develop, the state of exception increasingly implies the lack of foundation, not just for those emergency suspensions of law but moreover for the prevailing legal norms from which they emerge. Michael Page, deputy Middle East and North Africa director at Human Rights Watch, describes a set of constitutional amendments finalized in Egyptian parliament which "aim to smother Egyptians' aspirations to live in dignity and under the rule of law" (Human Rights Watch, 2019). In this sense, one struggles to distinguish between constitution and exception, order and chaos, law and autocracy in the Egyptian case. The rotting of legitimate emergency—the reality of false emergency—in the impulse to autocracy has spread to the law in general. And every battle between the state of exception and those who counterpose a "true exception," a "real emergency" to the prevailing norm through their democratic resistance, reveals that the rotting norms of law are the realization that they rest on no higher order. They are instead merely the aims and actions of those who would proclaim themselves representatives of the law, referring only to their self-same use of force (McLoughlin 2016). Of course, one should not read Benjamin's "real emergency" as a rejection of law altogether. Rather, as McLoughlin (2016) suggests, this is not an end point but a process of drawing into expanding question the foundational claims of those gate keepers and representatives of order. Perhaps, as Benjamin pushes, this also requires a reconsideration of the history of law more broadly. And to this end, as in walls, pipelines, and spy centers, the drive to imagine a new order that cannot yet exist must begin with a radical questioning of the buildings and environments through which we remake ourselves. This, on one hand, implies a demand for a right to the communicative environments of the urban process as a whole. On the other hand, it also implies a right to design and redesign them. This is opposed to that history of what we might call "unruly law" and instead imagining critical infrastructures of a desired future of dignity and anti-autocracy.

Notes

1. See *Pike v. Southern Bell, 1955.*
2. See People v. Brophy, 1992.
3. This and subsequent quotes from BART are from Bart.Gov., (2011), "A letter from BART to our customers," http://www.bart.gov/news/articles/2011/news20110820
4. Kevin Fagan, "Man shot to death by BART officer identified," *SFGate,* July 7, 2011, https://www.sfgate.com/crime/article/Man-shot-to-death-by-BART-officer-identified-2355477.php

5. See here Williams discussion of "need" in the first chapter of *Television* (1975) and his discussion of determination in *Marxism and Literature* (1977, eg., p. 87).

6. David Harvey's recollection of Robert Park's early 20th century comments on "the city": "indirectly, and without any clear sense of the nature of his task, in making the city man has remade himself" (quoted in Harvey, 2008, p. 23). This social relation of cities has advanced with the development of media necessarily. Not only have the infrastructure of media, the labor of their production, and their management collected in urban environments. But, likewise, the development of commercial capital, of industrial capacity, and of marketing solutions are central elements and innovations in the growth of cities and media/communications worldwide.

7. See Shaw and Graham (2017) for an excellent expanded discussion of this issue.

8. This references a broader philosophical discussion of Walter Benjamin's state theory, which we can only reference briefly later. For more on the discussion of Walter Benjamin's "true exception" in his "Theses on the Philosophy of History" (2006) see among many others Agamben (2005), McLoughlin (2016), and Abbott (2008).

9. Facebook has been the subject of scrutiny around this counter-revolution as well in the PBS Frontline documentary, *The Facebook Dilemma* (2018) in which activist Wael Ghonim explains,

   "There was a page – it had like hundreds of thousands of followers. All what it did was creating fake statements. And I was a victim of that page. [*subtitle*] Wael is a spy for the Israeli intelligence. They wrote statements about me insulting the army, which puts me at serious risk because that is not something I said. I was extremely naive in way I don't like, actually, now, thinking that these are liberating tools. It's the spread of misinformation, fake news, in Egypt in 2011."

References

Abbott, M. (2008). The Creature Before the Law: Notes on Walter Benjamin's Critique of Violence. *Colloquy: Text Theory Critique*, (16), 80–96.

Ackerman, S. (2011, February 3). Egypt hacked Vodafone to send pro-regime texts. *Wired*. Accessed November, 2018, from https://www.wired.com/2011/02/egypt-hacked-vodafone-to-send-pro-regime-texts/

Agamben, G. (2005). *State of exception*. Chicago, IL: University of Chicago Press.

Ahmed, W. (2012). From militant particularism to anti-neoliberalism? The anti-Enron movement in India. *Antipode*, 44(4), 1059–1080.

Allinson, J. (2019). Counter-revolution as international phenomenon: The case of Egypt. *Review of International Studies*, 45(2), 320–344.

BART.gov. (2011). A letter from BART to our customers. *BART.gov*. Accessed November 5, 2018, from http://www.bart.gov/news/articles/2011/news20110820

Beinin, J. (2009). Workers' protest in Egypt: Neo-liberalism and class struggle in 21st Century. *Social Movement Studies*, 8(4), 449–454.

Benjamin, W. (2006). *Walter Benjamin: Selected writings, 1938–1940*, volume 4. Boston, MA: Belknap Press.

Bonnett, A. (2014). *Unruly places: Lost spaces, secret cities, and other inscrutable geographies.* New York, NY: Houghton-Mifflin Harcourt.

Boykoff, J. (2007). Surveillance, Spatial Compression, and Scale: The FBI and Martin Luther King Jr. *Antipode, 39*(4), 729–756. https://doi.org/10.1111/j.1467-8330.2007.00549.x

Brown, A. (2019, May 23). Pipeline Opponents Strike Back Against Anti-Protest Laws. Retrieved September 9, 2019, from The Intercept website: https://theintercept.com/2019/05/23/pipeline-protest-laws-louisiana-south-dakota/

Carpentier, N. (2016). Beyond the ladder of participation: An analytical toolkit for the critical analysis of participatory media processes. *Javnost—The Public, 23*, 70–88.

Castells, M. (2015). *Networks of outrage and hope: Social movements in the Internet age.* Cambridge, UK: Polity Press.

D'Arcus, B. (2003). Protest, scale, and publicity: The FBI and the H Rap Brown Act. *Antipode, 35*(4), 718–741.

Feld, H. (2011, August 29). Petition of public knowledge et al. for declaratory ruling that disconnection of telecommunication services violates the Communications Act. *Federal Communication Commission.* Accessed on November 10, 2018, from https://www.public-knowledge.org/files/docs/publicinterestpetitionFCCBART.pdf

Galperin, E. (2011, August 12). BART pulls a Mubarak in San Francisco. *Electronic Frontier.* Accessed on November 10, 2018, from https://www.eff.org/deeplinks/2011/08/bart-pulls-mubarak-san-francisco

Glanz, J., & Markoff, J. (2011, February 15). Egypt leaders found "off" switch for internet. *The New York Times.* Accessed November, 2018, from https://www.nytimes.com/2011/02/16/technology/16internet.html

Gregg, A., & Sonne, P. (2019, September 7). Projects defunded for Trump's border wall include military buildings with 'life safety violations' and hazmat concerns. *Washington Post.* Retrieved from https://www.washingtonpost.com/business/2019/09/07/projects-defunded-trumps-border-wall-include-military-buildings-with-life-safety-violations-hazmat-concerns/

Gumpert, G., & Drucker, S. (2008). Communicative cities. *International Communication Gazette, 70*(3–4), 195–208.

Hardt, M., & Negri, A. (2011). *Commonwealth.* Cambridge (USA); London: Belknap Press of Harvard Univesity Press.

Harkness, T. (2016, September 8). How Oakland almost became an Orwellian surveillance city—and citizens stopped it from happening. *AlterNet.* Accessed November, 218, from https://www.alternet.org/books/how-oakland-almost-became-orwellian-surveillance-city-and-citizens-stopped-it-happening

Harvey, D. (2007). *A brief history of neoliberalism.* Oxford, UK: Oxford University Press.

Harvey, D. (2008). The right to the city. *New Left Review, 53*, 23–40.

Human Rights Watch. (n.d.). Egypt. Retrieved September 9, 2019, from Human Rights Watch website: https://www.hrw.org/middle-east/n-africa/egypt

Human Rights Watch. (2019). "Egypt: Constitutional Amendments Entrench Repression." *Human Rights Watch.* Retrieved September 11, 2019 (https://www.hrw.org/news/2019/04/20/egypt-constitutional-amendments-entrench-repression).

Madlena, Chavala. (2011). "Telecomix: Tech Support for the Arab Spring." *The Guardian*, July 7.

Marx, K. (1992). *Capital: Volume 1: A critique of political economy*. (E. Mandel, Ed., B. Fowkes, Trans.) (Reprint edition). London; New York, NY: Penguin Classics.

McLoughlin, D. (2016). The Fiction of Sovereignty and the Real State of Exception: Giorgio Agamben's Critique of Carl Schmitt. *Law, Culture and the Humanities, 12*(3), 509–528. https://doi.org/10.1177/1743872112469863

Mitchell, D. (1995). The end of public space? People's Park, definitions of the public, and democracy. *Annals of the Association of American Geographers, 85*(1), 108–133.

Mitchell, D. (2003). *The right to the city: Social justice and the fight for public space*. New York, NY: Guilford Press.

Mitchell, D. (2005). The SUV model of citizenship: Floating bubbles, buffer zones, and the rise of the "purely atomic" individual. *Political Geography, 24*(1), 77–100.

Mitchell, D. (2016). The liberalization of free speech: Or, how protest in public space is silenced. In W. Nicholls, B. Miller, & J. Beaumont (Eds.), *Spaces of contention: Spatialities and social movements* (pp. 47–68). New York, NY: Routledge.

Mitchell, D., & Rosati, C. (2006). The globalization of culture: Geography and the industrial production of culture. In D. Conway & N. Heynen (Eds.), *Globalization's contradictions: Geographies of discipline, destruction and transformation* (pp. 144–160). New York, NY: Routledge.

Mitchell, D., & Staeheli, L. (2005). Permitting protest: Parsing the fine geography of dissent in America. *International Journal of Urban and Regional Research, 29*(4), 796–813.

Mitchell, T. (1999). No Factories, no problems: The logic of neo-liberalism in Egypt. *Review of African Political Economy, 26*(82), 455–468.

Klein, N. (2007). *The shock doctrine: The rise of disaster capitalism*. New York, NY: Metropolitan Books/Henry Holt.

PBS/Frontline. (2018). *The Facebook Dilemma* [Documentary]. Retrieved from https://www.pbs.org/wgbh/frontline/film/facebook-dilemma/

Richtel, M. (2011, January 28). Egypt cuts off most internet and cell service. *The New York Times*. Accessed on November 10, 2018, from https://www.nytimes.com/2011/01/29/technology/internet/29cutoff.html

Rushkoff, D. (2017). *Throwing rocks at the Google Bus: How growth became the enemy of prosperity*. New York, NY: Portfolio.

Sen, A. (2000). *Development as freedom*. New York, NY: Anchor.

Shaw, J. and M. Graham. (2017). "An Informational Right to the City? Code, Content, Control, and the Urbanization of Information." *Antipode* 49(4):907–27.

Williams, R. (1975). *Television: Technology and cultural form*. New York, NY: Schocken Books.

Zwitter, A. J. (2013). Arab Spring State of Emergency and Constitutional Reform. *SSRN Electronic Journal*. https://doi.org/10.2139/ssrn.2369374

PART III

REDISCOVERING LOST SPACES IN GERMANY

The following chapters explore communicative strategies for the democratization of unruly spaces that are shaped or influenced by the global forces described in Part II. In particular, these chapters examine strategies utilized in two German cities to draw attention to lost spaces in the physical environment. These lost spaces had proven problematic, as scholars and writers had written extensively about the negative psychological and emotional impacts of the bland and blasé architecture that arose following the Second World War. Feelings of isolation and angst were a constant threat to the communicative qualities of these cities, and held the potential to feed growing feelings of resentment. In Chapter 5, we introduce the strategy of transformative memory revival, which was accomplished through the installation of historical markers into the physical environment. These markers drew attention to lost spaces, and called for citizens to explore environments they would otherwise avoid. In Chapter 6, we demonstrate a substrategy called transformative memory modification. Specifically, we examine one museum in Berlin that uses exhibits and acoustic organization of space to emphasize the importance of sites tied to Germany's socialist past. Overall, Part II of the book accomplishes the following:

1. Explains and demonstrates the concept of transformative memory revival, and the related substrategy of transformative memory modification.
2. Explains the relationship between mediated texts and the construction of identity.
3. Explores the organization of space in the construction of public memory.
4. Demonstrates the flaws and drawbacks in the use of these strategies for the democratization of space.

· 5 ·

MEMORY REVIVAL IN MANNHEIM

The previous two chapters have illustrated the significant problems that have fueled austerity in contemporary society, and how emergent policies have degraded, or further degraded, physical environments in society. Despite the problems that have arisen from unruly spaces, they do not fully constitute cities or regions altogether. Oftentimes, policies of austerity, as well as feelings of resentment, lead to the isolation and avoidance of communities stricken by the problems associated with unruliness. Other parts of a city, however, may flourish, or continue to act as communicative components that facilitate democracy, and give rise to hope and dignity. As years and decades pass, spaces that were once communicative become unruly and degraded, while sites that were deemed unruly or wild become gentrified or altered through finance capital. The early insights of scholars like Hall (1969), Jacobs (1963), and Mumford (1962) help to demonstrate that cities are not static forms, but rather organic environments that are shaped by the movement, technologies, and communicative practices of people over time. Unruly spaces, like in the cases of Flint, Cairo, and the Bay Area, have detrimental impacts on communities and the lives of the people therein. However, the fact that cities are always in flux, and shaped by the communicative practices and technologies of people over time, provides hope for average citizens (or government—should they be so inclined) to take control over such unruliness. Recent scholarship, inspired by those early efforts, further demonstrates the ways in which communication can shape the ways in which bodies pass through problematic, unruly material environments.

For instance, Mautner (2012) and Olofsson (2013) examined signs positioned throughout urban spaces; they explored the ways that signs alter perceptions about material environments, which in turn shapes the ways in which people travel through spaces. Mautner studied warning and prohibition signs placed throughout urban sites, which organized language, law and space in a way that constrained movement through material environments. Olofsson examined changeable highway message signs altered by hackers to include strange or nonsensical messages; the bizarre alterations destabilized perceptions about streets and highways and changed the ways in which people moved through sections of cities. For the most part, these studies demonstrated the use of signs to navigate problematic unruly spaces within cities or other areas. However, these studies have focused on the use of signs and markers to move people through unruly spaces within the logics of neoliberalism (in the case of Mautner), or in a way that distracts from such policies (as in Olofsson). In these cases, the installation of signs provided no new knowledge—at least, no critical knowledge—that would shape identity or influence performances of people as they passed through or by unruly spaces. The use of such signs would not constitute a strategy for the democratization of space.

Nevertheless, research that I (Atkinson) conducted in the city of Mannheim demonstrates that the mere installation of signs into the physical environment could serve as democratization of space. Such signs could create new knowledge, which in turn, could shape identity and performances within physical sites described in Chapter 1. This chapter demonstrates the installation of such markers into the material environment of certain sites as a strategy for communicative democratization of unruly spaces within a city, which we call transformative memory revival. Essentially, this strategy entails the installation of signs or other media into physical environments in order to highlight lost spaces that have been forgotten. In many cases, these lost spaces exist as material parts of environments that have largely been ignored over the years, or in the case of many cities in Germany, were designed to be featureless and bland so that they would be ignored altogether. Such spaces are passed by, or through, with little or no thought, which can create a sense of psychological isolation. In many cases, such spaces inspire feelings of unease or disquiet, and create an identity for people passing through in which they feel compelled to hurry through; they may even come to feel as though they should avoid those areas of a city altogether. Needless to say, such perceptions can disrupt the communicative qualities of cities.

In addition, we have also come to understand that there are significant limitations to the use of such physical installations into material, built environments. We feel that such a communicative strategy can potentially create boundaries that may lead to multiple shifts in people's identities as they pass through or interact with other people. The installation of media into the environment creates "knowledge pockets" in the city, which will lead people to shift back and forth between different performances within the material environment. Indeed, this communicative strategy, when used in only certain sites throughout an urban environment, can potentially fracture a cityscape and give rise to performative boundaries. Such boundaries could give rise to another form of unruly space discussed earlier in Chapter 2: the enclave. The initial research that produced the concepts in this chapter was introduced in an article published in *Explorations in Media Ecology* in 2017. In the following pages, we describe a qualitative case study of the cityscape of Mannheim, Germany, which is similar to a study carried out by Papen (2012) in Prenzlauer Berg outside of Berlin and the study described in Chapter 2.

Signs, Media & Identity

As noted in earlier portions of this book, research has demonstrated that communication build knowledge about spaces and material environments; through such communication, people come to understand how to move through and interact with those environments. However, in the studies concerning signs conducted by Mautner (2012) and Olofsson (2013), such knowledge was limited to specific spaces and demonstrated minimal influence on the larger cityscape. Mautner's examination of warning and prohibition signs demonstrated how those messages shaped the ways in which people redirected their pathways through specific environments. Olofsson's examination of hacked road signs illustrated how the confusion created by the strange messages momentarily made people more aware of portions of the built environment that they had typically ignored. More importantly, there was no real shift in identity involved in those studies, as the information conveyed by the signs merely altered the ways in which people moved through the material environment; the knowledge cultivated by signs fostered passive identities at best.

Conversely, case studies by Carpentier (2008), Sadler and Haskins (2005), and our own research concerning DetroitYES! (described in Part IV) demonstrate that the images and information conveyed through broadcast and interactive media not only transformed perceptions about larger material environments and entire cities, but also changed the ways in which people engaged with those environments. The implication has been that a transformation of cityscape, similar to the cases of the postcard effect and contested city identities, requires electronic forms of media, while the construction of some forms of participatory engagement is dependent on the presence of interactive media platforms. Does this mean that interactive media platforms are necessary for all communicative democratization of unruly spaces? Indeed, Gumpert and Drucker (2008) and Carpentier (2008) explain that as media technologies advance, they play a greater role in the construction of knowledge about material environments than the other features in the city. Carpentier contends that the development of media technologies give rise to contested city identities. The case of Carpentier's research is particularly interesting in this regard, as he explored the role of alternative media in the communicative city. He examined Wi-Fi networks in Antwerp, Belgium that were used by various state and activist groups to link interactive media together. The Wi-Fi network stood as a form of alternative media that existed in a rhizomatic form; such a form of alternative media created a crossroads in civil society, permitting linkages between movements, markets, and states that would not have otherwise existed. Such linkages allowed for differing visions of the city and material environment to come into contact, giving rise to a contested identity for Antwerp. For the most part, Carpentier hints that such a rhizomatic form of alternative media that allows for a contested city identity is only possible because of the emergence of interactive media technologies over the past two decades. In the case study of cityscape that I (Atkinson) conducted in Mannheim, however, we came to understand that simple signs had the potential to foster identity in the ways discussed by Carpentier, as well as construct a form of participatory engagement on the part of the citizenry who read them. In short, simple signs had the potential to be used in the democratization of unruly spaces.

Mannheim, Germany

Mannheim is located in the federal state of Baden-Wurttemberg at the confluence of the Rheine and Neckar rivers. This particular position was an important strategic and economic site for the County Palatinate of the Rheine in the Holy Roman Empire from 1607 until 1802. The city was unique in 17th Century Europe in that it was built on a grid system to facilitate the movement of products and troops to various stations along the two rivers (Keller, 2000); streets were never named, and blocks were noted according to a system of numbers and letters (e.g., block L2; block D6). This grid-like site became referred to as the Quadrate (Quadrant). The site became so important that Elector Palatine Karl Philip III moved the Palatinate capital from Heidelberg to Mannheim in 1720 where he began construction of one of the largest baroque palaces in all of Europe, and he initiated an influx of philosophers, scientists, musical composers, actors and artists into the city. After the siege of Mannheim during the Napoleonic Wars, however, the city lost the status of capital (Fiedler, 2013). Sitting at the convergence of the Rheine and Neckar rivers, however, the city still held importance within the Germanic states. As industrialization spread throughout Europe, Mannheim's geographical position made it an ideal location for manufacturing, and the city became one of the important industrial centers of the unified German Empire. In fact, the city was instrumental in the production of weapons and war machines that would be utilized by the German army during the first Great War and by the Third Reich in the second. This, of course, made the city a prime target for Allied bombers in the Second World War. As in the case of Berlin, Munich and other large German cities, most of the infrastructure, manufacturing, and housing were destroyed by 1945; many accounts claim that nearly ninety percent of buildings in Mannheim were destroyed (Diefendorf, 1992; Keller, 2000).

Like other parts of Germany, Mannheim became embroiled in a process of reconstruction that took decades because of the immediate needs at the end of the war. In order to address the widespread destruction, the new Federal Republic of Germany (FRG), with help from the Allies via the Marshall Plan, constructed cheap buildings that featured only the bare basics (bedroom, cooking area, bathroom); these buildings were constructed from pre-fabricated concrete slabs that were easily erected and assembled (Diefendorf, 1992; Leick, Schreiber, & Stoldt, 2010). This stage of reconstruction lasted until the late 1960s, when the majority of the problems from homelessness from the war were largely alleviated. At that point, the government noted that housing built in the immediate post-war years was far from ideal, and quite inadequate for the citizenry. The FRG engaged in a second wave of reconstruction and urban renewal by building better housing so that people could migrate out of the problematic post-war constructions.

There was a significant challenge that hindered the beginning of this second stage of reconstruction: what to build? Many in Germany wanted to distance themselves from the atrocities of the Third Reich. Others felt that their country had been wrecked forever and wanted no reminders of the glorious past that dated back to the fall of the Roman Empire. For these reasons, the nation engaged in the construction of housing and office buildings that were modernist in design; in particular, a form of modernist architecture called "brutalism" became popular (Hawley, 2010; Leick et al., 2010). This brutal architecture emphasized simplicity and conveyed little (if any) discursive meaning one might see explicitly in classical or modern architecture. The simplicity stood in stark contrast to the "heroic" architectural style of Albert Speer favored by Adolf Hitler, and it contrasted as well with the baroque and rococo styles that in many ways defined the nation's past. This brutal style helped some to build a sense of distance from the Nazi regime, and aided others in keeping cherished German history out of sight and mind (Hawley, 2010). This plain, simple architecture emerged all across the nation alongside the quickly constructed post-war housing projects. In many ways, the two were largely indistinguishable.

Figure 5.1 provides some sense of the change that took place in cities like Mannheim. The photograph shows the former Commodities Exchange Building at E4 in the Quadrate. Prior to World War II, most of the buildings in the Quadrate were built according to the style of historicism (otherwise known as eclecticism); this style recreated various historical styles within a single building. The basis of the historicist idea was to utilize elements of the past in order to build something for the future. Most of the historicist façade of the Commodities Exchange Building survived the war; this can be seen from the left of the photograph to the middle. However, the addition on the far right side of the building was designed according to the brutal style; this side of the building is flat with no ornament or decoration. Overall, the space of Mannheim, as well as many other cities across Germany, is dominated by these plain, simplistic, and utilitarian structures, with only a few older styles remaining. These structures stand in the place of architecture and buildings that were a part of the history of the city; the old architecture and buildings have become lost spaces.

As noted in Chapter 1, Bonnett (2014) has designated the lost spaces as one of his unrefined types of unruly spaces. These are spaces that were deemed

Figure 5.1. Building at E4 Mannheim, present day.

to be important or valuable in the past, but have largely been forgotten and come to be ignored; typically some kind of a cataclysm or revolutionary social change has occurred that altered meaning structures through which people experience the material environments. Bonnett offers the city of Leningrad as an example of lost spaces. He claims that the fall of the Soviet Union drastically altered the Russian states and cities at that time. As the old Soviet regime collapsed, people took down the major memorials and landmarks that shaped meaning structures for that era. However, many smaller symbols remained, like street names or decorative designs in the architecture. Without the major landmarks to anchor the meaning structures in the overall environment, those smaller symbolic spaces came to be lost. Sites in the city that were once important were ignored, and over time they were simply forgotten. Nevertheless, they were a part of the city, and passed by as people moved about their everyday lives. In many ways, lost spaces and hidden geographies are quite similar; for the most part, both involve physical environments that are out of sight and mind. When such sites do draw attention, they often elicit feelings of unease because they are different from the organized com-municative spaces of modern cities. The primary difference between these two types of spaces is that one (lost spaces) once had meanings ascribed to them, while the other (hidden geographies) typically did not. In the case of modern Germany, people passed by, and through, many cities like Mannheim, which were dominated by plain facades like the right side of the Commodities Exchange Building in Figure 5.1. The left side of that particular building still entailed those symbols that were connected to the past. However, because most of the environment came to resemble the right side of the building, those symbols had largely come to be ignored and eventually forgotten. What is more, many of the bland physical structures in the environment stood in the place of spaces associated with events and people of the past. These were the lost spaces of Mannheim.

For the most part, modern Mannheim met most of Gumpert and Drucker's (2008) criteria for communicative cities. That is to say, there were features that allowed for interactions between citizens and facilitated polit-ical communication. There was infrastructure that allowed for free move-ment of people and goods, as well as the circulation of local and national media. However, the plain, sterile façade of the initial reconstruction and the brutal style dominated the material environment; it had largely replaced the splendid architecture of Germany's past. For the most part, then, the old architecture and history connected to it was lost, as it had been replaced by the brutal architecture that now defines most modern German cities. The plain brutal architecture may not seem problematic, but much has been made of the psychological and emotional difficulties that such material space and infrastructure can create. In *Spiegel Online*, Leick et al. (2010) note that many psychologists of the 1960s and 1970s warned about problems that could arise from living in such "inhospitable cities."

> Unfortunately, the clean new suburbs and satellite towns didn't result in a better quality of life. Instead, the sterile environments elicited feelings of loneliness and boredom. Indeed, many of those who moved to these soulless ghettos were soon pin-ing for the familiar, chaotic confinement of their former cities. (p. 3)

Ultimately, the bland construction that had been erected around, and on top of, important sites tied to the history of Mannheim stood as unruly spaces that make the city seem depressing or unbearable for many residents. The city became a physical environment that was best hurried through, or ignored altogether. For these reasons, the lost spaces of Mannheim, and the brutal style architecture that came to dominate the cityscape, can potentially disrupt the communicative qualities of the city.

The Stadtpunkte of Mannheim

Given the problems stemming from the brutal and bland architecture that made up cities and communities, the German nation initiated a third wave of reconstruction and urban renewal that will again alter urban environments like Mannheim. One part of this renewal concerned perceptions about the existing material spaces. In particular, the city government in Mannheim installed historical markers, known as "stadtpunkt" on buildings and around parks that provided information about the city's past.[1] Each stadtpunkt was a glass plate that was attached to the side of a building, or to a post near a building or other notable space, which featured historical information with accompanying photographs or pictures. The stadtpunkte typically included information about the early city and its palace, migration and tolerance, industry or democracy. Overall, the information conveyed by the stadtpunkte were grouped into the following categories: past sites, past people, past events or history of a district. Essentially, the stadtpunkte drew attention to the lost spaces in the city of Mannheim.

The photograph in Figure 5.2 shows one such stadtpunkt that was located outside of the Rosengarten concert hall, adjacent to the park known as Friedrichsplatz. The stadtpunkt featured text and photographs explaining that the famous Berlin architect Bruno Schmitz oversaw construction of the baroque style Rosengarten structure between 1898 and 1903. This stadtpunkt also explained that the building was badly damaged during the Second World War, with only part of the façade still intact; the building was rebuilt in the 1970s and expanded around 2007. Essentially, the city of Mannheim installed historical and cultural information, conveyed through text and imagery, onto the material environment of the Rosengarten. Such an installation held the potential to revive memory about lost spaces throughout the city.

In the case study of Mannheim, the locations of stadtpunkte throughout the city were catalogued over a three and a half month period (August to December of 2014) as the different sections of the city were explored on foot. Each of the districts of Mannheim were visited at least one time during the three-month duration of my stay in the city. In each case, the walking tours of each district involved photography of the material environment and seeking out stadtpunkte wherever they could be found.[2] Whenever a stadtpunkt was discovered, it was

Figure 5.2. Stadtpunkt outside of the Rosengarten at Friedrichsplatz.

photographed and marked in Google maps for further examination; careful notes were also taken concerning the material environment around each stadtpunkt.[3]

In addition, oral histories were collected from the department of urban development. The three coordinators for urban development and planning met with me so as to explain the history of reconstruction and development in the city; these three individuals provided official information concerning the creation and placement of stadtpunkte.[4] According to the person in charge of the stadtpunkte, the markers were installed throughout the city in order to first and foremost educate the citizens of Mannheim about their history; tourists and visitors to Mannheim were a secondary audience. Through the oral histories, the coordinators for urban development also relayed that there was a committee that determined where to place stadtpunkte; the committee was composed of historians and city officials. Essentially, the committee would decide to place a stadtpunkt on or near a particular building or site in the city and approach the owners to ask their permission. It was noted during the oral history that there were instances in which people would refuse to allow the city to place any stadtpunkte on or near their property. Overall, this approach to the stadtpunkte and the city of Mannheim provided insight into the information available to people as they moved through the material environment. Such information helped to understand how that information could influence the interactions of people within the material environment.

Stadtpunkte: Where They Were Installed

The stadtpunkte in Mannheim were primarily found throughout the grid-like Quadrate at the center of the city. The installation of stadtpunkte throughout this part of the city came as little surprise, as major historical landmarks and nodes could be found throughout: the palace, the Jesuitenkirche (Jesuit Church, the largest church on the upper Rhein) and the baroque Wasserturm (Water Tower) at Friedrichplatz. The palace was located at the south central edge of the Quadrate with the Jesuitenkirche close-by, while the Wasserturm stood at the eastern central edge of the Quadrate. Each of these sites had at least one stadtpunkt on or near the physical structure, much like the example noted above in Figure 5.2. Interspersed throughout the Quadrate were stadtpunkte placed on or nearby many buildings. It was interesting to note that many of these buildings were physically bland, or even ugly, in their appearance. According to the coordinators for urban development, these buildings were typically built either according to the brutal style or from pre-fabricated concrete slabs after the war. Take for instance the building located at M1 in the Quadrate. The original structure that once stood at M1 prior to the Second World War had been built according to the style of historicism typical of the Quadrate at that time. That building was destroyed, however, and the structure that was built up in its place was rather unremarkable and bland; the modern building included some shops on the first floor and apartments above. On the side of the building, however, was a stadtpunkt that explained that the inventor of the motorcycle, Karl Drais, lived and worked inside the building that had once stood at this site. Such information on the glass plate notified people passing by that there was much more to this building than its blasé appearance.

In addition to being found on buildings, stadtpunkte could also be found at parks or other such empty spaces in the Quadrate where structures had once stood; in these cases, nothing had been rebuilt following the war. One such case was a post upon which two stadtpunkte were placed on either side. This post stood in the middle of an empty green space located at F7 in the north-eastern corner of the Quadrate. One of the stadtpunkte noted that the park had once been the Judischer friedhof (Jewish cemetery) in Mannheim; the Jewish community used the cemetery from the late 1600s until it was closed by the Nazi regime. The second stadtpunkt explained that the Nazis forced the Mannheim community of 6500 Jewish people from their homes. The stadtpunkt further noted that the 2000 people who remained were deported to eastern France, and later to Auschwitz; there were only forty-seven survivors who returned to Mannheim.

The Quadrate was not the only part of Mannheim where stadtpunkte were found. According to the coordinator in charge of the stadtpunkte, there were plans to place at least one stadtpunkt in all of the districts in the larger metro area. At the time of my research, stadtpunkte had been placed in the districts of Feudenheim, Jungbusch, Neckarstadt Ost & West, Schönau and Vogelstang. A single stadtpunkt was placed in the district of Schönau, which was a district located in the northwest corner of the Mannheim metro area populated by working-class people and immigrants (mostly from Turkey). The stadtpunkt was placed on the Schönauschule (Schönau School), one of the oldest schools in the districts surrounding central Mannheim. The building stood in the middle of a large immigrant community, with many homes all around. The stadtpunkt text began with a brief explanation of the current edges of the district (between Highway 6, the Mannheim-Frankfurt rail-line and the Frankenthaler road) and how the district developed and grew over the years. Following World War I, more settlers moved into the district due to a widespread housing shortage; around 1936 these settlements were formally recognized as a district of Mannheim. The stadtpunkt then turned to the Schönauschule, briefly explaining that the school was originally established as the Hans Schemm School. Finally, it was noted that prior to the Second World War, there were 4,669 inhabitants in Schönau, compared with over 13,000 inhabitants afterwards; over forty one percent of the post-war population of Schönau consisted of immigrants.

Two stadtpunkte were placed in the district of Neckarstadt-West, just south of Schönau. This district was located northwest of the Quadrate, across the Neckar River. Like the district to the north, mostly working-class immigrants populated Neckarstadt-West. The first of these stadtpunkte was placed on the wall of a store in the middle of a commercial section of the district. The marker explained the boundaries and history of the district, much like the one found in Schönau. Specifically, this stadtpunkt noted that Elector Karl Ludwig first established the district in 1679 and illustrated the boundaries that separate it from other parts of the metro area (the Neckar river and Max Joseph Strasse). The other stadtpunkt was located in the northernmost part of that district, placed on the exterior wall of an apartment building. The second stadtpunkt explained that the Mannheim GmbH company was established in 1926 and that it constructed "outstanding" social housing for the city; the three hundred ninety three apartments built were some of the best at that time for low and middle income families.[5] The stadtpunkt was the only notable feature on the flat, plain exterior of the building.

Directly to the east of Neckarstadt-West, two stadtpunkte were also placed in Neckarstadt-Ost. This district was different from the previous two discussed above, as the population consisted primarily of domestic-born Germans who were more middle to upper class. One of the stadtpunkte was placed at the University Medical Center (which served as the city hospital), while the other was placed at the Hauptfriedhof (main cemetery). The medical center was located in the commercial and economic center of the district, which was made up of shops, a brewery and a long park following the Neckar River. This stadtpunkt explained that the original city hospital located in the Quadrate proved too small for the growing population of the 19th Century. By 1889, plans were developed for a new hospital along the Neckar River, and construction began in 1913; the First World War slowed the project so that the building was not fully opened until 1922. The stadtpunkt at the Hauptfriedhof, located a short distance east of the medical center, explained that the site was originally a settlement of displaced people following the destruction of Mannheim during the Nine Years War; these displaced people called their settlement "New Mannheim." The wooden structures erected there quickly decayed and collapsed, and many people reclaimed homes and space in the old city following the war. In the 19th Century, the site was used as a small cemetery, and after 1900 it was used as the main cemetery for the entire city.

A single stadtpunkt was also placed in the district of Vogelstang, which was similar to Neckarstadt-Ost: a middle to upper class area populated primarily by domestic-born German people. This district was located in the far northeastern section of the metro area. The stadtpunkt was located at the tram station in the center of the district; the station had been converted into a small shopping center that included restaurants and various stores. The stadtpunkt explained that the city government had established the district in the late 1960s to be something different from the others that had been rebuilt and restored following the Second World War. At the time that the city initiated construction of buildings in Vogelstang, most other districts were composed of "social-housing" funded and built primarily by the federal government in order to address the homelessness following the war. City planners and leaders envisioned Vogelstang as a different kind of space; the district would be composed of high-rise housing built around a shopping center and a sports facility, all next to man-made lakes and surrounded by parks.

Overall, the exploration of the Mannheim cityscape over this three-month period revealed that stadtpunkte were either installed near already recognized landmarks (e.g., the palace, Wasserturm) or among common nodes in the city. Those that were installed on or near nodes proved to be particularly interesting, as the practice of installation held transformative implications for those sites. The stadtpunkte either connected the plain and uninteresting nodes to the recognized landmarks, or they conveyed information that made them worthy of landmark status themselves. Essentially, stadtpunkte were installed on or near the following kinds of nodes: (1) community nodes (e.g., apartments, homes, schools, places of worship), (2) commercial nodes with high traffic (e.g., shopping centers, downtown areas with multiple businesses) or (3) public nodes with high traffic (e.g., the hospital, tram stations). In many of these cases, the stadtpunkte were installed on or near otherwise bland looking structures or empty spaces, part of the material environment which people normally hurried by with little thought or inspection. With the installation of the markers into the material environment, however, people would stop to read the texts and thoughtfully study the area.

The installation of stadtpunkte in many cases, then, had the potential to highlight lost spaces and facilitate alternative knowledge about the city of Mannheim that could foster a form of participatory engagement. The act of reading these historical markers could make the material environment less unruly. As in the case of Wildcat Hollow, this participatory engagement was of the sociological variety, which entailed consumption and ritual. According to Carpienter (2016), one aspect of sociological participatory engagement is the consumption of media that help audiences to feel as though they are empowered. The act of reading and accumulation of new knowledge creates the sense of being part of a community, and initiates rituals that solidify those perceptions. In the cases of unruly spaces, the new knowledge and investigations of the environment create a sense of empowerment and control. Such was the case in Wildcat Hollow and Mannheim. However, unlike the case of Wildcat Hollow, the engagement with the stadtpunkte became a ritual in which people sought out new things in the physical environment. Rather than closing themselves off, citizens engaged in performances that involved the creation of new interactions (with the physical environment, at least).

The installation of the historical markers into the physical environment stood as a strategy of communicative democratization of space, which we call transformative memory revival. As citizens encountered a stadtpunkt that provided information about lost spaces nearby, they could engage with the environment in order to find it. They could then seek out other markers within a material environment that had typically held no significant meaning for them in the past. An alternative knowledge could emerge in which the brutal and blasé material environment could be viewed in historical terms of lost grandeur, brilliant artists and exceptional scholars. Such a context had largely been erased by the architectural necessities and choices following the Second World War and the Nazi regime. Essentially, as people walked through Mannheim, their gaze might turn from the paths in front of them to the lost spaces around them. As those nodes became viewed as connected to the existing landmarks, or actually important landmarks themselves (or at least the site of once important landmarks), people might stop to inspect and engage with the material environment—or with other people in the material environment. In many ways, seeking stadtpunkte out and actively building alternative knowledge seemed to be a sociological form of participatory engagement. That is to say, the act of consuming information on the glass plates initiated a ritualistic search of the lost spaces, which fostered a perception of the material environment as worthy of exploration rather than avoidance. The new, alternative knowledge about the city could, in turn, lead people to search out more information and engage further with other people and the material environment.

Stadtpunkte: Where They Were Absent

The examination of stadtpunkte in Mannheim also revealed where they were absent in the material environment. The best way to illustrate this revelation is to convey the story of the exploration of the district of Oststadt. The district was directly east of the Quadrate, past a commercial area around the Wasserturm and Friedrichsplatz. Overall, the district was comprised of upper middle class and upper class people of primarily native German decent. Unlike the Quadrate and other districts, there was no brutal architecture; the houses and buildings within Oststadt followed the historicism and baroque styles common to Mannheim's past, as well as other styles. After walking a few blocks into Oststadt, I encountered an enormous church called the Christuskirche (Christ's Church). This protestant church was constructed between 1907 and 1911 in the baroque style, and it survived the bombings of the Second World War largely intact. The Christuskirche appeared to be just as majestic of a city landmark as the palace or the Jesuitenkirche in the Quadrate. With thoughts of the major landmarks of the Quadrate in my mind, the Christuskirche was approached so as to seek out the accompanying stadtpunkt so as to photograph it and plot it onto the Google map of the city. However, no sign of any stadtpunkte was found outside or within. It seemed strange that such a structure within the city would be devoid of a marker that explained the history of the church or any special events in its past. Later, I found that someone had already marked the structure prominently on Google maps. Clicking on the church in Google maps provided access to a website wherein all of the historical information noted above was found.

With this absence of a stadtpunkt in mind, the walking tour of Oststadt led back toward the Quadrate along another street, until I came across a similarly impressive looking structure. Closer examination of the building revealed that it was the Tulla-Realschule (Tulla-Real School), a secondary school situated in the heart of the district. Through Google maps the website for the school was discovered. The website explained that the school was constructed in 1900 and opened in 1901. The Tulla-Realschule had been one of the few schools in Mannheim that took Jewish students during the time period between 1901 and the rise of the Third Reich. The school was closed for a few years following the Second World War, as the building was damaged during Allied bombing raids. As in the case of the Christuskirche, the area around the structure was thoroughly examined in order to find a stadtpunkt, with no success. Again, it seemed odd that an architecturally impressive building with an interesting history would have no such marker at all. In fact, at the time of the research, there was not a single stadtpunkt to be found throughout that entire district.

The lack of stadtpunkte on or near interesting or impressive structures was not confined to the district of Oststadt, as there were also remarkable structures in the district of Neckarstadt-Ost that were also devoid of any stadtpunkte. One of those structures was the Alte Feuerwache (Old Fire Station) near the Neckar River, situated beside a series of expensive high-rise apartment buildings. Again, the site had already been fixed into Google maps at the time of my research, through which it was possible to access the fire station's website. The website noted that it was built in 1910 and that it housed the city fire department until sometime in the 1970s, when a new fire station was constructed at another site in the city. After the building was decommissioned, disputes arose about how best to utilize the empty structure; a group of socialists wanted to make the building into a "municipal communication center," while a citizens group wanted to turn the building into a place for music and fun. The latter group prevailed in the debate, and the building was converted into a site for concerts and dancing. This new version of the Alte Feuerwache served as a location for people to come together, make music, collaborate on artistic projects and exchange ideas. Like the Christuskirche and Tulla-Realschule noted above, this site seemed to be worthy of a stadtpunkt, but the explorations of the physical environment turned up none.

Other such structures were discovered in the exploration of the different districts of Mannheim: impressive or historically significant buildings existed in Feudenheim, Neckarstadt-West, Schetzingerstadt and Vogelstang (as well as others), none of which had any stadtpunkte on display. In some cases (like Oststadt, Schetzingerstadt or Gartenstadt), my investigation determined that there were no stadtpunkte within the entire district. In other cases (like Feudenheim, Neckarstadt-Ost, and Vogelstang), there were one or two stadtpunkte in the district; these were typically located at commercial or public nodes with high traffic, but never within community nodes as in Schönau, Jungbusch or the Quadrate.

The issue of where stadtpunkte were installed, and where they were not, is no small thing. In the case of Schönau, a stadtpunkt was installed in an ordinary looking school in the midst of a conventional neighborhood. People passing by had the opportunity to engage with the text and learn about the school (and district) as a lost space that is important to the history of Mannheim. In the case of Jungbusch, a stadtpunkt was also installed at a community node: a church located in the middle of a similar neighborhood. Throughout the Quadrate, stadtpunkte were installed in or near community nodes that were far from commercial and public nodes with high traffic. These nodes in the blasé material environment, then, could be connected to existing landmarks (like the palace). Such connections allowed for the possibility of new knowledge that could serve as the basis for an alternative cityscape. Conversely, Oststadt and similar districts like Vogelstang had no such historical markers on or near any community nodes; the lost spaces remained ignored and forgotten by people passing through. In other words, districts populated primarily by working class and immigrant people had stadtpunkte installed in or near all types of nodes, whereas districts populated by upper class and domestic German people had either no stadtpunkte or only a few stadtpunkte in commercial rather than community nodes.

Such differences entailed obvious political and economic boundaries between districts, but additional performative boundaries also emerged due to the presence or absence of stadtpunkte. In certain parts of the city, knowledge was partly derived from information installed into the material environment and experiences of exploration. In other parts of the city, whatever knowledge was invoked for people passing by was constructed with little or no attention or engagement with the material environment. In terms of the first, the stadtpunkte could possibly draw the attention of people travelling along paths through the material environment; this is much like Sadler and Haskins' (2005) postcard effect described in Chapter 1. The information conveyed through the markers can potentially construct knowledge about specific nodes—no matter how bland or ugly the environment might be. The presence of the stadtpunkt can signal to people passing by that the material environment should not be bypassed quickly or resented, but rather experienced as an important site where one can feel good about spending time, shopping or living. In terms of the second part of the city, when people pass through the more affluent districts of Mannheim (e.g., Oststadt, Neckarstadt-Ost), little is actually marked by stadtpunkte. To be clear, outside of the Quadrate there are only a few stadtpunkte in any one district at best. However, in the case of the affluent districts, stadtpunkte have only been installed along high traffic pathways near commercial or public nodes. The same construction of knowledge noted above may very well take place for people passing through shopping centers and municipal sites in these districts, but it is confined to only those spaces. In other words, lost spaces in commercial and public nodes are transformed into historically significant landmarks, but not lost spaces near community nodes in affluent neighborhoods.

A performative boundary existed, then, between different parts of the city, in which different identities were called upon when passing through material environments. When one passed by community nodes in Oststadt or Vogelstang, there was little for someone to stop and examine, and little of civic value to cue a civic performative identity. Glimpsing lavish material goods, like cars and swimming pools, was the primary experience for people passing through those parts of the material environment. People could pass through such spaces in the same passive ways as described in the research of Mautner (2012) and Olofsson (2013). Conversely, the history installed in or near community nodes in working-class neighborhoods could hail people to stop and explore; one could potentially linger examining structures and learning how those nodes were lost spaces connected to the history of the city. Essentially, the presence (or absence) of stadtpunkte ascribed particular performances as appropriate or inappropriate and made the act of exploration acceptable or problematic. A person passing community nodes in affluent districts should be in motion; unless they were a resident, they should be moving through the material environment without stopping. If an outsider stopped to gaze at buildings and parks within these spaces, they became deviant.

Discussion

Ultimately, the stadtpunkte in Mannheim highlighted for residents lost spaces in the city that had been forgotten. These were sites that had been destroyed in the war, and later forgotten as reconstruction emphasized erasure of the past. The new physical environment constructed over the years was largely devoid of meaning, and had been noted as "inhospitable," often making people to feel isolated and alone. Typically, people did not want to linger in such blasé physical environments, which eroded some of the communicative characteristics and qualities of Mannheim. For the most part, Mannheim was a modern city, with adequate (or even excellent) roads and infrastructure that allowed for movement of people and products. The media and telecommunications in the city were as good as those in most other European cities. However, there were problems with the parks and public areas of the city, as people did not find them to be hospitable sites for congregation. The coordinators for urban development alluded to this in the oral history. Such a problem did not pose the same impediments for a communicative city as did the hidden geographies in Flint or Oakland, or in the city of Detroit, which is described in greater detail in Part IV. Nevertheless, the fact that residents of Mannheim often did not congregate in public spaces hindered the flow of ideas, public debate, and a sense of overall community. This made it all the more difficult for the development and implementation of local-level solutions to the global problems created by the austerity associated with modern societies and cities. Indeed, the presence of adequate (or robust) infrastructure and telecommunications meant there was high potential for national or European Union level forces to implement any such solutions. The addition of the stadtpunkte to the physical environment in the city alleviated this hindrance. By highlighting the lost spaces that have connections to the history of the city and nation, the coordinators for urban development provided an opportunity to the residents to explore their city and build an altogether different cityscape. Such opportunities can give rise to congregation, deliberation, and debate of ideas; citizens may find that the city feels like a community.

The analysis of the stadtpunkte in Mannheim revealed that there are significant variations in the installation of markers throughout the different districts and their material environments. During the oral histories conveyed by the coordinators for the department of urban development and renewal, particularly the person in charge of the stadtpunkte, questions were asked regarding the discrepancies noted above. These people noted that the committee charged with installation of the stadtpunkte was working to make sure that each district would have at least one, and that markers would be placed on important sites like the Christuskirche. However, the person in charge of the stadtpunkte also noted that there were multiple instances in which requests to place the markers on or near buildings were turned down by residents or owners. Such was the case with the Christuskirche. As of the time of the submission of this original essay to *Explorations in Media Ecology*, no stadtpunkt had been placed on that church. With that stated, the number of stadtpunkte throughout the districts of Mannheim grew significantly since the case study was conducted, as markers were added to Gartenstadt, Lindenhof, Neckarau, Sandhofen, Wallstadt and even Oststadt; additional stadtpunkte were also added to Schönau and Neckarstadt-West. However, subsequent examination of these stadtpunkte was conducted through records in the online stadtarchiv, and the sites where those markers were placed were examined by way of the street views accessible through Google maps and my notes/photographs of these different districts. Such subsequent examinations revealed that these new stadtpunkte were installed in the same kinds of nodes noted earlier.

Overall, the findings illustrated that interactive media platforms or broadcast media are not the only way to democratize unruly spaces, transform cityscape, or establish participatory forms of engagement on the part of the citizenry. Historical markers have the potential to transform spaces in the same ways as described by Sadler and Haskins (2005), and create a city identity described in research by Carpentier (2008). In the case of this study, the participatory engagement was created through the revival of memory about the spaces in the city. Such participatory engagement was constructed from the consumption of media texts and enactment of rituals that involved close examinations of the physical environment. For the most part, all of these fit with Carpentier's (2016) notion of consumption and ritual associated with sociological participatory engagement.

Unfortunately, if such installation practices are not universal or carried out in a systematized manner, a fractured alternative cityscape may emerge. The findings demonstrate that performative boundaries can emerge within the cityscape from such disparities. This can be particularly problematic as these fractures and boundaries can foster or reinforce existing socio-economic, political or racial divisions. Here, then, stood the problem in the democratization of lost spaces in Mannheim. The transformative memory revival utilized by the city government to highlight lost spaces and create participatory engagement potentially created new unruly spaces in the city. Rather than the problem of lost spaces, and the brutal style architecture built around them, there is now potentially the problem of the enclave described by Bonnett, which also existed in Wildcat Hollow in Chapter 2. As an unruly space, the enclave created confusion for people living in, and passing through, those sites. The rules for interaction and engagement are different, but unclear as the boundaries between districts or regions are never truly known—or they are influx. For the purposes of Mannheim and its lost spaces, the emergence of performative boundaries created a problem in which there are rules for engagement/interaction in some parts of the city that did not exist in others. This has the potential to create anxiety or tension for people who live in the city, as they cannot understand why certain performances are acceptable in some spaces, but offensive in others. Unless the government makes the stadtpunkte more widespread throughout the entire city, a new form of unruliness will take hold. Hopefully there will be stadtpunkte at more of the important, identity-building civic spaces, such as the Christuskirche and Alte Feuerwache, integrating their districts' lost spaces, and their districts' different racial and socio-economic populations, into one holistic, historically signifi-cant Mannheim cityscape.

Notes

1. Stadtpunkt is German for "city point." The plural form is "stadtpunkte."
2. The districts of Mannheim include Almenhof, Feudenheim, Friedrichsfeld, Gartenstadt, Ilvesheim, Jungbusch, Kafertal, Lindenhof, Luzenberg, Neckarau, Neckarstadt-Ost, Neckarstadt-West, Neostheim, Neuhermsheim, Niederfeld, Oststadt, Rheinau, Sandhofen, Schetzingerstadt, Schönau, Seckenheim, Vogelstang, Waldhof and Wallstadt.
3. The task of finding stadtpunkte was made easier when I met with the coordinators for urban development and renewal. The coordinator in charge of the stadtpunkte was able to provide a map of Mannheim with the placement of all of the stadtpunkte. In addition, he informed me that a record of the stadtpunkte existed online through the "stadtarchiv" (https://www.stadtarchiv.mannheim.de/stadtpunkte). With this information, I was able to seek out each of the markers, rather than relying on running across them. Nevertheless, I still engaged in an exploration of each of the districts of Mannheim.
4. When meeting with the three coordinators for urban development and planning, I simply asked them to tell me (1) the history of reconstruction in Mannheim following World War II, and (2) the history and processes of the stadtpunkte placement in the material environment.
5. Oddly, the narrative did not provide any explanation of a connection between the building and the Mannheim GmbH company. I have been led to assume, however, that the building was the site of the company headquarters.

References

Bonnett, A. (2014). *Unruly places: Lost spaces, secret cities, and other inscrutable geographies.* New York, NY: Houghton-Mifflin Harcourt.

Carpentier, N. (2008). The belly of the city: Alternative communicative city networks. *International Communication Gazette, 70*(3–4), 237–255.

Carpentier, N. (2016). Beyond the ladder of participation: An analytical toolkit for the critical analysis of participatory media processes. *Javnost—The Public, 23,* 70–88.

Diefendorf, J. (1992). *In the wake of war: The reconstruction of German cities after World War II.* Oxford, UK: Oxford University Press.

Fiedler, H. (2013). *Mannheim: Liebenswerte stadt im quadrat.* Gudensberg-Gleichen, Germany: Wartberg Verlag.

Gumpert, G., & Drucker, S. (2008). Communicative cities. *International Communication Gazette, 70*(3–4), 195–208.

Hall, E. (1969). *The hidden dimension*. New York, NY: Anchor Books.

Hawley, C. (2010, August 20). Living with sin: Germany comes to terms with its ugliest buildings. *Spiegel Online International*. Accessed on October 2, 2014, from http://www.spiegel.de/international/germany/living-with-sin-germany-comes-to-terms-with-its-ugliest-buildings-a-712535.html

Jacobs, J. (1963). *The death and life of great American cities*. New York, NY: Vintage Books.

Keller V. (2000). *Streiflichter aus alt-Mannheim*. Erfurt, Germany: Sutton Verlag.

Leick, R., Schreiber, M., & Stoldt, H. (2010, August 10). Out of the ashes: A new look at Germany's postwar reconstruction. *Spiegel Online International*. Accessed October 2, 2014 from http://www.spiegel.de/international/germany/out-of-the-ashes-a-new-look-at-germany-s-postwar-reconstruction-a-702856.html

Mautner, G. (2012). Language, space and the law: A study of directive signs. *International Journal of Speech Language and the Law, 19*(2), 189–217.

Mumford, L. (1962). *The city in history*. San Diego, CA: Harcourt, Brace & World.

Olofsson, J. (2013). "Zombies ahead!" A study of how hacked digital road signs destabilize the physical space of roadways. *Visual Communication, 13*, 75–93.

Papen, U. (2012). Commercial discourses, gentrification and citizens' protest: The linguistic landscape of Prenzlauer Berg, Berlin. *Journal of Sociolinguistics, 16*, 56–80.

Sadler, W. J., & Haskins, E. V. (2005). Metonymy and the metropolis: Television show settings and the image of New York City. *Journal of Communication Inquiry, 29*(3), 195–216.

· 6 ·

MEMORY MODIFICATION AT THE
DDR MUSEUM

In this chapter, we build on the concepts introduced previously by demonstrating the ways in which memory revival can also entail memory modification. Specifically, we focus on the DDR Museum as a site in which memory was modified in such a way that allowed for people to make sense of—and take control of—unruly urban spaces in eastern Germany. This particular museum was situated in the city of Berlin, and addressed the communist past of Germany associated with the Deutche Demokratische Republik, or German Democratic Republic (GDR)—the former socialist state of East Germany.[1] The democratization of space through the exhibits and materials in the museum helped people to rediscover lost spaces associated with East Berlin and the former state of East Germany prior to reunification of the nation in 1990. The museum aided in the manipulation of public memory, which influenced the overarching cityscape of Berlin and other East German cities. What is more, this form of democratization proved valuable as the fear and distrust caused by the East German government that might become associated with rediscovered lost spaces was shifted to the Soviet Union for many of the citizens who lived under the former socialist regime. In this way, then, Berlin (and other East German cities) could become a site for dialogue and reconciliation, rather than suspicion and resentment. However, this emergent vision of the lost spaces corresponded with Western nostalgia for the Cold War, and held the potential to influence the ways in which tourists engaged with historical sites throughout the city as well. The data that is the basis for this chapter was collected through research conducted at the museum in October of 2014. This analysis revealed manifest and latent meanings within texts, as well as the ways in which exhibits in the museum invited visitors into particular subject positions that reinforced those meanings. The concepts that emerged from the examination of the texts and exhibits were published in *Javnost—The Public* in 2016.

For more than a decade, numerous studies have explored the interrelationship between museums, public memory, and the construction of landscape or cityscape. Dickinson, Ott, and Aoki made numerous contributions to this ongoing discussion through their examination of the museums at the Buffalo Bill Center of the West (BBCW) in Cody, Wyoming (see Dickinson, Ott, & Aoki, 2005, 2006; Ott, Aoki, & Dickinson, 2011). Their research demonstrates that museums play a role in bringing together multiple diffused texts to construct an experiential landscape, which constitutes a knowledge about material and built environments (Dickinson et al., 2006). Such knowledge is important as it informs people how to interact with the environment, as well as other people within that environment. In many ways, this is similar to the mediascapes described in Chapter 1 (e.g., Appadurai, 1996), and was integral to the formation of performances in Wildcat Hollow and Mannheim. For Dickinson et al., however, past experience and personal memory play just as much a part of the construction of the backdrops for performance, as the media texts described by Appadurai (1996). Museums and other such places of memory act as both a personal experience, as well as a collection of mediated texts. One way that museums may play a role in the construction of landscape or cityscape involves the organization of exhibits in ways that invite visitors to occupy subject positions that structure sense making. The subject positions emphasize (and hide) meanings, which shape public memory; such memory is integral to the formation of landscape or cityscape.

The DDR Museum is similar to the BBCW noted above, in that both address controversial subjects of the past. The DDR Museum explored the communist past of Germany, while the BBCW illustrated the westward expansion of white settlers in the United States. In both cases, exhibits were utilized in ways that structured sense making about the past, and influenced public memory about the controversial issues in each nation. What is more, these subject positions did not allow for visitors to easily make textual associations beyond exhibits and structures of sense making provided for them. Visitors became enclosed within particular knowledges laid out for them; those knowledges, in turn, influenced their identity within particular material environments. The emergent knowledge and identity stood as a landscape (or cityscape) for those visitors. For the most part, this is similar to the ways in which different media narratives came together to construct knowledge that informs identity within the context of the physical environment of Mannheim. In the case of that city, new knowledges and rituals emerged from the consumption of information posted onto the stadtpunkte.

Within the BBCW the exhibits were organized in ways that constructed subject positions that structured the sense making processes for visitors. The five museums in the BBCW (Draper Museum of Natural History, Buffalo Bill Museum, Whitney Gallery of Art, Plains Indian Museum, and Cody Firearms Museum) presented exhibits that limited associations of white settlers in the west with genocide or colonial intentions, while portraying racial minorities (particularly Native Americans) as noble, yet simplistic. Essentially, visitors to the BBCW were guided to politically safe subject positions that reinforced hegemonic power structures, which constituted a cultural experience that could negotiate knowledge gaps about the changing demographics of the nation. In addition, these cultural experiences stood as knowledge that shaped the identity of people as they moved through, and interacted with the physical environment, of the American west. However, we do not consider the BBCW as a site that would facilitate the democratization of spaces in the west, as texts utilized in the museum do not facilitate any kind of participatory engagement; neither sociological or political, as described by Carpentier (2016). Through the BBCW, white visitors to the museum may have been able to reclaim a sense of dominance that could help them to feel in control of spaces that seemed unruly because of demographic changes to the United States. Minority visitors, however, potentially felt silenced or marginalized, which would do little to alleviate unease or address problems of austerity that impacted their communities.

The DDR Museum in Berlin accomplished many of the same functions observed at the BBCW, but also gave rise to the kind of democratization that could allow for multiple audiences to make sense of—and take control of—unruly spaces around them. Rather than reinforcing old hegemonic power structures threatened by activists or social change, the DDR Museum was utilized in such a way as to highlight lost spaces of the GDR that had become secondary to those other moments of the past. In particular, the DDR Museum was used to highlight the communist past of East Germany, which has often been overlooked in favor of historical examinations of the Nazi regime. The emphasis on Germany's Nazi past relegated many of the sites associated with the nation state of East Germany as lost spaces. Like Mannheim in Chapter 5, the city was largely obliterated in the Allied bombings during the Second World War. Like the cities in West Germany, reconstruction entailed prefabricated concrete slabs and simple architecture without decoration (Diefendorf, 1992; Leick, Schreiber, & Stoldt, 2010). Much of this drab construction from the communist era still existed throughout cities in eastern Germany, like Berlin, but they had come to be ignored and forgotten after the reunification of Germany in 1990. As in Bonnett's (2014) case study of Leningrad, those sites became the unruly lost spaces in the material environment.

In this place of memory, texts and materials highlighted unruly lost spaces associated with urban areas in the former communist state. Throughout the cities of eastern Germany there existed a variety of buildings and structures that were constructed by the GDR in the aftermath of World War II. Those buildings housed citizens, and played roles in the police state that emerged in the years of the Cold War. However, they have been forgotten, as they have no connection to the Nazi regime, or the confrontations between the United States and Soviet Union. The problem with these sites was that they did not facilitate the congregation of citizens because of their blasé and physically ugly condition, so that people often passed by them without notice. In many ways, this was similar to the problem associated with Mannheim noted in Chapter 5. Cities like Berlin are vibrant, but some of their communicative characteristics and qualities are eroded because of the nature of physical sites built in the reconstruction years following the Second World War. The museum provided a way of understanding the role of communism, and authoritarian police structures, in those lost spaces. To be sure, some sites in the city of Berlin associated with the GDR past were remembered and have become tourist landmarks; they were physical sites that were structured and organized to facilitate the flow of people and ideas. For instance, the remnants of the Berlin Wall and Checkpoint Charlie were both physical sites in the city that had strong connections to the past of the city and nation related to the GDR. However, both of these sites were portrayed through texts and memorials as important to the confrontations between the United States and the Soviet Union. These sites reinforced the modern, neoliberal order that has dominated the logics of space and cities over the past sixty years. Markers or texts installed at those sites convey little (if any) information about the

Stasi, Politburo, or other socio-political topics related to the nation-state of the GDR. If anything, those organizations or aspects of the GDR were portrayed as secondary.

Ultimately, I (Atkinson) engaged in a qualitative content analysis of the exhibits and texts of the DDR Museum (e.g., Altheide & Schneider, 2013; Atkinson, 2017; Mayring, 2000). In particular, I engaged in an inductive analysis, wherein the examination of the exhibits and texts gave rise to categories (e.g., Mayring, 2000). Through a close reading of these materials, I developed categories of spaces and actions within the museum. We came to understand that the museum created a transformative memory modification, as it revealed lost spaces of the physical environment to visitors. Like the overarching strategy of transformative memory revival, this stood as Carpentier's (2016) sociological form of participatory engagement, as it entailed the consumption of texts and enactment of new rituals around lost spaces. In order to successfully accomplish this memory modification, exhibits in the museum portrayed the former citizens of the GDR as juvenile alongside other materials about the socio-political structure of the socialist regime. These exhibits structured sense making and manipulated public memory concerning the people of the former socialist state, by representing them as easy dupes for external Communist forces; such a memory held both positive and negative implications. On the one hand, this public memory could help East Germans to navigate generational concerns and conversations regarding the atrocities of the Ministry of State Security, otherwise known as the Stasi. Indeed, such a public memory could help to avoid feelings of resentment that persist in the aftermath of reunification over twenty-five years ago. Conversely, the representations of those people who lived under the rule of the GDR Politburo for over forty years could easily be interpreted as simplistic and condescending. There was some similarity in this case to the Plains Indian Museum at the BBCW described by Dickinson et al. (2006), as that site entailed condescending and negative representations of Native Americans in the western United States. However, the case of the Plains Indian Museum (which is described in the following pages) was different in that the condescension was latent, hidden under manifest representations of Native Americans as noble. At the DDR Museum, the negative representations of the GDR citizenry were both manifest and latent. These problematic representations passed unnoticed, however, due to the process of acoustic participatory camouflage, in which the spaces within the museum guided visitors to participate in actions that normalized and reinforced otherwise condescending representations. Such an overly simplistic—and condescending—representation of citizens of the former GDR corresponded with western nostalgia for Cold War sites in Berlin and around East Germany, like at the Berlin Wall and Checkpoint Charlie. This practice is not inconsequential, as it can play a role in the formation of the cityscape of Berlin.

In the case of the DDR Museum, then, the arrangement of materials within the site drew visitors into subject positions that invited them to engage with exhibits in a way that drew attention to lost spaces in the city of Berlin. The subsequent public memory first reminded visitors of the connection between East Berlin and the GDR, and then wiped that memory clean of political meanings. The sites of East Berlin and the GDR were then populated by simplified vision of German people of the past. Such a public memory shaped a cityscape that was politically safe for people who were once citizens of the GDR, yet fun and exciting for foreign tourists seeking to insert themselves into history while on vacation in Berlin. For tourists, the museum played well to a consumer-oriented experience of history as meanings oppositional to the dominant structures of capitalism were also sanitized. The following pages provide insight into literature concerning museums and landscapes, as well as description of my inductive qualitative content analysis of materials from the DDR Museum.

Museums & Landscape/Cityscape

Museums do not simply exhibit items for visitors to view, but rather bring together multiple texts (e.g., objects, recordings, activities) so as to structure knowledge in ways that manipulate public memory, and in many cases shape landscapes or cityscapes. This is accomplished by regulating the movements and performances through the space of the museum, which stands as an experience of political "truth" for visitors (Bennett, 1995). Research by Dickinson et al. demonstrates the structuring of sense making and manipulation of public memory, while research by Davis (2013) and Woods, Ewalt, and Baker (2013) illustrates the influence of museums on landscapes and perceptions about physical environments. The research of Dickinson et al. demonstrates that museums bring together texts and experiences connected as exhibits; visitors engage with those texts in such a way that they build knowledge about a particular subject matter. In the case of the Plains Indian Museum at the BBCW, Dickinson et al. (2006) note that visitors were able to explore exhibits made up of displays, recorded oral histories, and anthropological notebooks. These texts placed the visitors into a particular subject position that helped them to make sense of the Native American people of the western United States as noble people, but also uncivilized.

Ott et al. (2011) also note that the organization of the physical spaces within museums is just as important (if not more so) as the texts utilized in the exhibits. The organization of space is important because it creates a way of experiencing the exhibits, and impedes association with alternative texts or experiences; the physical space of the exhibits gives rise to an understanding about the subject matter (e.g., Bennett, 1995). Essentially, Ott et al. drew upon McLuhan's (1988) work concerning media and space, in which there are two forms of space that ground human experience: visual and acoustic. According to McLuhan, visual space refers to organization of space so that subjects can be seen and experienced from a distance. Conversely, the notion of acoustic space entails organization of space that is "multisensory, participatory, and immersive" (Ott et al., p. 218); acoustic organization of space entails multiple senses working together to build a holistic experience. The Plains Indian Museum would be an example of acoustic organization of space, as visitors utilized multiple senses as they moved through the physical environment. In the museum, visitors' visual and auditory experience of displays played an integral role in making sense of Native Americans. Their sense making was also influenced by the participatory experience of handling and touching anthropological notebooks. The Cody Firearms Museum at the BBCW, conversely, utilized visual space to help visitors make sense of guns and their role in the west. By placing the guns behind glass, visitors viewed them from a subject position that was distanced, objective, and rationale; guns appeared as works of art, never associated with violence or bloodshed. Essentially, the way in which the texts were displayed within the physical environment of both museums structured visitors' sense making, and effectively sanitized public memory about settlers' role in the genocide of Native Americans.

In addition, these structures of sense making and manipulation of public memory stand as the foundation of perceptions of physical environments that give rise to landscapes and cityscapes. Research by Davis (2013) examined exhibits presented in two Civil War museums in the southern United States, which helped to foster alternative memories about the conflict; those memories challenged cityscapes shaped by resentment festering in many southern cities. The exhibits at the two Civil War museums featured representations of slavery that were different from those utilized for generations, and constructed negotiated memories about the Civil War and the Confederacy;

inclusion of slave narratives, alongside Union and Confederate materials, challenged public memory about the "Lost Cause" of the South. Those museums altered meanings associated with landmarks dedicated to Confederates and slave owners found throughout southern cities, and effectively influenced the cityscapes.[2]

Exhibits in museums can also shape landscape and cityscape by bringing together parts of larger networks of places, texts, and experiences. The association of different exhibits or texts with specific parts of a network can have profound implications for the sense making and manipulation of public memory. For instance, Woods et al. (2013) examined two exhibits at the Nebraska History Museum; the first emphasized a nostalgic history of Nebraska, while the second focused on the life of the lesbian writer Willa Cather. The second exhibit is particularly important as it featured a section entitled "the Shadow of Intolerance" about Brandon Teena, a transgender person who was murdered in Nebraska in 1993. This exhibit not only involved texts and objects directly connected to Teena, but images and texts associated with the national level rather than the regional level of Nebraska. Images and sounds of Nazis, Ku Klux Klan members in Mississippi, and Wisconsin Senator Joseph McCarthy surrounded the discussion about Teena, thus creating distance between Brandon's brutal murder and the region, people, and traditions of Nebraska. The way in which these two exhibits about Nebraska nostalgia and Willa Cather were placed next to each other helped visitors to make sense about the context of the murder, and disassociate it from their home state.

The DDR Museum and Berlin

Opened to the public in 2006, the DDR Museum showcases exhibits that provide visitors a brief glimpse into the world of the GDR. The museum was the creation of Peter Kenzelmann and Dr. Stefan Wolle. Kenzelmann, who originally hailed from the south of Germany, was disappointed by the absence of any museums or information about East Germany in Berlin, which was the former capital city of that defunct state. According to Bernstein (2006):

> [Kenzelmann] was struck by the absence of an East German museum, and even more struck by the fact that there are East German museums, albeit very small ones, in some smaller German towns, in the Netherlands and even in Culver City, California. Kenzelmann decided to do something about that. He invested some money of his own along with some from friends. Other funds came from a bank loan.

Kenzelmann used these funds to appropriate a private museum in the middle of the city, right across the Spree River from the Berliner Cathedral on Museum Island. At once, he began collecting old artifacts that could be put on display and tell a story of that former socialist state. Aiding him in these endeavors was Dr. Stefan Wolle, who acted as the chief academic director of the museum. Dr. Wolle, a renowned historian who studied at Humboldt University in the 1970s, had worked with opposition and underground groups in East Berlin for a peaceful reunification of Germany (Federal Foundation of Public Law, 2018). After the fall of the socialist regime and the movement towards reunification, Wolle worked as an expert advisor on examinations of the so-called "Stasi Files" that were obtained from state and military offices (Eckhard & Schubert, 2015). It was Dr. Wolle who provided an academic and historical vision for the display of the exhibits at Kenzelmann's museum.

The museum was visited on two occasions in October of 2014, in which the exhibits and accompanying texts were examined and photographed. The ways in which people handled and interacted with exhibits and materials was also noted. The photographs and notes were a part of the process for an inductive qualitative content analysis (see Atkinson, 2017; Mayring, 2000) of exhibits and materials housed within the museum. The content analysis revealed that the museum helped to structure sense making about East Germany, which was much more debated (and debatable) than the history of Nazi Germany. Much of the public memory concerning the Third Reich has (justifiably) focused on the persecution of Jewish people and the Holocaust. This focus is manifest in the numerous places of memory throughout the nation like the Topography of Terror in Berlin and the Dachau concentration camp memorial outside of Munich (Ladd, 1998). Although there are Germans (and non-Germans) who deny that the Holocaust took place, and others who feel that too much has been made of it, the public memory of Nazi Germany has generally been singular and focused because of these sites. Such is not the case with the public memory of East Germany, as there are divided opinions and memories about that former state; some are still enraged or traumatized by memories of Stasi atrocities, while others have fond memories of a state that assured full employment and stability (Vaizey, 2015). In fact, this division threatened to sunder entire communities following the collapse of the East German state in 1989, as people were suspicious of one another for acting as Stasi informants. According to Koehler (2000), the Stasi employed over one hundred fifty thousand full time operatives and workers at any time that engaged in surveillance and gathered information on citizens. However, the organization also relied on an expansive "unofficial" network of informants who relayed information about their friends, family, and neighbors. It is not known how many people actually assisted the Stasi in this capacity, but Koehler notes that estimates range from five hundred thousand to two million. What is more, many of those informants acted out of a sense of civic duty, while others acted out of fear or even coercion. All of this made the arrest and prosecution of Stasi criminals challenging, as it was difficult to differentiate those officers and informants who were actively involved. Consequently, there has been great difficulty in making sense of the past, which has left public memory of the cities and spaces of the former socialist state unfocused and scattered. Such difficulties made it particularly easy for museums and memorials to pass over the GDR past in favor of historical examinations of the Nazis.

At the center of the German capital, just across the Spree River from Museum Island, was the DDR Museum. Museum Island sits in the middle of the Spree River, and is the location of most major German state museums. This location was important, as the museum was a private venture of Peter Kenzelmann that first opened to the public in 2006. The site specificity of the museum, however, hid the fact that this was not an official part of Museum Island and separate from state operated museums throughout the capital. According to Dickinson et al. (2005), space specificity is "the relation between the site of the gallery and the space unconfined by the gallery. Museums are fashioned by the contents and materials of their physical locations … and thus it matters where memory is activated" (p. 90). Essentially, the physical environment around a museum plays an important role in the sense making that takes place inside a museum. All of this corresponds with past research by Bennett (1995), who explains that public museums have the authority to develop relations to culture, and generate politics by exhibiting "truth" to visitors. In the case of the DDR Museum, the placement of the site near many of the state funded and operated museums at the heart of the German capital made the vision of Peter Kenzelmann and Dr. Stefan Wolle seem "official." This was particularly important as the guise of a public museum gave the DDR Museum credibility and political power it would not have otherwise held.

In reality, however, there was significant resistance to the opening of this private museum by Kenzelmann. Many people associated with the state funded museums and historical sites feared that success of a private museum would put their own funding at risk (Hickley, 2006). Despite misgivings and resistance, the DDR Museum became one of the most popular sites in all of Berlin, earning the European Museum of the Year Award in 2008. According to the Senate Chancellery of Berlin (2009), the museum became the eleventh most visited site in the capital by 2009, alongside state museums like the Topography of Terror site dedicated to the examination of Nazi atrocities, the German Historical Museum, and the Memorial to the Murdered Jews of Europe.

The DDR Museum entailed two primary sections; for the purposes of this chapter, these sections are referred to as "Everyday Life" and "Politics." A large wall separated the two sections, while the texts and objects that made up the exhibits in each of the sections were placed into partitions. Many of the exhibits had photographs or objects set into the partitions for visitors to view as they walked by. Figure 6.1 illustrates one such exhibit, which provided information about different jobs and occupations in East Germany.

In this example, pictures and objects that demonstrated ordinary work in East Germany could be seen within the partitions, while texts to the side described the work and income in both German and English. However, the museum did not rely solely on such visual organization of the physical environment, but also utilized exhibits that were organized in terms of acoustic

Figure 6.1. A typical exhibit set into a partition at the DDR Museum. ©DDR Museum, Berlin 2019.

space, as visitors were typically able to handle and touch many of the exhibits. For instance, one partition in the section on "Everyday Life" had a closet set inside, with clothes hanging from racks that visitors could rummage through and even try on. Other exhibits entailed small cabinet sized doors set into the partitions. Visitors could open the door to view an item or collection of photographs, and read a text that provided more description of that display. One example of this was in the section on "Politics," where upon opening the door visitors saw a gas mask. The text set within the door provided more description of compulsory national service in the East German army. Finally, some of the exhibits were rooms or areas wherein the visitors did not view items or displays, but rather stepped into the subject position of GDR citizens and engaged in activities. There was a Trabant P 601 car that visitors could get inside and drive around East Berlin via a video game set up in the windshield. There was also an "authentic" East Berlin apartment in which visitors could sit on the couch and watch television or dial the rotary telephone.

As visitors entered the museum, they immediately found themselves in the first section dedicated to the exploration of "Everyday Life" in the GDR. This section of the museum moved with a certain flow; the partitions formed a zigzag pathway from text to text, exhibit to exhibit. The very first exhibit that visitors encountered within this section entailed models and maps that depicted the Berlin Wall as it stood after its completion in 1961. This is particularly important because although the focus of the museum was the former state of East Germany, this exhibit situated visitors immediately within the position of East Berlin (as opposed to Dresden, Leipzig, or the East German countryside). After the Berlin Wall exhibit, visitors moved through exhibits that depicted occupations and jobs, clothing and style, entertainment and leisure, transportation, average GDR homes, and Stasi surveillance.

The zigzag formation of the partitions eventually led visitors into the second section dedicated to "Politics." As before, pictures and objects were installed into the partitions with descriptions to the side. However, these exhibits did not focus on the everyday lives of people, but rather national level economics, politics, military, and ideology. This second section was distinctly different from the former, as the partitions did not form a pathway that steered visitors' movements. Instead, visitors walked around the partitions, returning always to a central point. This central point was particularly interesting as it entailed an exhibit concerning bureaucracy in the GDR, which featured a large desk and chair, with portraits of Karl Marx, Fredrick Engels, and Vladimir Lenin mounted on the wall behind them. The portraits were three-dimensional and moved in ways so that it appeared as though those Communist figures were constantly trying to look over the shoulder of anyone who was sitting at the desk.

The inductive qualitative content analysis demonstrated that the two sections of the museum helped to structure sense making about the city, former state, and its citizenry in two particular ways. Specifically, the section concerning "Everyday Life" illustrated the spaces in the city as they had been in Berlin before the fall of communism—before they were forgotten, lost, and unruly. In addition, this section led visitors to understand ordinary people in the GDR who occupied those spaces as dupes who were juvenile and acted out of hedonism, while the "Politics" section helped visitors to see those people in the GDR military and bureaucracy as Soviet puppets. The emergent public memory helped people to see the lost spaces around them in cities like Berlin, and understand those sites' connection to the communist past. In addition, the structuring of the ways in which people lived in those spaces can potentially help to navigate the tricky issue of the Stasi, and the suspicions that linger about the secret police force to this day. However, this public memory was also condescending of East German people and simplifies the context of their lives, and played a role in making the cityscape of Berlin a site wherein foreign tourists often look to insert themselves into exciting and nostalgic notions of Cold War history.

Juvenile Dupes

The first of these concepts arises from many of the exhibits placed throughout the first section of the museum, as well as the ways they were presented to visitors for handling and viewing. Specifically, the Trabant car, the "authentic" East Berliner apartment, and the Stasi surveillance exhibit were crucial for understanding the people of the GDR as hedonistic juveniles. After moving past the Berlin Wall model described previously, one of the first things that stood out was the tiny Trabant car, which was one of the most affordable and utilized cars in the former state.[3] Visitors could approach the car and open up the trunk, so as to examine tools and equipment within. More importantly, visitors could also get into the car and "drive" it around East Berlin by way of a video game displayed on the windshield. The game itself was rather unremarkable, as the graphics were pixilated and boxy. However, the car gave visitors the opportunity to explore old East Berlin beyond the wall depicted in the model. The buildings (nodes) throughout this virtual city were grey and devoid of any detail, while the streets (pathways) were empty as no people could be seen. This was important as visitors' exploration of East Berlin through the Trabant exhibit depicted the topographical categories of the city as empty and without any real features. The emptiness of the city was particularly significant as later exhibits helped visitors to make sense of that grey place and give it form. It is also important to note that many visitors were observed purposely driving the Trabant on sidewalks and slamming into buildings or objects. Groups of visitors would gather around the car watching the erratic driving, laughing and encouraging the driver.

After the Trabant car, visitors could proceed along the established pathway through the museum viewing and handling materials. This pathway led to an exhibit depicting an "authentic" apartment in East Berlin, complete with living room, kitchen, and lavatory. The living room was made up of a couch and coffee table sitting in front of an entertainment center that contained an old television, a stereo with cassette tapes, and books. Visitors could sit and watch segments of old GDR broadcast news and entertainment programs on the television, pick up a telephone and listen to an operator in German, or go through the cabinets of the entertainment center. The latter proved most interesting, because opening the cabinets revealed information about the people who once inhabited such living rooms in the city. One such cabinet opened to a cocktail bar with empty liquor bottles and cocktail glasses. Inside of the door, a text had been attached with the title "A Land of Hard Drinkers," and stated:

> Alcohol was the drug of choice in the GDR. With an estimated per capita consumption of 17 litres of pure alcohol per year, the men and women of the GDR could drink all-comers under the table. 17 litres equates to some 286 bottles of beer and 23 bottles of spirits per person.

Beside the cocktail bar was another cabinet door, which provided even more insight about GDR citizens. Opening the door revealed multiple nude pictures of a woman's lower abdominal region and upper legs, with her legs crossed in such a way as to conceal her genitalia. Across her nude body were the words "Medusa-Pessar," which is the name of a brand of intrauterine device (a contraceptive commonly referred to as an IUD). In a transparent plastic box in the corner of the cabinet were numerous packaged condoms and packets of birth control pills. Like the cabinet before, a text was set inside the door with the title "Joy of Sex." This text described the dominant views concerning sex and sex education within the GDR, and the development of birth control over the years:

> The first contraceptive pill was dispensed in 1965. Marketed as the "planned baby pill," in 1972 it was made available without prescription and free-of-charge to girls over 16. A further measure to enable safe family planning was the legalization, in the same year, of abortions within the first three months of pregnancy. The wide-availability of the Pill reduced condom-usage and resulted in an increase in sexually transmitted diseases, including HIV.

As visitors sat on the couch and watched television, and interacted with materials about alcohol and sex, certain knowledge was laid out for them about the living nodes in the GDR. The apartment was not really any different from other urban dwellings between the 1960s and 1980s. However, visitors also learned about the citizenry of the GDR who occupied these nodes. The selective information provided by the museum, and the manner in which it is conveyed to visitors, helped them to mentally populate the empty spaces of East Berlin that they encountered earlier through the video game in the Trabant car.

The lavatory in the "authentic" apartment featured a toilet with a plunger to the side, a sink and mirror, and a bathroom scale. In this case, there were no texts to convey any information, and visitors were free to rummage among the materials. During the observation, people turned the faucet on and off (there was no running water), examined the mirror, and tried to flush the toilet. Interestingly, almost everyone who moved through the lavatory sat on the toilet, smiling and laughing to friends and fellow visitors. On more than one occasion people made flatulent noises while occupying that position. More than anything else, then, the bathroom provided a sense of levity to the overall exhibit. In fact, none of the materials in the apartment exhibit were particularly unusual or exotic, as any of those materials might very well have been found in homes in the United States or other western countries in the 1980s. Rather than showcasing items unique to East Germany, or strange to westerners, the exhibit provided representations of GDR citizenry based on selective information about debaucheries, or comical actions taken by the museum visitors.

The final important exhibit in this section, the Stasi surveillance exhibit, was by no means the last. Indeed, it was situated in a small corner out of the "flow" of the section, just past the Trabant car. In the first visit to the museum, this exhibit was missed completely on the way to the GDR apartment exhibit.

While making observations of the closet of clothes described earlier, someone wondered aloud about a "bug," and noted that people at the Stasi exhibit behind us might be listening. Apparently, there was a listening device hidden somewhere in the closet. During the course of the research, this listening device was never found, but this led to a re-examination of the exhibits back against the "flow" of visitors. The Stasi exhibit featured visual and audio surveillance equipment used by the Stasi during the latter years of the GDR, all placed upon a small wooden desk; above the equipment was a portrait of Erich Honecker, the last chairman of the National Defense Council of the GDR. Specifically, there was a monitor with an unknown video playing, and audio equipment with headphones for visitors to put on. A large notebook had been placed on the desk, beside the equipment. On a wall beside these items were numerous texts that explained different aspects of the Stasi and their surveillance of GDR citizenry. When visitors put on the headphones, they were able to listen to conversations of other visitors who happened to be looking through the clothing exhibit. As visitors listened, they could open up the notebook and leaf through various notes, documents, and photographs held within. The texts on the wall beside the surveillance equipment told the story of the Stasi over the years. The first, entitled "The Ministry," noted that the secret police force was formed in 1950, and effectively convicted over quarter of a million people of political crimes. In addition, the text explained that by 1989 the Stasi had grown to include ninety-three thousand full time agents and employees. Another text with the title "Surveillance" explained that the Stasi relied heavily on informants in order to gather information on citizens.

Overall, these exhibits helped to highlight the lost spaces in the eastern portion of Berlin that had come to be ignored because of the emphasis in history on World War II and the Nazi regime. In addition, visitors could come to understand that the average people who lived and worked in those nodes tended to be hedonistic and juvenile. The sense making began with the Trabant exhibit, which illustrated the nodes and pathways as empty and devoid of details. As visitors moved through the first section, then, they encountered texts that provided details about the people who once lived in East Berlin; the information in the cabinets in the "authentic" apartment portrayed those people as hedonistic. In fact, the information that addressed the spread of sexually transmitted diseases and binge drinking could easily lead visitors to understand the people of the GDR as irresponsible. The acoustic nature of some of the exhibits also allowed for the visitors to take the subject position of a citizen of the GDR. In these cases, the subject position of those people included sitting on toilets and making flagellant noises, rummaging through drawers and cabinets, playing with kitchen appliances, and driving recklessly; such actions were somewhat hedonistic, and a little immature. Taking those subject positions in such ways could reinforce for visitors the information conveyed through texts at the various exhibits; indeed, these actions helped to make the portrayals conveyed by texts and materials seem realistic and normal. This was particularly important within the context of the Stasi exhibit; the texts at that site explained how numerous GDR citizens were involved with the secret police force over the years. With a firm understanding of those people (developed at any point in the museum), visitors could make sense of citizens' compliance with the Ministry of State Security as hedonism run amok and juvenile behavior. Indeed, visitors' act of spying on others digging impulsively through the closet of clothes could only add to their sense making.

Puppets

In the second section of the museum dedicated to "Politics," visitors viewed and handled materials that helped them to make sense of the larger GDR political and economic structures. These exhibits frequently pointed to external forces in control of the former communist state. Essentially, the military and bureaucracy in East Germany were puppets controlled by external agents; the hedonistic and juvenile people of the GDR were dupes, and the Soviets and other communist ideologues were the ones guiding politics, economics, and military/security. For the most part, the materials and texts of these exhibits depicted the political regime as authoritative and oppressive. However, the notion of international manipulation emerged in large part from two key exhibits: the bureaucratic desk, and the Stasi interrogation room. In addition, the decorative graphics utilized on the partitions and walls also added to the knowledge about international manipulation.

The topic of the bureaucratic desk was covered previously in this chapter. Essentially, as visitors moved among the partitions viewing exhibits, they returned to a central area of the section. The text on the desk explained that the life of the GDR bureaucrat was typically dull:

> The everyday face of power was more boring than terrifying. Functionaries in creased suits, tired, unshaved and grey. With a cigarette in the corner of their mouths and a full briefcase under their arm, they hurried from meeting to meeting. Their life revolved around their desk: decisions were made, passed on via the grey telephone

and recorded in top secret files. The functionaries were mere cogs in the machinery
of power. Cheerless, anonymous, and efficient.

This notion of bureaucrats and functionaries as the face of power was important, as there was no face to be seen at the desk—save for any visitor who
happened to be sitting there. However, the faces of Marx, Engels, and Lenin
dominated this exhibit, as they peered menacingly over the shoulders of anyone seated at the desk. The desk, accompanying text, and portraits on the wall
could lead visitors to an understanding of power in the GDR. Specifically, the
bureaucrats and party functionaries were mere "cogs" serving Soviet masters
and Communist ideologues. This was particularly important as visitors kept
passing through this site; as they learned more about the authoritative and
oppressive nature of the GDR regime, they were reminded of the "everyday
face of power."

Something that emphasized this point was photographs and graphics that
decorated this section of the museum. Throughout the "Politics" section were
pictures and graphics that emphasized the relationship between the GDR and
the Soviet Union. For instance, one of the first things that visitors could see as
they entered was an image of a crimson Soviet flag waving in a virtual breeze
projected onto a wall. In another instance, one of the partitions in the section entailed a large photograph of former Soviet leader Mikhail Gorbachev
embracing Erich Honecker. In this particular photo, Gorbachev's face was
much more visible and recognizable, as he was facing the camera and the focus
of the image.

Aside from the desk exhibit and faces of Communist leaders, another
exhibit featured a person with no face at all. The Stasi interrogation exhibit
was set in a small room adjacent to the "Politics" section of the museum.
Outside of the room, visitors could read a text beside the doorway entitled
"You Will Talk!":

> "Don't worry, we have plenty of time," said the interrogator repeatedly. The same
> questions for hours and the monotonous tapping of the typewriter. The remand pris-
> oner was entirely helpless. Nothing to read, no visitors, no lawyer, sleep deprivation
> and strict isolation. Prisoners often felt the need to get everything off their chest. In
> fact, this was part of the strategy which the Stasi men learned at the Stasi University
> in Potsdam.

After reading the text, visitors could proceed through the doorway into the
interrogation room. The room was sparse, with a (presumably) one-way mirror on the wall and a small desk and chair in the middle. Behind the desk was

a black silhouette of a figure positioned as if they were sitting; this figure was supposed to be the visitors' Stasi interrogator. Visitors could sit in the tiny chair across from the faceless Stasi officer (See Figure 6.2).

Two dimples were set into the tabletop with instructions for visitors to place their elbows within them and cover their ears with their hands. This action allowed them to hear a recording of a Stasi interrogator speaking in German to a prisoner.

The faces, or lack thereof, were particularly important for this section of the museum. As noted previously, visitors moved back and forth through the partitions viewing materials that demonstrated cruelty and oppressive political practices in the GDR; always, however, they returned to one central exhibit that emphasized Communist ideologues and Soviet leaders looking over the shoulders of the "boring" "cogs" in the GDR power structure. When the visitors moved into the Stasi interrogation exhibit, they encountered a faceless character sitting at the desk. As Ott et al. (2011) note, experiences play an important role in viewing materials within museums; in some cases, the organization of space can repress personal and cultural experiences necessary for sense making. In this case, the observation of Russian faces in connection with GDR

Figure 6.2. Stasi interrogation room exhibit. ©DDR Museum, Berlin 2019.

"Politics" associated the Stasi silhouette more with the Soviet Union and outside Communist influences; past experiences and information concerning the socialist state were deterred for visitors. Overall, this section of the museum fostered public memory about the GDR in such a way that the problematic politics of the former state became associated with external states and ideologues, rather than the German people. As in the case of Woods et al. (2013) examination of the Brandon Teena exhibit at the Nebraska History Museum, images featuring external people helped visitors to separate Stasi violence and oppression (at least partially) from Germany and East German people.

Discussion

Ultimately, this examination of the DDR Museum illustrated the substrategy for communicative democratization that we call transformative memory modification. Like the memory revival described in the previous chapter, this substrategy reminded people about the material spaces and sites from the past; in many cases, those physical structures no longer existed. Nevertheless, people were reminded of what had once been in a region or area. This substrategy differs, however, in that the GDR and its authorities have not really been forgotten. Instead, they had been pushed to the side in favor of historical examinations of the Nazis. When the GDR or Stasi were remembered, or made a part of any discussion of the past, they were usually described in relation to the US and USSR. In this way, then, typical memories or discussions reinforced the neoliberal world order that emerged following the Cold War confrontations between those two superpowers. So this strategy did not just revive memory, but modified it. In this case, the GDR, Stasi, and Politburo were made to be important parts of the German past, rather than footnotes in neoliberal history. The spaces associated with them were henceforth worthy of examination and interaction, rather than ambivalence and avoidance.

In addition, the examination of the museum demonstrated the practice of acoustic participatory camouflage, in which simplistic and condescending portrayals were hidden and reinforced by the actions called upon by visitors passing through. We see the transformative memory modification/revival as separate from acoustic participatory camouflage; the two do not have to appear together. However, in the case of the DDR Museum, they were intertwined. The first was a strategy for the democratization of unruly spaces, while the second was the message conveyed by way of the strategy. Essentially, negative manifest and latent messages about GDR citizens were embedded into spaces throughout the museum, and organized in such a way to influence the sense making of visitors as they passed through. Many of those manifest meanings might very well have been labeled offensive by visitors, but were normalized through participatory actions guided by the arrangement of acoustic spaces. The acoustic spaces created an experience for the visitors, which called for actions that corresponded with negative manifest meanings. Visitors' participation in those actions could make such representations seem sensible and appropriate.

In this way, then, the DDR Museum deviates from museums illustrated in past research, which typically treated subjects with reverence and respect. In Davis' (2013) research concerning Civil War museums, the exhibits constructed a sense of respect for Union soldiers, Confederates, and slaves alike. The Plains Indian Museum, despite the emergent knowledge of those ancient peoples as uncivilized, led visitors to engage with materials about Native American tribes in thoughtful and respectful ways. This fostered a sense of admiration that sanitized the western US of colonial relations and genocide (Dickinson et al., 2006). Such was not the case at the DDR Museum in Berlin. The exhibits positioned visitors in such a way that they understood GDR citizens in terms of hedonistic or juvenile acts (e.g., binge drinking, unprotected sex), all the while the visitors themselves engaged in similar acts (e.g., sitting on the toilet, driving erratically). Condescension and insensitivity were conveniently disguised and made normal by the actions taken by visitors. In the case of the transformative memory modification, this message was important for shifting blame for past political crimes by the Stasi to the Soviet Union and other external forces.

Overall, the DDR Museum helped people to see the lost spaces associated with the GDR and communist East Berlin. Buildings could now have a past connected to these crucial moments in German history. What is more, they learned that the people who lived and worked in these nodes acted hedonistic and slightly immature, which made it all to easy for them to be duped by external political actors. As noted in the introduction of this chapter, this strategy of transformative memory modification is not inconsequential, as it holds two important implications for understanding public memory about the former state, and the cityscape of Berlin. First, this structured process of sense-making can actually aid ongoing conversations about the Stasi and efforts for reconciliation within Germany today. Making sense of the GDR has been much more divisive than making sense of the Third Reich, due in large part to the nature of Stasi records concerning informants; roughly one hundred fifty thousand people were recorded as Stasi informants. However, both Koehler and Vaizey have noted that many of those records were destroyed, and the Stasi regularly recruited informants who were never documented. Koehler (2000) estimates that there may very well have been one Stasi informant for every ten or six citizens. Suspicions abound to this day as to the roles that neighbors, family, and friends played in Stasi persecutions and arrests (Vaizey, 2015). However, most of these suspicions can never be substantiated, and even if they could be it can never be proved whether people collaborated out of a sense of civic duty or fear. The transformative memory modification relocated the focus of historical examination in the nation to the GDR and Stasi, but also placed the blame for atrocities outside of the city and nation. The emergent public memory of dupes and puppets, then, can make grappling with the past more manageable; people who have been duped can be forgiven.

As former citizens of the GDR rediscover the lost spaces of the physical environments of Berlin, they may navigate them with less suspicion of other East Germans with whom they may interact. The city may become a site for dialogue and learning, rather than rife with distrust; such a change in interactions (with people and the material city) may help to foster forgiveness and reconciliation. What is more, the city itself becomes interesting for many of the citizens who routinely ignore or avoid spaces in the physical environment. Public spaces throughout the city can potentially become more communicative, allowing for more debate and discussion at the local level—similar to the city of Mannheim described in Chapter 5. This may not be entirely beneficial, however, as the structure of this sense making can effectively shield guilty parties responsible for crimes and barbaric atrocities. The chief Stasi strategists have been tried and convicted, but many others responsible for atrocities may still be at large (Koehler, 2000; Vaizey, 2015).

In addition, making sense of the GDR through the frame of acoustic participatory camouflage conveyed through the museum shaped cityscape for foreign tourists visiting Berlin. Through sites like the DDR Museum, tourists could learn that the GDR citizenry had little connection to, or responsibility for, politics and actions taken by that former socialist state. Such was not the case with memorials and museums dedicated to the memory of the Nazis and their atrocities; those places built important public memory about the experiences of Holocaust victims, as well as German responsibility for those atrocities. In this way, then, tourists visited sites like the Topography of Terror and the Memorial to the Murdered Jews of Europe with a sense of respect and sorrow. Conversely, tourists made sense of sites associated with the Cold War past of the GDR, like the Berlin Wall or Checkpoint Charlie, in different ways. The public memory about the GDR and the socialist past of Europe built through places like the DDR Museum reinforced political views about Western dominance and capitalism, and emphasized the importance of the United States in world affairs. In a way, the memory modification helped to create new performative rules for sections of the urban environment associated with the GDR. A new unruliness potentially emerges from the differing performative rules: the unruliness of enclave, like in the case of Wildcat Hollow. Rather than interacting with those material sites connected to the GDR with a sense of respect, tourists inserted themselves into a nostalgic, historical spotlight. Those sites were not understood in terms of any suffering caused by the Stasi and Politburo, but rather the standoff between the Soviet Union and the United States. Tourists—especially American tourists—regularly snapped "selfies" at these historic places in order to demonstrate that they were at sites that were important to a political clash between two superpowers external to Germany. Groups could often be seen huddled together at these sights to take photographs, holding up victory/peace signs, and giving their best smile for the camera. These are not actions ever performed by tourists at the Memorial to the Murdered Jews of Europe.

Notes

1. The English abbreviation for the former East German state is "GDR," while the German abbreviation is "DDR" (pronounced Day-Day-Ahr). For the purposes of this chapter, we refer to the former socialist state with the English abbreviation, but refer to the museum with the German abbreviation. This is simply due to the fact that DDR is the name of the museum, and it is called such on the museum's English language website and in English language advertisements.
2. Unlike the Plains Indian Museum, we would consider the museums examined by Davis (2013) to correspond with the kind of transformative memory modification observed at the DDR Museum.
3. This information comes directly from the text at the Trabant car exhibit.

References

Altheide, D., & Schneider, C. (2013). *Qualitative media analysis*. Thousand Oaks, CA: Sage.

Appadurai, A. (1996). *Modernity at large: Cultural dimensions of globalization*. Minneapolis, MN: University of Minnesota Press.

Atkinson, J. D. (2017). *Journey into social activism: Qualitative approaches*. New York, NY: Fordham University Press.

Bennett, T. (1995). *The birth of the museum: History, theory, politics*. New York, NY: Routledge Press.

Bernstein, R. (2006, July 20). In Berlin, a museum under surveillance. *New York Times* [online]. Accessed May 7, 2018, from https://www.nytimes.com/2006/07/20/world/europe/20i-ht-stasi.2251763.html

Bonnett, A. (2014). *Unruly places: Lost spaces, secret cities, and other inscrutable geographies.* New York, NY: Houghton-Mifflin Harcourt.

Carpentier, N. (2016). Beyond the ladder of participation: An analytical toolkit for the critical analysis of participatory media processes. *Javnost—The Public, 23,* 70–88.

Davis, P. (2013). Memoryscapes in transition: Black history museums, new South narratives, and urban regeneration. *Southern Communication Journal, 78*(2), 107–127.

Dickinson, G., Ott, B., & Aoki, E. (2005). Memory and myth at the Buffalo Bill Museum. *Western Journal of Communication, 69*(2), 85–108.

Dickinson, G., Ott, B., & Aoki, E. (2006). Spaces of remembering and forgetting: The reverent eye/I at the Plains Indian Museum. *Communication and Critical/Cultural Studies, 3,* 27–47.

Diefendorf, J. (1992). *In the wake of war: The reconstruction of German cities after World War II.* Oxford, UK: Oxford University Press.

Eckhard, J., & Schubert, T. (2015). *Friedliche revolution und demokratie: Perspektiven nach 25 jahren.* Berlin, Germany: Christoph Links Verlag.

Federal Foundation of Public Law. (2018). *Die heile welt der diktatur? Herrschaft und alltag in der DDR.* Accessed May 7, 2018, from https://www.bundesstiftung-aufarbeitung.de/die-heile-welt-der-diktatur-%2363%3B-herrschaft-und-alltag-in-der-ddr-2354.html

Hickley, C. (2006, July 14). New Berlin museum portrays life in communist East Germany. *Bloomberg.com.* Accessed on June 2, 2015, from http://www.bloomberg.com/apps/news?pid=newsarchive&sid=a84zdFeQZkVk&refer=germany

Koehler, J. (2000). *Stasi: The untold story of the East German secret police.* Boulder, CO: Westview Press.

Ladd, B. (1998). *The ghosts of Berlin: Confronting German history in the urban landscape.* Chicago, IL: University of Chicago Press.

Leick, R., Schreiber, M., & Stoldt, H. (2010, August 10). Out of the ashes: A new look at Germany's postwar reconstruction. *Spiegel Online International.* Accessed October 2, 2014, http://www.spiegel.de/international/germany/out-of-the-ashes-a-new-look-at-germany-s-postwar-reconstruction-a-702856.html

Mayring, P. (2000). Qualitative content analysis. *Forum: Qualitative Social Research* [Online Journal], *1*(2). Accessed October 1, 2002, from http://www.qualitative-research.net/fqs-texte/2-00/2-00mayring-e.htm

McLuhan, M. (1988). *Laws of media: The new science.* Toronto, ON: University of Toronto Press.

Ott, B., Aoki, E., & Dickinson, G. (2011). Ways of (not) seeing guns: Presence and absence at the Cody Firearms Museum. *Communication and Critical/Cultural Studies, 8*(3), 215–239.

Senate Chancellery of Berlin. (2009, November 13). *Gedenkstätten und zeitgeschichtliche Museen bleiben im Aufwärtstrend.* Accessed on June 1, 2015, from http://www.berlin.de/rbmskzl/aktuelles/pressemitteilungen/2009/pressemitteilung.54980.php

Vaizey, H. (2015). *Born in the GDR: Life in the shadow of the wall.* Oxford, UK: Oxford University Press.

Woods, C., Ewalt, J., & Baker, S. (2013). A matter of regionalism: Remembering Brandon Teena and Willa Cather at the Nebraska History Museum. *Quarterly Journal of Speech, 99*(3), 341–363.

PART IV

EXPLORING A HIDDEN GEOGRAPHY IN DETROIT

The final chapters of the book entail our research concerning hidden geographies in Detroit, Michigan. In that research, we demonstrate one communicative strategy for the democratization of hidden geography, which we refer to as diffused intertextual production. This particular strategy entails the simultaneous presence of an intertextual frame with an interactive media platform. In the case of Detroit, we found that this strategy allowed for a group of citizens to reimagine the physical environment as inviting and interesting, which altered their pathways through—and interactions with—the city around them. In Chapter 7, we provide a detailed description of this communicative strategy, and how it was manifest in the web community. In Chapter 8, we illustrate the ways in which diffused intertextual production influenced the performances of the members of the community. Finally, Chapter 9 reveals the potential that this communicative strategy holds for the construction of bridges between communities separated by the hidden geography. Overall, Part IV accomplishes the following:

1. Explains and demonstrates the concept of diffused intertextual production.
2. Depicts the emergence of a participatory civic identity associated with the new knowledge that is constructed from diffused intertextual production.
3. Demonstrates the performance of standpoint by members of the web community, as they interact with the physical environment of Detroit.
4. Illustrates one case in which diffused intertextual production allowed for a community isolated in the hidden geography of Detroit to connect to other communities.

· 7 ·

DIFFUSED INTERTEXTUAL PRODUCTION

As demonstrated in the previous chapters, spaces in contemporary society are often made unruly because of the degradations that occur in the physical environment. The second part of this book provided detailed descriptions of the creation, or acceleration, of such degradation and unruliness of spaces in cities like Flint from austerity that stem from resentment and neoliberalism. However, we have found over the years that citizens are able to create a sense of control over such unruly spaces, as in the case of Wildcat Hollow and Germany. In those cases, and others like them, democratization, media environments, or mediascapes, were integral for the formation of alternatives to the physical environments that citizens encounter in their everyday lives. In the case of Wildcat Hollow, the traditional families in that region constructed a trust network in order to counter the unruliness that stemmed from the rural gentrification that had deeply eroded their agricultural economic base. The resistance performed by certain members of the trust network was grounded in the logic and worldviews espoused through conservative alternative media, which influenced the way in which they created a sense of control over the unruly enclave around them. In the cases from Germany, historical markers in Mannheim and the DDR Museum in Berlin both highlighted lost spaces in the urban environments. The consumption of texts utilized in all of these cases constructed new knowledges, which initiated ritualistic examinations of physical environments that had become unruly. In all of these cases, however, the democratization of unruly spaces adhered to the notions of sociological participatory engagement, outlined by Carpentier (2016).

In the remaining chapters, we examine and explore the communicative strategy that we call diffused intertextual production. As in the case of Wildcat Hollow and the German cities, such actions and performances on the part of citizens were informed and guided by media environments. The difference in this particular case is that rather than existing as passive consumers of mediated texts, the citizens in Detroit actively engaged in the co-production of texts integral to the construction of new knowledge and an alternative cityscape. What is more, citizens engaged in struggles over meanings, which shaped the ways that the physical environment was perceived. The strategy used here was much more participatory in nature, as it adhered to Carpentier's (2016) notion of political participatory engagement. All of this gave rise to a more vibrant form of democratization than the strategy utilized by traditional residents in Wildcat Hollow and the urban environments of Germany.

In the case that follows, communicative democratization was formed from mediascapes that gave rise to locally-oriented engagement and relational development (e.g., Carpentier, 2016; Howley, 2005). We call this particular strategy diffused intertextual production, as it entails the use of mediated platforms that provide users with intercreative access to most of the texts utilized in the formation of a mediascape. We introduced this concept in an article published in *Critical Studies in Media Communication* in 2012. In that article we illustrated the ways in which the simultaneous presence of intertextuality and interactivity allowed for members of a web community to build new knowledge about spaces and places around them in the city of Detroit. Such knowledge stood as the foundation for a new, participatory civic identity that helped them to understand that they could interact with the physical environment, and people within that environment, in different ways. Within this chapter, we provide an in-depth description of diffused intertextual production. In the following chapter, we explore how this concept—and the democratization of space associated with it—actually influenced performances of members of the community online and within the physical environment. Afterwards, chapter 9 provides insight into a substrategy of diffused intertextual production that we call creative narrative appropriation, which also proves useful in the democratization of space.

Much of the city of Detroit stands as a collection of unruly spaces, filled with seemingly wild or untamed sites that alter the ways in which people travel through, and interact with, the physical environment. In many ways, these unruly sites within the city stand as hidden geographies. As noted in the first three chapters, Bonnett's (2014) unrefined notion of hidden geographies hints at physical environments that are concealed from people as they move through their everyday life. Similar to lost spaces, these can be places or physical environments by which people move, or even through, without any knowledge that those sites are there—or they may only get glimpses of those hidden spaces as they move along. Conversely, hidden geographies may be spaces that people travel by with no notice, like the pipelines and waterways in Flint. In many cases, hidden geographies have typically been long abandoned, and no longer facilitate the movement of bodies or goods like spaces typically encountered in the everyday life of communicative cities. These sites often leach chemicals or other toxins into the environment, which degrades Sen's (2000) capabilities that provide hope and dignity for the citizenry. Whenever people notice those spaces, they often elicit feelings of confusion or trepidation. Indeed, the very presence of abandoned structures can feel ominous or foreboding, which similarly hampers hope or dignity, or other instrumental freedoms.

Sections of Detroit stood as similarly hidden geographies as those in Flint. And like many unruly hidden geographies, they were viewed with a sense of unease. Abandoned houses and factories dotted entire areas of the city, and people often traveled by those sites on foot or by car. An "urban prairie" of trees and brush had grown up over the years, leaving only parts of these spaces visible, and actually claimed some of those spaces entirely. As people traveled through this environment, they often felt worry or concern about who or what might dwell within those sites that were barely visible (or out of sight entirely); they felt the need to pass by quickly—to get away entirely. The very fabric of the physical environment had come to be reviled and despised for many citizens, as it had been incorporated into an ever-growing narrative of urban neglect and failure described in Chapter 3.

Despite this expansive problem, there were people in the city who worked to tame the unruly spaces and hidden geographies. They had banded around an online art project about the "fabulous ruins" of Detroit. The forums grew around an art project that stimulated discussion about the different spaces in the city, their current state and past, and potential futures. These discussions developed alternative knowledges about the city and aided in the construction of new identities that guided interactions with the physical environment, and people within that environment. This strategy for the communicative democratization of space was evident in the DetroitYES! web community dedicated to discussions about the history and current state of that city. In the following pages, we explain a basic history of Detroit, along with description of the competing cityscapes that have emerged over the past fifty years. We then provide an overview of the DetroitYES! web community and the Fabulous Ruins of Detroit Virtual Tour. Finally, we explicate the notion of diffused intertextual production, and demonstrate how it stands as one strategy for democratization of space.[1]

Detroit, Michigan

Detroit has been, perhaps, one of the most embattled cityscapes in the US, emblazoned in the national memory with its military occupation during the 1967 riots, and its destructive Devil's Night arsons in the 1980s and 1990s. It has become a national symbol of urban decay, post-industrial neglect, and criminality. However, the city was not always visualized in this way and, in fact the cityscape developed out of the institutions, labor, and capital-driven necessities of urban development (Zukin, 1991). The city's industrial might, employment, and standard of living all expanded as it shifted into its role as the "Motor City" after the expansion of trucking following the First World War, and then as the "Arsenal of Democracy" during the second.

Such a shared view or "way of seeing" Detroit (Berger, 1972) highlights, rather than hides, the grittiness of the actual city. In the past, the city was constructed as heroic and modern through numerous stories and depictions in popular media of Detroit as the "prosperous," "opulent," and "lucrative" home of the auto industry (Farley, Danziger, & Holzer, 2002; Sugrue, 1996). Today, the swirl of narratives found in American media constructs an altogether different image of Detroit. Newspapers describe the city as the "most murderous city" in America (Ewalt, 2007), with the highest poverty rate (Bouffard, 2015), and one of the highest rates of home foreclosures (Porter, 2008; Rooney, 2008). Movies such as *Narc* and *8 Mile* portray a city in which abandoned buildings and factories stand as the anchoring landmarks, while poverty, drug use, and violence frame its cityscape. In this way, the cityscape is often depicted for onlookers as dangerous. In the case of Detroit, the economic and political problems of the city become the mediated experience that one can visit without actually being there, or mediate how to perform within spaces found there. One can start to see the city of Detroit, then, in terms of the topographical categories of Sadler and Haskins (2005) described in Chapter 1. In reference to their notion of the postcard effect, one can easily imagine a postcard that contains shifting images of ominous burned out buildings filled with scowling criminals with an inscription at the bottom that reads: "Detroit: Where the Weak are Killed and Eaten!," a phrase that was depicted on popular t-shirts in the Detroit area at the time of our research.

Interestingly, this bleak urban landscape is contrasted with a new one—or, rather, an affirmation of the old one's constitutive opposite. With the construction of the GM Renaissance Center, Detroit was to be rewritten as a center of industrial power and corporate governance. Later, the People Mover monorail and several casinos were constructed to rewrite the Motor City as comfortable and accessible to tourists. The attempt to rebrand Detroit's dominant cityscape reflects a particular way of reading the old one. It is not just that Detroit should become a center of commerce, but like many cities around the world it should become a playground for the wealthy and a place of low-wage service jobs for those in the other side of the polarizing post–1960s economy. This narrative embodies the simultaneous reuse and reconceptualization of the spaces and built geographies of the post-industrial city. It is a re-landscaping of Detroit, both in terms of the functioning of the built environment and the image that it projects to audiences. Travel guides found at various stops along I–75 during the period of our research featured images of such a Detroit, often calling the site "Detroit Shop City."

What we found to be particularly interesting are the ways in which this "new and improved" cityscape is struggled over and contested by a project that was initiated by a group of citizens within the city and immediate area. While such struggle is always a feature of any dominant landscape (Cosgrove, 1985, 1988; Mitchell, 1996, 2000), what makes this group and their work interesting is that their counter-narrative revolves around the valorization of the city's "ruins"; those spaces in the physical environment that would stand as Bonnet's hidden geography. They are those factories that have been closed, houses that have become vacant, and churches and schools that have been abandoned. It is within the context of the simultaneously material and symbolic competing cityscapes described above—the city "where the weak are killed and eaten" and "Detroit Shop City"—that the DetroitYES! web community attempts to reframe the debate around a third cityscape: the exposure of the hidden geography, historical investigation of residual urban forms, preservation of ruined landscapes, and construction of new historical and experiential narratives.

We refer to this new one as an "alternative cityscape." Essentially, the website used by the group attempts to make what appears to be an unruly ghost town live again through discussion, exploration, investigation, and memory. In the following pages, we examine this alternative cityscape. Like Dickinson's (1997) examination of Old Pasadena described in Chapter 1, the two competing dominant cityscapes described above are built around legends. In the first case, "where the weak are killed and eaten" is a legend of danger and toughness, built from news stories and narratives of unemployment, crime, racial segregation, and rioting. It is distinctly less predictable and more hazardous than Dickinson's (2006) description of controlled risk in the film *Pleasantville*. Yet, as the t-shirt suggests, there is something vaguely romantic (if also a bit melancholic) in this legend, although it is romance that attracts "morbid curiosity" similar to the curiosity of people passing by a traffic accident, rather than Dickinson's (1997) "shopper's browse." Such a morbid curiosity could stand as one of Dickinson's (2015) rhetorical spatialities, warning people of the nightmares that await them if they do not live the "good life" of modern capitalism. In the second case, the Renaissance Center and casinos are based on the nostalgia of the old, powerful Motor City, channeling that legendary past to directly attract consumer capital. Yet, while it is founded on this legendary past, it functions through the erasure of the residual elements—"decrepit," "blighted," "abandoned," "dereliction"—of the old city. As we will show, the alternative is not so much outside the two competing dominant narratives of Detroit, but rather contained—or domesticated—within elements of both as a third cityscape that is built from nostalgia generated by interactive and intertextual components within a web-community. The alternative cityscape that is constructed corresponds to the two competing cityscapes in that it has one eye on the past defined by "decline" (as in the case of the city "where the weak are killed and eaten"), while at the same time looking to future revitalization (as in the case of "Detroit Shop City"). The unruly spaces in Detroit's cityscape are not simply an issue of representation and narrative, but a question of how people live, work, and interact within the city. In this case, the "cultural power" (Mitchell, 1994) of the Detroit cityscape mediates the ways in which people will in the future interact within the city, as well as how they will interact with the city itself.

DetroitYES! and the Fabulous Ruins

The counter narrative emerged in 1997 with the advent of a website called "the Fabulous Ruins of Detroit" and is now accompanied by other similar websites dedicated to defunct buildings and crumbling landmarks. The website was created by a local photographer and artist, Lowell Boileau, and is part of a larger Detroit digitally networked meet-up group called "DetroitYES!" This organization is situated in an even broader movement of "urban exploration" that has developed in the United States and Europe over the past decade. In conjunction with framing the city, narrating it, and constructing a hegemonic totality through texts, myths, and codes—who are insiders/outsiders, what are good/bad neighborhoods—various interests (with varying configurations of power) struggle to create this shared vision through the built environment. The DetroitYES! website, as well as other such sites (e.g., Deadmalls.com), features two important components that are documented and explored in literature concerning online communication: intertextuality (e.g., Collins, 1992; Warnick & Heineman, 2012; Ott & Walter, 2000; Warnick, 1998, 2007) and interactivity (e.g., Atkinson, 2010; Endres & Warnick, 2004; Warnick & Heineman, 2012; McMillan, 2002; Meikle, 2002; Warnick, 2007; Warnick, Xenos, Endres, & Gastil, 2005).

At this juncture, it would be appropriate to fully discuss these important concepts in detail. Intertextuality has proven to be a tenuous topic, as Ott and Walter (2000) have demonstrated how past research has conflated two distinct definitions: a reference to the unconscious ways audiences create meaning when reading a text (e.g., Fiske, 1987), and "a textual strategy consciously incorporated by media producers that invites audiences to make specific lateral associations between texts" (Ott & Walter, 2000, p. 430). Essentially, the second definition entails media producers utilizing references, allusions, and appropriations from other texts, and "infusing" them into their own text; such a textual strategy broadens the scope of the producers' text (Collins, 1992; Warnick & Heineman, 2012; Ott & Walter, 2000; Warnick, 1998, 2007). The second definition is the basis for our discussion in this chapter as such strategies can be observed on the DetroitYES! website. Together, Ott and Walter (2000), Warnick (2007), and Warnick and Heineman identify specific intertextual strategies such as parodic allusion, creative appropriation, self-reflexive reference, cross-reference, and explicit play with social texts. Parodic allusion is the juxtaposition of one text along with another text in order to emulate, embellish, or critically comment on the original text (Ott & Walter,

2000; Warnick, 2007). Creative appropriation refers to an author's splicing of fragments from one text and incorporating them into their own text (Ott & Walter, 2000). Self-reflexive reference is a literary style in which a text producer will refer to other texts in an attempt to comment on the culture and history associated with the producer's text (Ott & Walter, 2000). Cross-reference refers to the practice of mentioning or alluding to specific popular films, songs, or other such texts (Warnick, 2007; Warnick & Heineman). Finally, explicit play with social texts is a strategy in which the producer juxtaposes different social situations that have been portrayed in popular media, news, or historical accounts to explain a particular issue to an audience; such juxtaposition often takes the form of satire (Warnick, 2007).

Interactivity has proven to be an even more slippery subject, as scholars such as Landow (2006) and Meikle (2002) have argued that the term has been misused and misrepresented to the point that it no longer holds any meaning. Some communication and media scholars have defined interactivity in terms of responses or reactions that are directed toward the sender of a message (e.g., Rafaeli, 1988; Turow, 1977), while others have addressed interactivity as stimulating elements found within a text (e.g., Endres & Warnick, 2004). In our research, we relied on definitions of interactivity provided by McMillan (2002) who outlined three interactivity typologies that have emerged in communication and media literature: user-to-system, user-to-user, and user-to-document. User-to-system interactivity constitutes interactions between media users and media systems, as in the case of the use of websites like Amazon.com. (e.g., Kiousis, 2002). User-to-user interactivity refers to interactions between multiple media users through interactive media systems, such as Facebook or Skype (e.g., Warnick et al., 2005). Finally, user-to-document interactivity entails modification or additions to a text by audiences through either technological systems (e.g., Kidd, 2003; Meikle, 2002) or through the provision of feedback to text producers (e.g., Atkinson, 2008; Atton, 2002; Eliasoph, 1988).

In the case of the DetroitYES! web community, the concepts of interactivity and intertextuality are both present. In reference to interactivity, the co-production of media texts, or what McMillan calls "user-to-document interactivity" is evident. In addition, the juxtaposition of social situations within texts, or what Warnick calls "explicit play with social texts" is also evident. These concepts can be observed in two important parts of the DetroitYES! website: the Fabulous Ruins of Detroit virtual tour, and the discussion forums. Boileau created the virtual tour in 1997 to showcase his photographs and artistic renderings of abandoned Detroit landmarks. As the site developed, intertextual strategies such as allusions to ancient Athens and Rome were added to enhance and "guide" Boileau's tour of the artwork featuring the city. To complement the guided tour, he added an interactive discussion forum in 1999, allowing visitors to post comments about the photographs and artwork found in the virtual tour. According to the DetroitYES! website, both the virtual tour and the discussion forum were developed by Boileau as an attempt to answer very difficult questions about the city of Detroit: how could this have happened, and what is to be done?

> The DetroitYES! Project takes on these questions by providing a setting where an audience of those who care can meet, discuss, and carry forward the evolving portrait of Detroit, far beyond the artist who started it, and guide the socially cutting edge city and region forward [to] its uncertain future.

Ultimately, the DetroitYES! web community was constructed from two intertwined aspects: one intertextual, the other interactive. We explored this community by engaging in qualitative content analysis of the intertextual aspects of the web community (the Fabulous Ruins Virtual Tour) and the interactive aspects (the discussion forums). In addition, we also engaged in postmodern interviews (see Atkinson, 2017; Gubrium & Holstein, 2003) and focus groups with numerous members of the web community. Those interviews are much more relevant in the following two chapters concerning standpoint and narrative appropriation. In terms of the qualitative content analysis, we engaged in a deductive analysis (see Atkinson, 2017; Mayring, 2000) in which we searched for themes that emerged from depictions of the topographical categories (e.g., Sadler & Haskins, 2005) that we found within the virtual tour and the discussion forums. We noted how the different topographical categories were depicted in photographs and narratives provided by Boileau in the virtual tour, as well as through stories, anecdotes and attachments (e.g., YouTube videos, MapQuest references) provided by users in one hundred sixty two of the threads posted on the forums. The following pages explain our findings related to both the intertextual and interactive aspects of the web community.

Fabulous Ruins of Detroit

The intertextual component at the heart of the DetroitYES! website was the Fabulous Ruins of Detroit virtual tour. In the case of the virtual tour, the site producer, Lowell Boileau, juxtaposed "popular" ruined cityscapes such as

Rome and Athens with the current cityscape of Detroit, which allowed for an alternative commentary about the city in which the hidden geography was exposed and portrayed as marvelous and beautiful. Such juxtaposition of ruins was evident in Boileau's introduction to the virtual tour. The virtual tour opened with a photograph of the demolition of Hudson's Department Store in 1998, which was one of many buildings within downtown Detroit that had been abandoned in the latter half of the 20th Century. The photo was followed by the following commentary by Boileau:

> Zimbabwe, Ephesus, El Tajin, Athens, Rome. Now, as for centuries, tourists behold those ruins with awe and wonder. Yet today, a vast and history laden ruin site passes unnoticed, even despised, into oblivion. Come, travel with me, as I guide you on a tour through the fabulous and vanishing ruins of my beloved Detroit.

The concept of such ruins became the frame around the hidden geography—buildings and architecture featured in the photographs that comprised the "exhibits" in the virtual tour. Sites such as the abandoned Michigan Central Railroad Station and the Michigan Theatre, now converted into a parking lot, had been photographed in their crumbling state, and Boileau provided his own commentary about those sites. The commentary was the instrument used to "superimpose" the legend of ancient Athens and Rome over the photographs of present-day Detroit. Such intertextuality allowed for the transformation of different topographical categories depicted in present-day Detroit. In particular, the intertextuality of the virtual tour captured abandoned and burned out architecture that stood as edges that framed the city, pulled them to the center of attention, and transformed them into potential landmarks by reminding users of how they were important nodes or districts in Detroit's "ancient" past.

In the instance of the railroad station, as users moved through the tour they encountered an exterior image of the crumbling architecture. The photograph showed an enormous arched window with large majestic pillars on either side; the window was made up of multiple panes of glass, many of which were seen to be broken. Below the large window, a doorway could be seen, with a person peering out from the darkness within. Underneath this photograph was a description, which read: "Gateway to immigrants and visitors to Detroit for decades, Michigan Central Railroad Station saw millions of people pass through its doors. Now a massive ruin of eerie proportions, it houses a single visitor." The commentary described the important role of the structure long ago, and noted that it was left in ruins with only a single man who could barely be made out in the photograph. Below Boileau's commentary, one link offered users the option to either move on to the next ruin in the tour, while a second link offered more "exhibits" of the railroad station. Taking the second link, users found interior photographs of the building, many featuring wild plants growing throughout the structure, graffiti, and damage from the elements. Underlying each of these photographs was commentary provided by Boileau about either the past, or the current state of the building. On one page, the commentary read: "The vaulted interior courts of the Michigan Central Railroad Station maintain their cavernous majesty in spite of years of decay and vandalism." This commentary was found beside a photograph of the interior of the station, which depicted the grand size of the chamber and its vaulted ceiling, as well as the crumbling stone masonry. On the next page, users found another photograph featuring the old boarding platforms of the train station with large ferns and other plants growing from the tracks around them. Boileau provided the following commentary: "The gargantuan platforms of the Michigan Central railroad station now succumb to the forces of nature." On the page after that, users could find yet another image of the wrecked interior of the building, with commentary that read, "Where thousands of trains transported millions of passengers yearly, only stripped automobiles, graffiti artists and the intrepid now dare to enter."

Throughout the online tour of the Michigan Railroad Station, the photographs captured that hidden geography in its crumbling and burned out state; a geography that was rarely seen and concealed from people passing through the area. Such images of crumbling architecture were typically the frame for nodes and districts in decline, which contributed to the cityscape of "where the weak are killed and eaten." However, the commentaries provided by Boileau moved structures like the railroad station away from the edges, where they had been hidden and consigned in the images circulated through mainstream news and entertainment media, and into the center of attention. The movement was accomplished by framing those structures within the intertext of ruins in Athens and Rome, which are depicted in "popular" historical accounts and literature about travel. Such depictions frequently entail legends of Emperors, senators, and wars that constitute a nostalgic history that draws the tourists' gaze. Like Athens and Rome, Boileau suggested that Detroit similarly held an ancient past that was vibrant and exciting, and that the past, as well as the present, was worthy of such nostalgia. In addition, the commentary described a vague cataclysm that occurred long ago to drive away the ancients, as well as the millions of people who traveled through the railroad station regularly. Now only "intrepid" people risk the journey into the shadowy ruins, where the shadows and risk created a sense of mystery that was precarious, but not too dangerous, which made the historic nostalgia more authentic. Throughout every site and exhibit featured in the virtual tour, a link at the bottom of each page allowed users to enter the Forums so that they could provide their own commentary about the Fabulous Ruins. The Forums constituted the interactive aspect of the website, and proved to be an integral second component in the democratization of unruly hidden geographies in the city of Detroit.

DetroitYES! Discussion Forums

Through the interactive Forums site of DetroitYES!, users were able to start threads about various topics relating to the city of Detroit and post commentary into those threads. Such posting regularly involved the attachment of pictures, videos, and hyperlinks to news stories and different websites. Our deductive content analysis revealed four categorical roles that were played out by the users of DetroitYES! through their threads and posts concerning the topographical components and hidden geography of the city: Historian, Indigenous Urban Planner, Storyteller, and Explorer. Interestingly, these roles were fluid and not static, as many users would move from one role to another; the roles that users assumed were often dependent on the subject of the thread.

One role taken by DetroitYES! members was that of the Historian; a role in which users delved into old documents and texts in order to make discoveries about hidden geographies in the city as they existed before they were made unruly. Typically, users who assumed the role of Historian possessed a variety of decades old documents and data about the city, such as old photographs and maps, or were in a position to locate such materials. Essentially, the Historians engaged in discussions about a particular part of the city that was usually abandoned and/or in severe decay. Using the decades old materials at their disposal, the Historians investigated "the story" of that part of the hidden geography as it existed in the 1920s or the 1950s—back during Detroit's "better" days. In many ways, the Historians set out to find what "the ancient records" could reveal about "the lost world" of the Fabulous Ruins of Detroit, before the ravages of time and economic cataclysms had taken their toll. Take for instance a thread called "Continental Plant on Jefferson." At the beginning of the thread, a user asked others if anyone knew about the current ownership of a structure on "the northeast corner of Jefferson and Conner" that had been the

Continental automobile plant at one point in time. Other users clarified that the structure was no longer an automobile plant, but was used by Continental to manufacture aluminum as the auto plant had been torn down "years ago." In order to further demonstrate this point, another user scanned a postcard of the Continental plant from 1915 and attached it into a posting in order to provide a visual image of what the auto plant had looked like before being torn down and replaced with the aluminum plant. The discussion that ensued on the thread entailed the use of city and state records from the early 1900s to the 1940s in order to properly identify several of the manufacturing plants in the area of Jefferson and Conner that had been "lost" to abandonment and decay over several decades. Yet another user provided photographs of various auto plants in Detroit during years when they were still in operation, and the user who had scanned the postcards later provided photographs of the Aerocar plant on Mack Street from 1905. In each these cases, users identified the building and its location in the city through investigation of details in the photographs that had provided. In one case, the person responsible for the postcards and photographs went so far as to scan and post a section from a 1947 map of the city in order to show the location of the Warner Aircraft plant. Through the use of such documents and texts the Historians provided other community members an understanding about what the nodes and districts (e.g., the Continental plant and the Aerocar plant) were like in the past. In addition, the Historians provided information about abandoned and forgotten buildings tied to religious communities, sports franchises of Detroit, and Motown music. With such an understanding of the ancient cityscape, as opposed to the two competing cityscapes, community members were able to engage in lively discussions and debates about what life had been like long before cataclysmic events befell the city.

Another role played by members of the DetroitYES! community was that of the Indigenous Urban Planner. This was a role in which users engaged in debates about the future of the hidden geographies of Detroit. Such users would argue whether decayed and burned out edges that had once been districts and nodes, such as the Aerocar plant, should now be considered a landmark worthy of rehabilitation and celebration. Often, the debates among the Urban Planners relied on evidence: photographs of sites in the city, and narratives collected from those who live in or around that site. Take for instance the thread entitled "Brush Park." In the initial post, one user asked whether Brush Park, a Victorian style district that had once been an opulent residential area until its fall into disrepair over several decades, was worth rehabilitating. According to this user, Brush Park was not getting "the group hug" that industrial nodes and districts around the city—areas that were now burned out edges—were receiving from members of the DetroitYES! community. A debate emerged among several of the users concerning the fate of Brush Park, which evolved into two positions: allow developers to tear the remnants of the Victorian houses down, or inject some revenue into the residential area in order to restore the once great houses. Those users who advocated for the first position presented photographic evidence of the ruined condition of those houses. For instance, one user attached photographs of buildings that were not only in disrepair, but were near total collapse; the user claimed that such buildings posed a serious threat to public safety. Conversely, other users wove narratives about the people who lived in Brush Park at the time of this online debate. Those narratives stood as a rationale for the city or other agencies to introduce some forms of revenue to renovate and revitalize the homes therein. Such stories described the efforts of residents to fend off urban decay, crime, and developers from many of the homes in the district; the stories called for the DetroitYES! community to support those efforts in some capacity. One user conveyed a story of a homeowner in Brush Park whose house had been scheduled for demolition without her knowledge:

> [The owner] chatted up some guy on a bulldozer, and he pointed out her house as one to go the next week. She told him he was wrong, but he had a list with her house on it. She attended a meeting to seek help, and a police officer stepped in to resolve the misunderstanding.

Such a narrative demonstrated the harsh realities facing many of the people who remain in Brush Park, and valorized their actions as they protected the crumbling district. Ultimately, through these photographs and narrative evidence, the Indigenous Urban Planners presented evidence that helped users to conceptualize certain parts of the city as either burned out edges, as they existed at that time in the cityscape constructed through mainstream news and media, or as landmarks that needed to be renovated in some way. Through the use of pictures, stories, and personal experiences in Detroit the users either swayed the entire DetroitYES! community to one vision of an area of the city or, as with the case of the "Brush Park" thread, established competing perspectives about that area.

A third role that played out through the forum threads was that of the Storyteller, in which certain members related narratives about themselves or others set in Detroit's "distant" past. Oftentimes, a user would start a thread by naming a node or landmark in Detroit, like Tiger Stadium or the Grand Army of the Republic building, and ask people to share their memories about that place. One such thread called for users to share their memories about the Book-Cadillac Hotel in downtown Detroit. The Book-Cadillac, once the glamorous gathering place of celebrities and industrial leaders, had been forced to close its doors in 1986. Several members' recounted personal experiences at the hotel, such as meeting political figures like Lady Bird Johnson and sports heroes like Lou Gehrig. In one interesting post, a user discussed her experiences at "the Book" in 1949:

> We often walked [to the Book-Cadillac] after school. It was safe then! In those days the entertainers (singers, big bands, etc) always stayed at the "Book." Whenever famous people came to town we teenagers loved to see if we could see them. I tried to get an interview with a famous singer called Tony Martin. Even Frank Sinatra stayed there . . . The Book was a very exciting place to just walk into!

Meanwhile, other users recounted stories passed on to them by their parents and grandparents from even further back in time. One particular user explained how his grandparents met and fell in love while working in the Book-Cadillac kitchen, and another told how his grandmother lied about her age to take a job at "the Book" the year it opened in 1924 in order to support her family. Essentially, the Storyteller was a role in which DetroitYES! users reminisced about the people, either themselves or those to whom they were close, who lived, worked, and loved in the nodes and districts throughout Detroit, long before the city had fallen into ruin.

The final role that emerged from our deductive qualitative content analysis was that of the Explorer; a role in which certain members of the web community went out to the physical sites in the hidden geography that had been discussed on the forum in order to investigate them. Explorers would take it upon themselves to actually enter the sites—often illegally—discussed and debated about on the Forums, and bring back some "relics" to help others to understand the Fabulous Ruins. In many ways, the Explorers were people who took on Indiana Jones-like personas, in which they braved the dangers and hostile natives of the hidden geography to bring back relics in the form of photographs and narratives about the burned out edges and other concealed spaces. An interesting example of the Explorer role was found in a thread entitled "Apocalyptic St. Cyril's—A Final Look." The purpose of the thread was to examine St. Cyril's, a large Catholic church situated northeast of downtown Detroit, prior to its demolition later that year. Many of the users discussed how they "entered" the dilapidated structure and explored its crumbling interior. According to one such user:

> The front door is now unpadlocked so I gave in to temptation and had a look around inside. Water puddles on the floor, cold damp atmosphere, light streaming in through broken windows, birds startled by a human coming into their abode.

Such narratives created a sense of romanticism concerning the node turned burned out edge of the cityscape. Romanticism in this case was analogous to the legends of Lewis and Clark setting off into an unknown wilderness, or of Hiram Bingham discovering the ruins of Machu Picchu. The expeditions of Lewis and Clark, Bingham, and other "real-life" explorers were fraught with real and concrete hardships like disease, starvation, and natural disasters. Nevertheless, stories and history books describe each as intrepid men boldly following their curiosity and travelling into a mysterious frontier devoid of "civilized" people. Within the interactive Forums, the Explorers described activities that, under other contexts, would simply be called "breaking and entering" or "loitering." Narratives like the one above, however, were set within the context of Boileau's intertext, which recast these activities so that the Explorers appeared to other users of the Forums as adventurers stepping into a mysterious and exciting hidden geography. Users built on such romanticism in two ways: explanation of risks and photographic relics. First, users who assumed the role of Explorer often discussed some of the risks associated with entering the Fabulous Ruins, as in the case of one user who explained the dangers posed by icy floors in St. Cyril's. In another instance, a user provided the following warning to others who might enter the ancient church: "To anyone interested in checking out this site, I encountered hypodermic needles while sneaking around so BE CAREFUL!" The potential threats found within the wild and mysterious ruins enhanced the sense of romanticism that had emerged in the initial stories of exploration. As one user explained: "Boy, you guys are adventuresome. My husband and I went over there a week ago to shoot a few pictures. We did notice that the padlock was off the door, but decided that our safety was above our curiosity!!" Words such as adventuresome and exciting were often used to describe the risky efforts of such intrepid Explorers.

Explorers also built on the romanticism of their endeavors by sharing photographic "relics" from their journeys into the ruins. One such user returned from the trip into the heart of St. Cyril's with several photographs that showed the interior in shambles. Such photographs illustrated a broken alter surrounded by shattered glass, and pews in disarray about the main chamber. For all intents and purposes, the interior of St. Cyril's appeared to be wrecked or destroyed. These photographs elicited not only awe and praise from many of the other users, but also investigation. Several of the users noted that a foreign language was inscribed over the altar of the church, and began to debate what language was depicted in the photograph. One of those users claimed that it was Polish, while another insisted that the language was in fact Slovakian. The second user went so far as to track down the new St. Cyril's, and approached the church's new priest about the inscription. That user was able to find that the language was in fact Slovakian, and that it read: "We bow before the eternal holiness of the altar."

As explained previously, the users were never locked into a single role within the discussion forums; roles tended to be fluid as members would switch from one to another (e.g., Storyteller to Explorer). In addition, threads were not based on one particular role, and it should be noted that usually only two or three of the roles appeared in any given discussion thread. The four roles existed as a symbiotic relationship that brought discovery, debate, exploration, and sharing into the Forums, which simultaneously constructed and reinforced an alternative cityscape that was constantly in flux as new materials were introduced and discussed by the users. Essentially, Historians built on the nostalgia associated with the virtual tour by explaining how a burned out or hidden edge (e.g., an abandoned factory, a crumbling building from Motown's past) was once a node or a district where people had gathered to work or engage in cultural activities that had built the city into an affluent metropolis. In this way, edges that were once hidden nodes could become landmarks. The Storytellers contributed nostalgia as well, through tales about glamorous celebrities like Frank Sinatra and Tony Martin who populated many of the historic nodes within the hidden geography that had fallen into ruin and been abandoned to the edges of the city. Storytellers also added another layer of nostalgia through accounts of grandparents and relatives working at such nodes, falling in love, and building their futures. All of this nostalgia was in flux, however, as materials presented by Historians and tales woven by Storytellers could refute or contradict earlier postings, and even question some aspects of Boileau's Fabulous Ruins.

The Indigenous Urban Planners complicated nostalgia even further through their debates about sites that have been discussed and described by Historians and Storytellers, and featured in the virtual tour. The research of the Historian, the debates of the Indigenous Urban Planners, and the memories of the Storyteller, constructed ever-shifting, alternative spaces with thrilling pasts and presents that diverged from the competing cityscapes of Detroit created from swirling images circulated in the news media and popular entertainment. The Explorers, then, took it upon themselves to leave this divergent space developed through the Forums, and into the architecture that was the subject for portrayals and discussions in the web community. The photographic relics and stories of dangerous (but not too dangerous) adventure brought back to the Forums by Explorers reinforced the vision of the Fabulous Ruins of Detroit, and further invigorated the research and debates within the discussion threads. For instance, in the thread "Continental Plant on Jefferson" discussed previously, not only did Historians provide information about the history of the plant and identify other factories and plants in the area, but Indigenous Urban Planners also debated whether the site should be rehabilitated for some new use (e.g., rave parties) or if industrial contamination in the area had rendered the site useless. In addition, Explorers travelled to the Continental plant and took photographs of interesting architectural features that were a part of the remaining design that had not been destroyed. Together, the Historian and Urban Planners constructed knowledge about a node that had decayed and become an outer edge, which helped to transform that site into a landmark that had been integral to the rise and affluence of the ancient city. This landmark, then, stood as an image that aided in the construction of the overarching alternative cityscape that was ripe for exploration. The photographic relic brought back to the Forum by an Explorer added to users' understanding and excitement about the specific landmark, and the larger alternative cityscape.

Ultimately, our analysis illustrated that the Fabulous Ruins and the DetroitYES! web community aided in the construction of a nostalgia-laden alternative cityscape in which Detroit stood as the hidden remnants of an ancient empire. Boileau superimposed the legend of Athens and Rome over the city of Detroit through his photographs and narratives on the virtual tour, but that alone did not constitute the construction of a larger alternative cityscape. The interactive Forums allowed for users to expand on the intertextual legend introduced by Boileau as they provided additional images, narratives, and material through the four roles. Essentially, the intertextual virtual tour constituted an anchoring legend, while the interactive Forums served as a fluid site for exchange of ideas and the generation of additional nostalgia. The emergent alternative spaces and cityscape transformed the dilapidated architecture of Detroit, while hiding many of the problems associated with the contested cityscape (e.g., racial segregation, riots, high unemployment).

Diffused Intertextual Production

Our examination of the Fabulous Ruins Virtual Tour and DetroitYES! Forums brought together past research concerning the topics of intertextuality and interactivity, and illustrated the communicative strategy of diffused intertextual production. We contend that this particular strategy can be used to democratize unruly spaces. This strategy could be used to domesticate and democratize not only hidden geographies or lost spaces, but also enclaves like Wildcat Hollow or spaces of exception, as in Cairo or the San Francisco Bay area. Past research by Ott and Walter (2000), Warnick (2007), and Warnick and Heineman (2012) demonstrates intertextuality as a strategy used by media producers to "play" with multiple texts in order to build a "frame" around a particular issue. In addition, past research illustrates interactivity as a process for the "co-production" of texts (e.g., Atkinson, 2010; McMillan, 2002; Warnick, 2007; Warnick & Heineman). The current chapter demonstrates how both intertextuality and interactivity, when utilized simultaneously, stand as a communicative strategy that allows for users to discover hidden environments, so as to envision different uses for those environments. The interactive components allow for participatory audiences to add to an intertext so that it expands and grows from their interaction, participation, and contribution.

Diffused intertextual production, in turn, proves crucial for the construction of alternative spaces, which coalesce together into a larger alternative cityscape like the one associated with DetroitYES! This concept is particularly evident when looking at the role of the Explorer in the Forums, as such individuals journeyed into the physical cityscape of Detroit in order to discover and investigate the hidden geographies depicted in the virtual tour. The relics that they brought back became integral components for the Forums, as well as the stories about how those relics were obtained. The interactive elements of web communities, such as the Forums, allowed for users to add to overarching intertexts, which generated nostalgia and additional production/contribution from other users. In this way, then, ordinary people were able to take control of those unruly hidden geographies that seemed so different and disorganized; they plotted ways through the physical environment, interacted with that environment, and interacted with others within it. In addition, people had the power to diverge from the visions of the city perpetuated by economic and cultural elites, which often play on the unruly perceptions. They could take an active role in the production and circulation of images and stories that could influence knowledge and perceptions about physical environments. Even though such images and stories were not dominant "mediations" of the "everyday life" of society as described by Debord (1994), the emergent alternatives had the potential for profound impacts on those environments, and the people who lived and worked therein.

The constant fluctuation of the alternative spaces and the alternative cityscape created an open-ended past, present, and future that allowed for the emergence of a participatory civic identity. According to Denzin (1997), participatory audiences engage with performances they observe, often in media texts, "as co-performers or critics" (p. 101). Participatory audiences often build on performances and media texts through their own performance with other people; they perform as if they are a part of the media text. Co-performance with media texts provides audiences with a knowledge about the world around them and how to perform within the world (e.g., Abercrombie & Longhurst, 1998; Appadurai, 1996); such knowledge, in turn, locates the person within the world and influences their identity (e.g., Burgin, 1996; Dickinson, 1997, 2006). What is more, this manner of performance involved a struggle over the meaning structures that has defined the city, and in many cases, the lives of the community members. This brings diffused intertextual production in line with Carpentier's (2016) notion of political participatory engagement. Their performances within the online community assimilated the negative meaning structures concerning the city, and built a more equitable vision of Detroit. The diffused intertextual production that stems from the simultaneous presence of intertextuality and interactivity within web communities, like in the case of DetroitYES!, constitutes such a co-performance and political participatory engagement.

Discussion

In the case of the contested cityscape that was torn between the city "where the weak are killed and eaten" and "Detroit Shop City," people performed within the background of dominant texts that located them within a city that was either imprisoned in the past dominated by unruly spaces formed by policies driven by resentment and neoliberalism, or a city that fled from that stagnant past to a post-industrial future that was based in gambling and consumption. Both of these competing cityscapes represented false opposites that were seen by many as catastrophic and unchanging. The abject evacuation of capital from the city, which constituted the first cityscape, became the defining condition for the "reversal" associated with the second cityscape. Conversely, the knowledge that emerged from the diffused intertextual production associated with the Fabulous Ruins virtual tour and the DetroitYES! Forums located the members of the community within a city that was crying out for exploration and engagement, rather than a dilapidated crime-ridden city that should be avoided, vacated, or consumed. Contesting the hegemonic power of Detroit's dominant dual cityscapes, the intertext of "ruins" served as an "instrument of cultural power" (Mitchell, 1994) that fractures the false choice and the myth that the city was totally constituted by its economic value, no matter how foundational those material limits. Within this contested form, then, members of the web community developed a participatory civic identity that was potentially more egalitarian and empowered than identities influenced by the images and stories associated with the contested cityscape, in that they came to understand that it was important to look for historical materials, weave stories, debate information, and explore the landmarks and edges of Detroit. Indeed, the participatory civic identity in this case was more egalitarian and empowered than identities constructed through other forms of democratization in Wildcat Hollow and Germany. Essentially, diffused intertextual production constructed an experience of the hidden geography that empowered the members of the community so that they engaged, rather than avoided, the physical city.

For activist and citizen groups of this kind who are wrestling with unruly spaces in their own communities, the mutually constitutive performative curiosity imbedded within diffused intertextual production brings together multiple elements (e.g., relics, histories) of the physical environment, which allows for those actors to actually feel a sense of control over those spaces. As these elements are brought together, they engage the growth of an intertextual phenomenon (e.g., the Fabulous Ruins, DetroitYES!), which allows for those actors to imagine routes through, and uses of, a space that was once hidden or reviled. The discovery of relics and histories, and the subsequent discussion and debate through the Forums, diverges from the dominant visions of the past and present, and opens in such a way as to construct new possibilities for engagement with the city in the future—mired as those cities might be in the instrumentalist demands of the present. Thus, through diffused intertextual production, activists and citizens bored at work, alike, are able to engage with their community in such ways as to create alternative spaces full of possibilities, which can, in turn, potentially transform the physical cityscape through civic interest and involvement. Over time, those actors can revitalize the communicative qualities of portions of the city, and even reinvigorate the capabilities that provide hope and dignity to citizens. Such is the case, as we further examine Detroit and DetroitYES! in the following chapter.

Note

1. This chapter contains passages adapted from "DetroitYES! and the Fabulous Ruins Virtual Tour: The Role of Diffused Intertextual Production in the Construction of Alternative Cityscapes" by J. Atkinson and C. Rosati, (2012), *Critical Studies in Media Communication*, 29(1), 45–64. Reprinted by permission of the publisher (Taylor & Francis, http://www.tandfonline.com)

References

Abercrombie, N., & Longhurst, B. (1998). *Audiences: A sociological theory of performance and imagination*. Thousand Oaks, CA: Sage.

Appadurai, A. (1996). *Modernity at large: Cultural dimensions of globalization*. Minneapolis, MN: University of Minnesota Press.

Atkinson, J. D. (2008). Towards a model of interactivity in alternative media: A multilevel analysis of audiences and producers in a new social movement network. *Mass Communication and Society*, 11(3), 227–247.

Atkinson, J. D. (2010). *Alternative media and politics of resistance: A communication perspective*. New York, NY: Peter Lang Publishing.

Atkinson, J. D. (2017). *Journey into social activism: Qualitative approaches*. New York, NY: Fordham University Press.

Atton, C. (2002). *Alternative media*. Thousand Oaks, CA: Sage Publications.

Berger, J. (1972). *Ways of seeing*. New York, NY: Penguin Books.

Bonnett, A. (2014). *Unruly places: Lost spaces, secret cities, and other inscrutable geographies*. New York, NY: Houghton-Mifflin Harcourt.

Burgin, V. (1996). *In/different spaces: Place and memory in visual culture*. Berkeley, CA: University of California Press.

Bouffard, K. (2015). Census bureau: Detroit is biggest poor city in the US. *The Detroit News* [online]. Accessed July 19, 2019 from https://www.detroitnews.com/story/news/local/michigan/2015/09/16/census-us-uninsured-drops-income-stagnates/32499231/

Carpentier, N. (2016). Beyond the ladder of participation: An analytical toolkit for the critical analysis of participatory media processes. *Javnost—The Public*, 23, 70–88.

Collins, J. (1992). Television and postmodernism (2nd Edition). In R. Allen (Ed.), *Channels of discourse reassembled: Television and contemporary criticism* (pp. 325–353). Chapel Hill, NC: University of North Carolina Press.

Cosgrove, D. (1985). *Social formation and symbolic landscape.* Totowa, NJ: Barnes & Noble Books.

Cosgrove, D. (1988). Geography is everywhere: Culture and symbolism in human landscapes. In T. Oaks & P. Price (Eds.), *The cultural geography reader* (pp. 176–185). New York, NY: Routledge.

Debord, G. (1994). *The society of the spectacle.* New York, NY: Zone Books.

Denzin, N. (1997). *Interpretive ethnography: Ethnographic practices for the 21st century.* Thousand Oaks, CA: Sage Publications.

Dickinson, G. (1997). Memories for sale: Nostalgia and the construction of identity in Old Pasadena. *Quarterly Journal of Speech, 83*, 1–27.

Dickinson, G. (2006). The *Pleasantville* effect: Nostalgia and the visual framing of (white) suburbia. *Western Journal of Communication, 70*(3), 212–233.

Dickinson, G., (2015). *Suburban dreams: Imagining and building the good life.* Tuscaloosa, AL: University of Alabama Press.

Eliasoph, N. (1988). Routines and the making of oppositional news. *Critical Studies in Mass Communication, 5*(4), 313–334.

Endres, D., & Warnick, B. (2004). Text-based interactivity in candidate campaign websites: A case study from the 2002 elections. *Western Journal of Communication, 68*(3), 322–343.

Ewalt, D. (2007). America's most murderous cities. *Forbes* [online]. Accessed November 8, 2010, from http://www.forbes.com/2007/11/08/murder-city-danger-forbeslife-cx_de_1108mur-der.html

Farley, R., Danziger, S., & Holzer, H. (2002). *Detroit divided.* New York, NY: Russell Sage Foundation.

Fiske, J. (1987). *Television culture.* New York, NY: Routledge.

Gubrium, J., & Holstein, J. (2003). Postmodern sensibilities. In J. Gubrium & J. Holstein (Eds.), *Postmodern interviewing* (pp. 1–20). Thousand Oaks, CA: Sage.

Howley, K. (2005). *Community media: People, places & technologies.* Cambridge, UK: Cambridge University Press.

Kidd, D. (2003). Indymedia.org: A new communications commons. In M. McCaughey & M. Ayers (Eds.), *Cyberactivism: Online activism in theory and practice* (pp. 47–70). New York, NY: Routledge.

Kiousis, S. (2002). Interactivity: A concept explication. *New Media & Society, 4*(3), 355–383.

Landow, G. (2006). *Hypertext 3.0: Critical theory and new media in an era of globalization.* Baltimore, MD: John Hopkins University.

Mayring, P. (2000). Qualitative content analysis. *Forum: Qualitative Social Research* [Online Journal], *1*(2). Accessed October 1, 2002, from http://www.qualitative-research.net/fqs-texte/2-00/2-00mayring-e.htm

McMillan, S. (2002). Exploring models of interactivity from multiple research traditions: Users, documents, and systems. In L. Lieverouw & S. Livingstone (Eds.), *The handbook of new media* (pp. 163–182). Thousand Oaks, CA: Sage.

Meikle, G. (2002). *Future active: Activism and the Internet.* New York, NY: Routledge.

Mitchell, W. J. (1994). *Landscape and power.* Chicago, IL: University of Chicago Press.

Mitchell, D. (1996). *Lie of the land.* Minneapolis, MN: University of Minnesota Press.

Mitchell, D. (2000). *Cultural geography: A critical introduction.* New York, NY: Blackwell Press.

Mitchell, W. J. (1994). *Landscape and power.* Chicago, IL: University of Chicago Press.

Ott, B., & Walter, C. (2000). Intertextuality: Interpretive practice and textual strategy. *Critical Studies in Media Communication, 17*(4), 429–446.

Porter, L. (2008). Detroit: Highest home foreclosure rate in US. *World Socialist Web Site.* Accessed February 20, 2018, from http://www.wsws.org/articles/2008/feb2008/home-f20.shtml

Rafaeli, S. (1988). Interactivity: From new media to communication. In R. Hawkins, J. Wiemann, & S. Pingree (Eds.), *Sage annual review of communication research: Advancing communication science: Merging mass and interpersonal processes, 16* (pp. 110–134). Beverly Hills, CA: Sage.

Rooney, B. (2008). Rust and sun belt cities lead '07 foreclosures. *CNNMoney.com* [online]. Accessed February 13, 2018, from http://money.cnn.com/2008/02/12/real_estate/realtytrac/index.htm

Sadler, W. J., & Haskins, E. V. (2005). Metonymy and the metropolis: Television show settings and the image of New York City. *Journal of Communication Inquiry, 29*(3), 195–216.

Sen, A. (2000). *Development as freedom.* New York, NY: Anchor.

Sugrue, T. (1996). *Origins of the urban crisis: Race and inequality in postwar Detroit.* Princeton, NJ: Princeton University Press.

Turow, J. (1977). Another view of "citizen feedback" to the mass media. *Public Opinion Quarterly, 41*(4), 534–543.

Warnick, B. (1998). Appearance or reality? Political parody on the Web in campaign '96. *Critical Studies in Media Communication, 15,* 306–324.

Warnick, B. (2007). *Rhetoric online: Persuasion and politics on the World Wide Web.* New York, NY: Peter Lang.

Warnick, B., & Heineman, D. (2012). *Rhetoric online: The politics of new media.* New York, NY: Peter Lang Publishing.

Warnick, B., Xenos, M., Endres, D., & Gastil, J. (2005). Effects of campaign-to-user and text-based interactivity in political candidate campaign web sites. *Journal of Computer-Mediated Communication, 10*(3), article 5.

Zukin, S. (1991). *Landscapes of power: From Detroit to Disney World.* Berkeley, CA: University of California Press.

· 8 ·

STANDPOINT PERFORMANCE WITHIN
THE INTERTEXT

Diffused intertextual production proves to be a valuable communicative strategy that allows for people to make sense of, and feel like they have control over, unruly spaces in society like hidden geographies. This communicative strategy stands as a political form of participatory engagement as it allows for people to engage in a focused collaboration within online environments, so as to build new knowledge about physical environments. Essentially, diffused intertextual production effectively helps people to build new knowledge about unruly spaces, and reconceptualize them as alternative spaces that feel safe—or at least manageable. In the case of Detroit, the addition of new information anchored to the intertext of "fabulous ruins" gave rise to a different knowledge of the city. The new knowledge from the intertext led people to see the spaces in and around the city as interesting or worthy of exploration, which stood in stark contrast to typical descriptions or narratives about Detroit. Those typical visions of the city were grounded in the logics of resentment and neoliberalism, which elicited emotions of fear, dread, or anger. What is more, the interactivity of the forums allowed for engagement and the capacity for co-construction of the new, alternative vision of the city, which proved was integral to the construction of participatory civic identity.

However, the research described in the previous chapter only provided insight concerning the construction of new knowledge, perceptions, and identity. Our understanding about the web community and diffused intertextual production raised questions as to whether the new knowledges and identity had any influence on the ways in which people actually interacted within the hidden geography when they were offline. Essentially, we were curious as to whether the democratization of space through online environments shaped performances by members when they interacted with, or around, those hidden geographies that they had rediscovered through their participation in the web community. Did the construction of new knowledge and perceptions actually change anything for the members of that community when they travelled into the physical environment? Did it impact their own performances when they were physically in those spaces? At the end of our initial research concerning the web community, we were confident that the interactive and intertextual components would give rise to identity that would influence the interactions with the physical environment in the city. Following our analysis of the virtual tour and forums, we conducted a focus group with five users of the forums as a member check. One of the members relayed to us a story concerning a discovery that she had made with her boyfriend; she was a frequent user of the forums, whereas he had no connection to the community. The two were planting an "urban garden" in a vacant lot in downtown Detroit—a project that had been discussed and promoted on the forums—when they happened to unearth a particularly ancient looking brick with a strange emblem and insignia stamped on the side. The boyfriend, who had minimal interest in the work on the urban garden, took little notice, but she was instantly intrigued. The boyfriend suggested that they Google the insignia on the brick in order to find out more, to which she responded, "Fuck that! I'm DetroitYESing this shit!" She told us that it would be important to bring this discovery to the attention of the "diggers" to see what they would have to say; the "diggers" were those members who "dig up" documents from the 1940s and 1950s, scan them, and post the images within threads. Such users were essentially the Historians described in the previous chapter.

In order to fully understand diffused intertextual production as a strategy for the democratization of unruly spaces, it is important to conceptualize the role of the DetroitYES! forums in the performance of community members. This chapter provides more insight into how the communicative democratization of space changes the ways in which people engage with the hidden geography, and with each other in that environment. In particular, we explored whether diffused intertextual production and the emergent participatory civic identity qualified as a standpoint that people in the web community could enact in their everyday lives. We felt that if such a standpoint were to emerge, then we could build on past literature concerning Audience Performance, and indeed introduce the concept of standpoint performance as a component of the democratization of unruly spaces. We posed these questions and introduced the concept of Standpoint Performance in an article published in *Communication, Culture & Critique* in 2012. In that article, we demonstrated that the diffused intertextual production utilized within the DetroitYES! web community called forth three different performances of the members who participated in the site. One of these performances entailed a standpoint that had been constructed through their involvement in the DetroitYES! forums. What is more, our research demonstrated the ways in which this Standpoint Performance was protected by administrative practices in the forums; without those practices, the dialogue necessary for the construction of standpoint could not have occurred. Indeed, it is our contention that such administration was necessary to make the enterprise of diffused intertextual production successful.

Past audience research has demonstrated two forms of audience co-performance within mediascapes constructed from mediated texts: Spectacle Performance and Resistance Performance. Spectacle Performance is illustrated in Abercrombie and Longhurst's (1998) book *Audiences*, in which they explicate the different theories of audience that had emerged in media and audience research throughout the latter half of the twentieth century. Spectacle Performance emerged from research concerning spectacle and performance developed by scholars like Appadurai (1996), Debord (1994), Hebdige (1979), and Schechner (1993). Under this view, audiences co-perform with spectacle-laden, consumption-oriented images that they find in the media, which transforms their experience of "everyday life." Resistance Performance was developed through research concerning anti-war activism in 2003–2004 (Atkinson & Dougherty, 2006), and later refined in the book *Alternative Media and Politics of Resistance* (Atkinson, 2010); this line of research utilized the same notions about performance in order to build on alternative media research of journalism and media scholars such as Atton (2002), Downing (2003), and Meikle (2002). Resistance Performance developed from interviews with activists and qualitative content analysis of alternative media, and demonstrated how critical worldviews, interactions with alternative media, and communicative resistance shaped the performances enacted by activists who sought to address problems that stem from dominant power structures (i.e., corporations, government). Both forms of audience co-performance fit well within the literature concerning mass media audiences (e.g., Couldry, 2004), as well as alternative media and activism (e.g., Atton, 2002; Downing, 2003).

Interestingly, it has been noted that Spectacle Performance and Resistance Performance are not mutually exclusive, but are in fact part of the same paradigmatic view concerning audiences that could be called Audience Performance (Atkinson, 2010). It was also suggested that Standpoint Performance could also be a part of this Audience Performance Paradigm. One place to explore the possibility of Standpoint Performance was the alternative cityscape of Detroit constructed from the diffused intertextual production associated with the DetroitYES! web community. As noted in the previous chapter, diffused intertextual production is a reference to the development and extension of an intertextual framework from the interactive co-production between producers and audiences. The previous chapter demonstrated how the simultaneous presence of intertextuality (see Ott & Walter, 2000) and interactivity (see Warnick & Heineman, 2012; Warnick, 2007) stood as a communicative strategy that allowed for community members to construct a fluid "knowledge" about the hidden geographies of Detroit that was considerably different from representations of the city in news and popular media. This alternative cityscape—as well as the performances of community members within that virtual site—stood as an excellent opportunity to observe and explore the possibilities for Standpoint Performance. In the following chapter, we illustrate concepts related to Audience Performance and standpoint, and provide a description of our research procedures and findings.[1]

As noted in the previous chapter and Chapter 1, we engaged in qualitative content analysis (see Altheide & Schneider, 2013; Atkinson, 2017; Mayring, 2000) of discussion threads on the DetroitYES! forums. In this case, the content analysis was inductive, similar to the research described in Chapter 6. We read through the different threads on the forums that entailed discussions about race, which allowed for the formation of categories from those materials. In addition, we engaged in postmodern interviews (Atkinson, 2017; Gubrium & Holstein, 2003) with eighteen members of the DetroitYES! web community in order to explore their use of the websites, their interactions with one another, and their performances in the city of Detroit. The data that we collected provided much more insight into diffused intertextual production and alternative cityscape than in the previous chapter. Ultimately, our research helped us to demonstrate (1) the different performances engaged in by members of the DetroitYES! community, (2) the emergence of standpoint within one of those performances, and (3) how that emergent standpoint was maintained. The findings from the interviews were important as they provided insight into how the communicative strategy of diffused intertextuality actually impacts performance within the physical environment of unruly spaces. What is more, the findings also built on past media research. In particular, the following pages help to build on Audience Performance by demonstrating a new performative category that fits alongside Spectacle Performance and Resistance Performance.

Audience Performance

The idea for an Audience Performance Paradigm first emerged from the writing of Abercrombie and Longhurst (1998), in which they conducted a meta-analysis of past audience research. They found that audience research had moved through three paradigmatic shifts: Behavioral Paradigm, Incorporation/Resistance Paradigm, and Spectacle/Performance Paradigm. The Behavioral Paradigm is rooted in media effects research (e.g., Lazarsfeld, Berelson, & Gaudet, 1948); media content serve as a stimulus, while changes in audience attitudes or behaviors constitute a response. For instance, the social scientific research on cultivation conducted by Gerbner, Gross, Morgan, and Singorielli (1980) stands as an example of the Behavioral Paradigm. In those studies, the researchers demonstrated that people who watch high levels of violent television develop negative perceptions about the world around them. In the case of cultivation, there is a cause effect relationship as the television content acts as a stimulus, whereas the changes in perceptions stood as a response. The Incorporation/Resistance Paradigm emerged from critiques of audience agency associated with the Behavioral Paradigm, as well as research that explored the interpretation of texts by audiences (e.g., Fiske, 1987; Hall, 1980). For instance, Lindlof (1988) explained that people read and understand media content from their respective interpretive communities. Such communities could be their religious affiliation (a church or mosque), or political alignment (membership in a party or activist organization). The interpretive communities to which people belong teach different interpretive strategies through which they may create meaning within texts as they read or use them. In this way, then, people from different interpretive communities can read the same text, but take away different messages. Essentially, audiences are incorporated within different structures of meaning that they use to understand texts. Take for instance a conservative and a liberal reading a news story about the issue of Russian meddling in the 2016 election; one would read it as "fake news", while the other would read it as an indictment of the Trump Administration. The ways in which they read the text would create different meanings.

The Spectacle/Performance Paradigm described by Abercrombie and Longhurst is based largely on the work of scholars who focused on the consumption of media content, cultural practices, and pleasure (e.g., Appadurai, 1996; Debord, 1994; Ruddock, 2001). According to Abercrombie and Longhurst, there are three different forms that the audience can take under Spectacle/Performance: the simple audience, the mass audience, and the diffused audience. The simple audiences are those who adhere to strict rules about the division between audience and the observed performance within a mediated text. One could think of an audience at a (typical) movie theatre sitting in their seats as an example of the simple audience. Mass audiences are those who are exposed to media content, but push the texts into the background so that they may attend to other things around them; they pay partial attention to the media content. Talking to friends at the bar while ESPN Sports Center plays on a television is a good example of the mass audience. The foundational concept of the Spectacle Performance Paradigm (and in fact, all forms of Audience Performance from this point forward) is the diffused audience, which refers to an audience that blurs the line between their own position and the mediated performances in society that they witness. The notion of diffused audience addresses the concept of mediascape described by Appadurai (1996), which was briefly discussed in Chapter 1. Essentially, the diffused audience exists at the intersection of "everyday life" and the multitude of media messages around them. At this intersection, fragmented spectacle and images meld into a mediascape in which the audience engages in performance.

> So deeply infused into everyday life is performance that we are unaware of it in ourselves or in others. Life is a constant performance; we are audience and performer at the same time; everybody is an audience all the time. Performance is not a discrete event. (p. 73)

The diffused audience pieces together a mediascape from all of the different fragments of spectacle and imagery swirling about, and come to perform as a part of the "gang" on It's Always Sunny in Philadelphia or one of the survivors led by Rick Grimes on Walking Dead. They perform as a member of an NFL team by buying the jersey of their favorite quarterback. That is not say that audiences will see themselves as Danny Devito or Tom Brady, but the images and narrative components from those mediated stories are incorporated into their performances of everyday life. The images and narrative components serve as a backdrop for those performances. Such performance is narcissistic, in that the blurring of the line between audience and performance contributes to the inability of the audience to differentiate between themselves and the outside world; the diffused audience view the world as an extension of themselves, or vice versa (see Porter & Catt, 1993).

Although Abercrombie and Longhurst's Spectacle/Performance Paradigm provided valuable insight into the performances of affluent audiences of mass media within the context of a thriving capitalist system, critiques have been leveled about its value for the examination of groups who resist dominant power structures. Specifically, I (Atkinson, 2010) raise the argument that this vision of the audience largely ignores power and resistance to institutions that manufacture/circulate spectacle-laden images. Essentially, such "audiences seem to become part of the dominant structure without question; the more involved they are in spectacle, the more narcissistic they become" (p. 32). To counter this problem of power and resistance, the notion of Resistance Performance was developed from observations of audiences who used alternative media (e.g., *Adbusters* magazine or Breitbart news website) grounded in critical worldviews as the foundation for their mediascapes and performances (Atkinson, 2010; Atkinson & Dougherty, 2006). Essentially, this line of research explores performances of alternative media audiences—typically political activists—that express their cultural and individual identity as they attempt to draw the gaze of others (e.g., Schechner, 1993). The research illustrates how the performance of resistance emerges from five categories: (1) critical worldviews, (2) interactions with alternative media content, (3) communicative resistance, (4) intercreative capacity, and (5) narrative capacity.

The first three categories focus on the audiences and their actions. Audiences of alternative media often demonstrate critical worldviews in the way they talk about dominant power structures in society; those worldviews range from radical to reformist. Such audiences also engage in interactions with alternative media texts; such interactions range from passive to participatory (e.g., engagement with texts through co-production or feedback to producers). Finally, communicative resistance entails strategies audiences deem to be necessary to counter the dominant power structures in society; these strategies range from legal to militant. Ultimately, these first three categories emerge against a backdrop of fragmented alternative media content about power structures, power, and resistance; such fragmented narratives are passed about and shared within activist networks in local level communities. As activists learn these narratives they begin to form critical worldviews, and engage with additional texts to learn more. The more participatory their engagement—or interaction—with those texts, the more they solidify critical worldviews (see Atkinson, 2010; Huesca, 2001; Meikle, 2002). Those audiences who are more "participatory" in their use of alternative media are more confident of their worldviews, and more likely to engage in public performances of communicative resistance. The latter two categories deal with activist organizations, networks, and their connections to the world around them. Intercreative capacity focuses on the interactivity between producers and audiences at the local level, and between the local level with the global level. Narrative capacity, finally, entails the ability of activist networks in a local community to come together and form protests and public resistance. Overall, the Resistance Performance concept illustrates the integral role of certain alternative media in the development and enactment of public performances of protest and dissent.

At this point, we would like to note that spectacle is still a part of this Resistance Performance view; spectacle is, however, bifurcated as activists separate good spectacle (e.g., content in *Adbusters*) from bad spectacle (advertisements for Apple's newest iPhone). In this way, the "good" spectacle found in alternative media content solidifies the audiences' critical worldviews, and mobilizes them against "bad" spectacle. The community of Wildcat Hollow in Chapter 2 stands as an excellent example of Resistance Performance. In that case, some of the members of the trust network in the enclave interacted in a passive way with alternative media produced by conservative activists at the national level. The national level texts that they consumed described abstract visions of resistance against liberalism and "elites" within the United States (see Atkinson & Berg, 2012). Such interactions shaped the critical worldviews of the alternative media visionaries, as well as their tactics for communicative resistance. Essentially, these members of the trust network engaged in tactics of resistance that were dictated by the backdrop of alternative media that they consumed. The abstract concepts of "purity" and sorting "good" from "bad" within the texts were made concrete, and shaped the construction of knowledge about the enclave. Although this did democratize the enclave to an extent, it also left the trust network enclosed away from neighbors and other communities; their resistance could not spread beyond their immediate physical environment.

In part, some of the enclosure of the Wildcat Hollow trust network was tied to the nature of the media content from which they used to construct the backdrop for their performances of resistance. However, it is also important to note that within the context of Resistance Performance the alternative media visionaries were passive consumers of activist media produced at the national level. The lack of engagement with media (e.g., production or provision of feedback to producers) left the visionaries and others in Wildcat Hollow without a strong political identity. Huesca (2001), Meikle (2002), and others (e.g., Atkinson, 2010) have noted that interactivity with alternative media—by way of open publishing or commentary—helps in the formation of political identity and solidification of critical worldviews; this, in turn, gives rise to increased political participation. For these reasons, then, we see Spectacle Performance and Resistance Performance (at least that which is grounded in passive interactions with alternative media) as inadequate starting points for democratization of unruly spaces. Instead, we feel that Standpoint Performance would offer the most robust mediascape wherein strategies for democratization of spaces could be developed.

Standpoint

As we were conducting our deductive qualitative content analysis described in the previous chapter, we became interested in the possibility for Standpoint Performance by the members of the DetroitYES! community. The diffused intertextual production gave rise to alternate paths through—and interactions with—the unruly hidden geographies of Detroit. In many ways, this emergent knowledge and identity is similar to the establishment of standpoint that is described in communication literature, but divergent on one important aspect. According to feminist standpoint scholars, a standpoint is a shared location that emerges from recognition of material circumstances; this location aids people in the process of interpretation (e.g., Hartsock, 1998; Harding, 1993). In the most general sense, standpoints constitute a way of looking at and understanding the world:

> Generally, standpoint theories provide an analytical framework for understanding how individuals or groups view the world. Standpoint theories provide a method for discovering how a set of historical, material, and lived experiences culminate in an analytical framework or standpoint epistemology. (Richardson & Taylor, 2009, p. 250)

This general sense, however, does not truly grasp the full extent of a standpoint. The notion of standpoint is not merely a matter of how groups view the world, but how they build that understanding and use it to interact with the world around them. According to Hartsock (1998), "A standpoint is not simply an interested position (interpreted as a bias) but is interested in the sense of being engaged" (p. 107); that is, standpoint is not a preconceived worldview that people take up, but is an engagement with others in order to build community and understand the world. Standpoint is achieved through the recognition of different material conditions within varying cultural locations, as well as the power and subsequent oppression associated with relations between and within those locations (e.g., Dougherty 2011; Harding, 1993; Hartsock, 1998). It should be noted that the notion of standpoint has also fallen under critique for its assumption of the essential connection between subjectivity and a particular identity position (see Butler, 1990). Such essentialism has been demonstrated as incomplete (see Hall, 1996). But, so has—within this same critique of essentialism—the opposing notion that all individuals have unfettered agency in their choice of identity positions. Our use of standpoint acknowledges the non-essential nature of identity, as well as the mediated construction of community through multiple discourses within which subjectivities are produced. That is, the construction of standpoint is, itself, also constructed out of the limits and pressures (Williams, 1977) that at once constrain and fracture so as to make identities multiple (see Deleuze & Guatari, 1977). However, even where our emphasis intersects with the physical material of the city, we conceptualize this intersection as one that opens up and closes down potential subjectivities and performativity, rather than constituting some special position of knowledge or subjectivity outside of forms of discursive mediation. Through discourse and narratives, people share their different perspectives on those locations and power relations until they reach a collective experience about their own material condition and oppression (e.g., Allen, 2000; Sloan & Krone, 2000).

For example, men and women, whites and African-Americans, rich and poor all constitute different cultural locations that hail subjectivities into identifications and forms of performativity and, as such, entail differing resources and social capital that constitute power. Power relations between these different locations often lead to oppression by one location, although that oppression is oftentimes hidden through discursive closures (e.g., Clair, 1998). As Hall (1996) notes, all such locations entail a process of being "hailed" into specific identity positions, which are neither completely external nor simply internal to an individual. That is, both oppression and domination are discursive projects, which construct the subjectivities of all such positions. This, obviously, is not necessarily mutually exclusive with a nuanced view of feminist standpoint. For instance, as Mitchell, Marson, and Katz (2004) and other cultural geographers (e.g., Mitchell, 2000; Olwig 2002) have emphasized, the morphology and use of the built landscape do not exist outside of dominant systems of meaning and relations of power. Materiality, so central to feminist standpoint, can never exist outside of discursive production, nor can discourse ever not be material. The material environment is a political project within which dominant, residual, and emergent social formations interact. Our argument is that discourse and materiality are mutually constitutive, which is something that has been developed by Williams (1977), and expanded through the research of cultural geographers such as Mitchell et al. (2004), Mitchell (2000), Olwig (2002), and Cosgrove (2008).

An oppressed group can build a standpoint to establish an alternative cultural location through the sharing of narratives; such sharing allows for the construction of a collective experience that can enable people to see through the discursive closures established by the dominant group. The sharing of narratives and construction of a collective experience applies to the diffused intertextual production, alternative cityscape, and participatory identity described in the previous chapter. However, one important point made by feminist standpoint scholars is that the collective experience that emerges through discourse also provides a voice for those who are oppressed, through which they can address the dominant power structures responsible for their oppression and find some form of liberation (Dougherty, 2011). It is important to note that just because a standpoint is developed does not mean that it is done evenly or democratically. And, certainly, voice is not equivalent to unhindered agency among those participating. What voice can be, however, is an alternative rhetorical strategy against dominant narratives and the discursive production of oppressive social locations. Such voice is not addressed in the content analysis of the DetroitYES! web materials, and is the primary deviation from standpoint literature. Establishment of Standpoint Performance rests in the illustration and exploration of any "voice" that emerges from the knowledge and identity associated with the alternative cityscape of Detroit.

Performances and the Intertext

As we interviewed the members of the DetroitYES! community, we were interested in two specific issues in relation to their engagement in the city: their "voice" (i.e., what they did in the city and with whom they interacted) and race (which will be discussed in greater detail in the next chapter). The interviews revealed that there were three different performances that were grounded in the voice of the members. In some cases, voice was not present, whereas in others there was a voice that could be associated with the emergence of a standpoint. The following pages describe the different performances that were noted in the interviews.

Performance

The interviews with the DetroitYES! community members, as well as the inductive qualitative content analysis of the forums, revealed three categorical performances: performance outside of the intertext, performance against the intertext, and performance within the intertext. The first of these categories, performance outside of the intertext, involved discourse and actions that did not reflect or embrace the vision of Detroit as an ancient ruins portrayed in the Fabulous Ruins Virtual Tour. That is not to say that such performances rejected or challenged the frame established in the tour, like those discussed further below, but rather ignored this intertextual component altogether. In postings on the forums and in one-on-one interviews, some community members talked about sports and politics outside of the frame that had been established by Boileau. In these instances, the community members reflected the "mainstream" unruly notions of the cityscape. That is to say, they discussed Detroit within contexts established through mainstream media outlets (e.g., high crime rate and unemployment, government interventions in the auto industry). Within this context, the hidden geographies of the city remained concealed from site and largely unknown. Those sites continued to be dangerous or scary for those members of the community. They focused, instead, on the music scene in Detroit or the chances for the Red Wings winning the Stanley Cup.

The second performance that emerged from the interviews and focus groups, performance against the intertext, involved discourse and actions that challenged the original intertextual strategy employed by Boileau; such performance typically took place online in the discussion threads. Essentially, members of the community would question Boileau's notion that Detroit was the "fabulous ruins" of a once mighty empire toppled by some unknown cataclysm; such individuals often posted their own theories and opinions concerning the problems plaguing the city. For instance, one community member, who was a black activist, claimed that Detroit was a city battered and ravaged by white racism. As black people in the city demanded accountability of the police and city government in the 1960s and 1970s, white flight to the suburbs increased. This flight from the city reduced the number of jobs, as well as tax revenue that was necessary for integral services. In fact, he claimed that the DetroitYES! community was nothing more than a "white" project aimed at reclaiming the city from blacks for those white communities that fled decades ago; he often noted that most of the community members were white people who lived in the suburbs: "I think whites dominate here, the whole chat … they're comfortable, they think they're progressive, they think they've done great things for Detroit." Another community member told us about how he had made claims on the forum that Detroit was ruined by black people who have created a "black holocaust of abortion."

> I may have referred specifically to the published stats that show African-Americans currently abort fifty-eight percent of all their pregnancies, with that number soaring to ninety percent in some inner-city areas. Since Detroit is over eighty percent African-American and is publicly pleading for more residents, it made sense to suggest starting at home in the quest for more people.

According to the community member, this "holocaust" leaves black families broken and more dependent on government aid. Needless to say, such challenges to the intertextual frame did not go unnoticed. In both cases, these members explained that Boileau banned them from the forums and completely erased their comments from all of the threads; both individuals essentially ceased to exist within DetroitYES! In our interviews with him, Boileau admitted to banning the black activist from the community, and had some memory of banning the other individual. The banning and erasure of comments from threads plays an important role in the maintenance of standpoint, described below.

The final performance illustrated from the interviews and qualitative content analysis was the performance within the intertext. Of the three performances, only the performance within the frame entailed the expression of collective experience and speaking out against oppressive practices associated with the theory of standpoint outlined above. Online, many of the community members posted commentary about their actions in and around the city of Detroit. Such posting is not in and of itself resistive in a traditional sense, in which oppression and resistance entail confrontation within public view (see Aptheker, 1987; Clair, 1998). In such postings, the community members often talk to one another about their vigilant observations watching over important landmarks and nodes within the city; in some cases these individuals even acted as an eyewitness reporter. For instance, in a thread entitled "Tiger Stadium Elevator Tower to Fall," several members of the community kept watch over the slow demolition of the old baseball stadium near downtown. One of the last parts of the stadium to be demolished was the elevator used to take reporters up to the press booth in the past, before the stadium was replaced by the new one at the Tiger's new home at Comerica Park. In one post, a member noted that the demolition of the elevator had not yet occurred:

> Was at the ballpark yesterday, and one of the guys said they had just put in permits to close Michigan Avenue so they could raze the rest the elevator tower, et al on the corner of Michigan and Cochrane. Said they'd be working at night. I'm stuck at work during nights. Has anyone driven by in the last few hours? I'll drive by around 12:30 myself. Sure would be nice to get video and/or photos of that tower falling.

Later, another member reported the following about the elevator tower: "I was at the Tiger Stadium site at 8:30 a.m. today (Friday) and found no demolition workers on site. Could it be that they are getting their rest now so they can work tonight?" Later still, another member decided to follow through on the first member's desire for photographs of the elevator; he posted pictures into the thread. These photographs demonstrated the demolition that had taken place to the site over the course of a day. In the first photograph, the old elevator tower and the building at the bottom could be seen still largely intact. The Detroit Tigers logo was still on the side of the building, with a few holes visible in the walls. The second picture showed the building later, completely demolished. All that remained in the second photo was the elevator itself, standing above the ruins of the building.

Similar to the performance concerning Tiger Stadium, another community member noticed a Bangladeshi festival taking place a few blocks from his house. He started a thread on the discussion forum about this event, and then, taking on the guise of an "intrepid reporter" went out to the festival to observe. The notion of intrepid reporter was evident in the way that he signed off in his posts (e.g., "this is your reporter, reporting from the eye of the storm";

"Your daring reporter, risking it all for you"). Throughout the day, he posted a series of "on the scene reports" in the thread about the activities, people, sights and smells that he discovered:

> 12:20 pm: Booths still empty. No people. But music is emanating from the band shell at the end of the street. Life stirs . . . . 1 pm: The vendor booths are still empty. Lite jazz starts to play.

These "reports" served as a kind of online "community watch" that was concerned with keeping track and narrating changes in the alternative cityscape; such narration was similar to "coping and survival."

In past research, Aptheker (1989) and Clair (1998) examined forms of resistance that were alternative to the "traditional" notions of resistance that emphasized ideology, liberation, and power shifts. Aptheker examined the resistance of Jewish women in the Nazi controlled ghettos, and noted that retelling traditional stories and enacting rituals brought hope to a community that knew only despair. Utilizing such a view, I deemed some oral histories told and retold in Zapatista autonomous communities in southern Mexico to be resistance through coping and survival: "Such resistance did not so much challenge the balance of power in the region, so much as it was an activity that could function as a source of hope and dignity for a community that existed under siege" (Atkinson, 2009, p. 21). In the same way, then, the narratives and rituals of some community members celebrated the city's historical buildings against—even if simultaneously within—the dominant discourse of those buildings being "ugly," "wasteful," and "unproductive." Essentially, this narration envisioned those parts of the hidden geography in a manner that is alternative to the dominant visions about the city as devoid of upkeep and abandoned. These instances stood as a new knowledge that engaged voice and thus, constituted a standpoint against the dominant oppressive view of the city as destroyed and without physical value.

In addition, many of the community members whom we interviewed described events and actions in the physical cityscape that grew out of discussions on the forums. For instance, one community member explained that he often joined with a group of DetroitYES! community members to play softball at Riverside Park in Detroit. The softball games were a ruse for the community members to get in the way of workers who were planning the construction of a new toll bridge that would destroy the park. The community members felt that the bridge was only being constructed to increase the incomes of wealthy elites in the city.

> There were a bunch of us, we went down there in full view as [construction work-ers] showed up ... we [organized] this on Detroit Yes ... So this initial thing ended up leading to other demonstrations here in the park where people just went in and decided to go in and use the park. You can't kick me out.

Another community member, whom we call Guy, read about the concept of community gardens in the DetroitYES! forums and decided to start a major cooperative garden in his neighborhood.

> Everyday I was putting stuff on the forum about what I was doing. Soon, [members of DetroitYES!] came out and helped me till and map out the plots of where we're going to plant. [One person] brought out his tiller ... That was our first official work day game from DetroitYes! people.

Guy noted that the garden not only provided fresh fruits and vegetables to people who had little access to such things, but also created a sense of commu-nity pride. Yet another community member explained that she worked with other community members to provide historic tours of downtown Detroit. The tours were designed to educate the community about the hidden geography of downtown, as well as its rich history and role in the region. Much of the infor-mation that she and the other tour guides passed on to people came directly from the discussions on the forums. In another instance, a community member became part of an urban gardening project in which people grew food in vacant lots. She used the project not only to grow food, but also as an opportunity to explore the city. As noted earlier in this chapter, she found some interest-ing items as she worked with her boyfriend in the gardens. They unearthed a brick with an emblem that she did not recognize, which she later took to the forums for discussion. Finally, another community member explained that she had worked in an office in the city until 1981, but refused to cross Eight Mile Road again after she retired. She claimed that she was often frightened of the people and problems in Detroit; she avoided the city as much as she could. However, after she found the Fabulous Ruins of Detroit and involved herself in discussions on the forums, she took a different view of the city. Through the forums, she became involved in an urban gardening project, as well as a non-profit group that works to restore and preserve parts of the city.

Ultimately, we contend that the performance within the intertext consti-tuted performance of standpoint, which arose in large part because of the use of diffused intertextual production. Such production stood in stark contrast to the passive consumption of media texts, which is often the basis for the construction of mediascapes under Spectacle Performance and Resistance Performance. The standpoint arose from the expression of a collective experience in the postings in the forums and the commentary provided by many of the community members in the interviews. In addition, this also stood as Standpoint Performance because of the newfound "voice" to oppose oppressive practices around them, which was demonstrated in many of the interviews. First of all, the postings of many community members exhibited a collective experience concerning the hidden geographies within the city. This collective experience involved the nostalgic-laden history that came from the intertextual frame described in Chapter 7. As the city was enriched with history and nostalgia, rather than crime and danger associated with unruliness, many within the DetroitYES! community considered it to be worthy of rediscovery and exploration. In many instances, like in the case of the retiree who would not cross Eight Mile Road, there was the notion of a "sea change" concerning the perception of the city. Before she was involved in DetroitYES! she was apprehensive of the city; after she became involved she sought to engage with the city.

> After I stopped working in the city in 1981, I became one of those suburbanites who would *never* cross Eight Mile Road and go to the city. It seemed the older I got the more afraid I became. Then when I got involved with the non-profit, I found myself going into the City all the time .... I am more interested in the City itself now ... for years I didn't care at all.

Other community members also described a significant transformation of their perceptions about the city and the surrounding region. The activities of community members like the intrepid reporter chronicled on the forum, as well as their commentary in our interviews, reflect both a collective experience about the ancient ruins and coping and survival as a form of resistance (see Aptheker, 1987; Atkinson, 2009; Clair, 1998). As many community members developed a new knowledge about their community, they took part in activities that would demonstrate to people that Detroit is not the crime-infested burned out industrial shell often represented in popular media. The tours of the city, the work conducted by multiple people in the different urban gardens in the city, and the work with the non-profit groups constituted such resistance. In their own ways, their actions stood in contrast of the dominant cityscape of Detroit built from popular media and mainstream news, which build a perception of the spaces in the city as unruly. These actions also helped to reestablish Sen's (2000) capabilities necessary for dignity and hope to the vacant lots and crumbling parts of the city—the hidden geography of Detroit. It should be noted, however, that such actions can also constitute hegemonic resistance, as described by Mumby (1997). Such resistance can be deeply counterproductive in that the actions reinforce the dominant ideologies and power structures; in the cases above, the actions of the community members draw attention to problems that are often the focus of mainstream media, and even trivialize them in some cases.

Maintenance of Standpoint

Not only did the interviews demonstrate the performance of standpoint described above, but also the process for the maintenance of that standpoint. The interviews revealed one interesting fact: that Boileau, the site creator and administrator, regularly banned people who crossed him from the forum and erased all of their past comments. On the surface, this sounds particularly authoritarian and contrary to the notion of standpoint establishment described in past research (e.g., Dougherty, 2011; Harding, 1993; Hartsock, 1998). This seemed particularly problematic as the first person we discovered that Boileau had banned was the black activist discussed earlier. In his interview, the black activist claimed he would enter the forum and begin calling out the racist nature of comments on the discussion threads, and especially point to the racist nature of Boileau's virtual tour and administration of the forums. These comments, he claimed, led to his banishment, after which he would then create a new account and return to the forums. Interviews with other people removed from the community, as well as with Boileau himself, provided more insight into this practice. Members of the community like the black activist and the member who spoke about the "black holocaust of abortion," who was also described previously, all performed against the intertext and were banned. The black activist made challenges through his vivacious postings, while the other challenged the intertext through his racially charged explanation of the role of abortion in the collapse of Detroit. Other members also had similar experiences and reprimands. Two in particular were older members of the community who had engaged in performances against the intertext, and were banned at one point or another by Boileau. One of those older members challenged Boileau's authority by telling him to "blow it out his ass" in the middle of a debate about proper etiquette on the forums. The other, whom we call Pearl, also made a challenge by sticking her tongue out at Boileau using an emoticon (:P) during a similar debate. Boileau admitted to us his practice of banning people and their IP addresses from the forums in a second interview that we conducted with him. However, Boileau defended these actions by noting that the people who were typically banned from the forums and DetroitYES! community were "trolls" looking to create problems for people. Trolls could either create obvious problems (e.g., calling people vulgar names), or derail discussion threads through their "one trick pony" antics:

> Somebody who really gets into a one trick pony. That means, they got something they were on to. This one guy was on to mass transit and he would come into threads that had nothing to do with mass transit and he would say the same thing basically over and over. It was completely about that . . .. Lots of people get annoyed by that.

For Boileau, such banning was absolutely necessary in order to maintain the integrity of the discussions, and he cited other forums (in Detroit and elsewhere) in order to demonstrate his point. He explained that the "nastiness" of "trolls" often "infuriates other people and derails the discussion." A forum that was dedicated to knowledge and the democratization of unruly spaces could quickly fall apart if an administrator did not act often and decisively; democratization of the hidden geographies would be virtually impossible. This idea of derailment was mirrored in comments made by the urban gardener described at various points in this chapter—the one who found the brick. She explained that the DetroitYES! community had once gone through some "tough times", when "thread rippers" regularly "trolled" the forums insulting people and making racist/disrespectful comments about Detroit. In those days, she was not particularly active in discussion or activities in the physical cityscape.

Ultimately, the interviews and commentary of community members demonstrated how standpoint established through online settings needed to be hierarchical and a little authoritarian. Commentary provided by many of the members, like the one noted above, demonstrated how the stability of the community was threatened before Boileau utilized his strategy of banning and erasure. In addition, many of the community members told stories about other forums concerning Detroit that did not establish a shared or collective vision of the city; one community member described such forums as "mob rule." Within such a chaotic context it would difficult to establish any kind of collective experience, or the coping as resistance described above.

Discussion

Ultimately, this chapter provides a fuller picture of the DetroitYES! web community, and diffused intertextual production as a strategy for the democratization of unruly spaces. Specifically, the materials presented in this chapter demonstrate that those individuals who accepted and took part in the inter-text established through the virtual tour engaged in Standpoint Performance. This Standpoint Performance entailed community members' engagement with the hidden geographies in the city, as well as their interactions with other people in or around those hidden geographies. Integral to those engagements and interactions was the knowledge and participatory civic identity described in the previous chapter. Essentially, the intertextual frame was necessary for the emergence of a collective experience for audiences/users of a particular medium, similar to the shared experiences described in past standpoint research (e.g., Allen, 2000; Sloan & Krone, 2000). Those individuals who "accepted" the intertextual frame and performed within that context were more likely to share such a collective experience. Those audiences/users who did not accept it did not share any such experience, and in many cases challenged the frame.

It should be noted, however, that the intertextual frame was only one part as interactivity, such as documenting activities or posting stories, also played an important role. These actions helped to solidify the collective experience associated with the intertextual frame and gave rise to the participatory identity that was described in the previous chapter, and also demonstrated in the past research of Carpentier (2016) and Denzin (1997). In this way, then, those community members who accepted the intertextual frame and engaged in interactive use of the forums were able to establish a new understanding of their city, as well as a "voice" that corresponded with past standpoint research (e.g., Dougherty, 2011). This allowed those community members to utilize coping and survival to bring order and control the unruly nature of the dominant, hidden geographies of Detroit. This was something that was sorely missing in Wildcat Hollow, as the alternative media visionaries there were primarily passive consumers of alternative media. It seemed that the active engagement with media associated with diffused intertextual production was integral to the formation of the participatory civic identity, which gave rise to the establishment of standpoint and "voice." Indeed, the more passive engagement with alternative media in Wildcat Hollow, and historical markers in Germany, resulted in rituals and actions that could create the problems of unruly enclaves (or amplify those problems). In the case of that rural community, the performance did not create new knowledge, but rather led to reliance on outdated knowledge of the curators that could not address the economic problems at the root of the regions unruliness.

It should also be noted that the Standpoint Performance observed in the case of DetroitYES! required centralized, hierarchical maintenance. This is significant as past standpoint research alludes to the construction of standpoint as an egalitarian event with little or no hierarchy or guidance (e.g., Allen, 2000; Dougherty, 2011). Such lack of hierarchy or guidance stems from the fact that past research focused on the construction of standpoint in face-to-face organizational settings. In those settings marginalized individuals can identify allies and threats, which allows for them to shift the sites for communication from one point to another when need be. For example, if a group of women in a corporate setting were meeting in the break room to discuss sexual harassment within the organization, they could relocate their discussion if an assemblage of men entered the room. In the case of DetroitYES! and other online environments, anonymity and the possibility for multiple user identities makes such identification of allies and enemies difficult—almost impossible. In addition, the discussion forums and threads are public space that is available to all audiences, including those who are not actually members of the community. For these reasons, then, it becomes necessary for a centralized figure or group to engage in maintenance of the intertextual frame that drew people to the site and community. Boileau's banishment and censorship of performances against the intertext maintained the integrity of the Fabulous Ruins from the attacks of "trolls," and allowed others to construct and perform standpoint.

We would like to emphasize that this does not mean that spectacle and narcissism associated with Spectacle Performance, or critical worldviews and communicative resistance associated with Resistance Performance, held no place within the DetroitYES! community. On the contrary, all of the concepts associated with those forms of Audience Performance arose in our observations of the forums and interviews with community members. There was a narcissistic quality to the postings provided by community members, and the actions of community members at Riverside Park constituted legal forms of communicative resistance. However, diffused intertextual production held the potential for a different kind of Audience Performance from the frameworks of Spectacle Performance or Resistance Performance. In the case of both, the mediascape in which audiences performed was created for them by powerful economic and cultural elites (e.g., network executives, social movement leader, organic intellectuals). In the case that we examined for this research, the audience constructed that mediascape through their own interactivity framed within an intertextual component; the performance, then, took place within a mediascape truly negotiated with the audience. This was different from the communicative resistance under Resistance Performance, as cultural elites created a bifurcated mediascape of good versus evil; such resistance (militant or legal) adhered to the more traditional forms of resistance described by Aptheker (1987) and Clair (1998) (e.g., public confrontation). Within the DetroitYES! community, audiences worked together to build alternative knowledge that gave rise to a new voice through which stories were told and rituals engaged. We should also note that the performances of audiences in this community were fluid, so that individuals were not locked into a singular form of performance; people engaged in multiple forms of Audience Performance within the context of our research. Depending on the situation or topics of conversation, community members' mediascapes shifted, followed by the nature of their performance. The Standpoint Performance, however, was strongly tied to the use of the interactive media platforms of DetroitYES! The performance of standpoint emerged from the democratization of space that was accomplished by way of the diffused intertextual production by community members.

Note

1. This chapter contains passages adapted from "The Performance and Maintenance of Standpoint within an Online Community" by J. D. Atkinson and C. Rosati (2012), *Communication, Culture & Critique*, 5, 618–635. Reprinted by permission of the publisher (Oxford University Press).

References

Abercrombie, N., & Longhurst, B. (1998). *Audiences: A sociological theory of performance and imagination*. Thousand Oaks, CA: Sage.

Allen, B. (2000). "Learning the ropes": A black feminist standpoint analysis. In P. Buzzanell (Ed.) *Rethinking organizational and managerial communication from feminist perspectives* (pp. 177–208). Thousand Oaks, CA: Sage.

Altheide, D., & Schneider, C. (2013). *Qualitative media analysis*. Thousand Oaks, CA: Sage.

Appadurai, A. (1996). *Modernity at large: Cultural dimensions of globalization*. Minneapolis, MN: University of Minnesota Press.

Aptheker, B. (1989). *Tapestries of life: Women's work, women's consciousness, and the meaning of daily experience*. Amherst, MA: University of Massachusetts Press.

Atkinson, J. D. (2009). Networked activists in search of resistance: Exploring an alternative media pilgrimage across the boundaries and borderlands of globalization. *Communication, Culture, and Critique*, 2, 137–159.

Atkinson, J. D. (2010). *Alternative media and politics of resistance: A communication perspective*. New York, NY: Peter Lang.

Atkinson, J. D. (2017). *Journey into social activism: Qualitative approaches*. New York, NY: Fordham University Press.

Atkinson, J. D., & Berg, S. (2012). Narrowmobilization and tea party activism: A study of right-leaning alternative media. *Communication Studies, 63*(5), 519–535.

Atkinson, J. D., & Dougherty, D. S. (2006). Alternative media and social justice movements: The development of a resistance performance paradigm of audience analysis. *Western Journal of Communication, 70*, 64–88.

Atton, C. (2002). *Alternative media*. Thousand Oaks, CA: Sage.

Bonnett, A. (2014). *Unruly places: Lost spaces, secret cities, and other inscrutable geographies*. New York, NY: Houghton-Mifflin Harcourt.

Butler, J. (1990). *Gender trouble: Feminism and the subversion of identity*. New York, NY: Routledge.

Carpentier, N. (2016). Beyond the ladder of participation: An analytical toolkit for the critical analysis of participatory media processes. *Javnost—The Public, 23*, 70–88.

Clair, R. P. (1998). *Organizing silence: A world of possibilities*. Albany: State University of New York Press.

Cosgrove, D. (2008). Geography is everywhere: Culture and symbolism in human landscapes. In T. Oaks and P. Price (Eds.), *The Cultural Geography Reader* (pp. 176–185). New York: Routledge.

Couldry, N. (2004). Theorising media as practice. *Social Semiotics, 14*(2), 115–132.

Debord, G. (1994). *The society of the spectacle*. New York: Zone Books.

Deleuze, G., & Guattari, F. (1977). *Anti-Oedipus: Capitalism and schizophrenia*. Paris, France: Les Éditions de Minuit.

Denzin, N. (1997). *Interpretive ethnography: Ethnographic practices for the 21st century*. Thousand Oaks, CA: Sage.

Dougherty, D. (2011). *The reluctant farmer: An exploration of work, social class, and the production of food*. London: Troubador.

Dougherty, D., & Krone, K. (2000). Overcoming the dichotomy: Cultivating standpoints in organizations through research. *Women's Studies in Communication, 23*, 16–39.

Downing, J. (2003). Audiences and readers of alternative media: The absent lure of the virtually unknown. *Media, Culture & Society, 25*(5), 625–645.

Fiske, J. (1987). *Television culture*. New York, NY: Routledge.

Gerbner, G., Gross, L., Morgan, M., & Signorielli, N. (1980). The mainstreaming of America: Violence profile #11. *Journal of Communication, 30*(3), 10–29.

Gubrium, J., & Holstein, J. (2003). Postmodern sensibilities. In J. Gubrium & J. Holstein (Eds.) *Postmodern interviewing* (pp. 1–20). Thousand Oaks, CA: Sage.

Hall, S. (1980). Encoding/decoding. In S. Hall, D. Hobson, A. Lowe, & P. Willis (Eds.), *Culture, media, language* (pp. 128–138). London: Hutchinson.

Hall, S. (1996). Who needs "identity"? In S. Hall & P Du Gay (Eds.), *Questions of cultural identity* (pp. 1–17). Thousand Oaks, CA: Sage.

Harding, S. (1993). Rethinking standpoint epistemology: What is "strong objectivity"? In L. Alcoff & E. Potter (Eds.), *Feminist epistemologies* (pp. 49–82). New York, NY: Routledge.

Hartsock, N. (1998). *The feminist standpoint revisited and other essays.* Boulder, CO: Westview Press.

Hebdige, D. (1979). *Subculture: The meaning of style.* London: Pluto Press.

Huesca, R. (2001). Conceptual contributions of new social movements to development communication research. *Communication Theory, 11*(4), 415–433.

Lazarsfeld, P., Berelson, B., & Gaudet, H. (1948). *The people's choice: How the voter makes up his mind in a presidential campaign.* New York: Columbia University Press.

Lindlof, T. (1988). Media audiences as interpretive communities. In James A. Anderson (Ed.), *Communication Yearbook,* 11 (pp. 81–107). London: Sage.

Mayring, P. (2000). Qualitative content analysis. *Forum: Qualitative Social Research* [Online Journal], *1,* 2. Accessed October 1, 2002, from http://www.qualitative-research.net/fqs-texte/2-00/2-00mayring-e.htm

Meikle, G. (2002). *Future active: Media Activism and the Internet.* New York: Routledge.

Mitchell, D. (2000). *Cultural geography: A critical introduction.* Malden, MA: Blackwell.

Mitchell, K., Marston, S., & Katz, C. (2004). Life's work: An introduction, review, and critique. In K. Mitchell, S. Marston, & C. Katz (Eds.), *Life's work: Geographies of social reproduction* (pp. 1–26). New York, NY: Blackwell.

Mumby, D. (1997). The problem of hegemony: Rereading Gramsci for organizational communication studies. *Western Journal of Communication, 61*(4), 343–375.

Olwig, K. (2002). *Landscape, nature, and the body politic: From Britain's renaissance to America's new world.* Madison, WI: University of Wisconsin Press.

Ott, B., & Walter, C. (2000). Intertextuality: Interpretive practice and textual strategy. *Critical Studies in Media Communication, 17*(4), 429–446.

Porter, W. M., & Catt, I. (1993). The narcissistic reflection of communicative power: Delusions of progress against organizational discrimination. In D. Mumby (Ed.), *Narrative and social control: Critical perspectives* (pp. 164–185). London: Sage.

Richardson, B., & Taylor, J. (2009). Sexual harassment at the intersection of race and gender: A theoretical model of the sexual harassment experiences of women of color. *Western Journal of Communication, 73*(3), 248–272.

Ruddock, A. (2001). *Understanding audiences: Theory and method.* Thousand Oaks, CA: Sage.

Schechner, R. (1993). *Future of ritual: Writings on culture and performance.* New York, NY: Routledge.

Sen, A. (2000). *Development as freedom.* New York, NY: Anchor.

Sloan, D., & Krone, K. (2000). Women managers and gendered values. *Women's Studies in Communication, 23,* 111–130.

Warnick, B. (2007). *Rhetoric online: Persuasion and politics on the World Wide Web.* New York, NY: Peter Lang.

Warnick, B. & Heineman, D. (2012). *Rhetoric online: The politics of new media.* New York, NY: Peter Lang.

Williams, R. (1977). *Marxism and literature.* Oxford, NY: Oxford University Press.

· 9 ·

CREATIVE NARRATIVE APPROPRIATION

The previous two chapters have demonstrated diffused intertextual production as a political form of participatory engagement that was used to tame and democratize unruly hidden geographies in the city of Detroit. The first of those chapters illustrated how the strategy emerged from the simultaneous presence of intertextuality (e.g., Ott & Walter, 2000) and interactivity (e.g., McMillan, 2002) within web communities like DetroitYES! Afterwards, the subsequent chapter demonstrated how this communicative strategy influenced some of the everyday life performances of community members within the unruly spaces of the physical environments of cities like Detroit. In the case of the DetroitYES! web community, some of the members rejected the meanings associated with the virtual tour and performed outside of, or against, the intertext. However, we determined that a significant portion of the community did in fact accept those meanings, and engaged in performances that corresponded with the intertext. The performance of standpoint within the intertext was a result of the members taking part in the diffused intertextual production employed by the web community for the purposes of exploration and dialogue about hidden geographies near and around them. This is important as discovery and construction of knowledge about a hidden geography shapes identity and performance therein (see Burgin, 1996; Dickinson, 1997).

While we were in the process of examining the construction and performance of standpoint, we were struck by the absence of discussion about race in members' discussions about the web community and city of Detroit. In fact, as we looked back at all of our qualitative content analyses of the virtual tour and the discussion forums we realized that race was a topic that rarely came up in any significant way. This led us to ask about the topic of race in many of the interviews that we conducted with the members; we started asking them about race and race relations in the city and web community. What is more, we conducted another inductive qualitative content analysis of the discussion forums, this time looking for conversations and postings about race or race related issues. Interestingly, our analysis revealed that race was often avoided in the forums, and only discussed among the members offline in idealistic or inferentially racist ways. Our findings demonstrated a system of discursive closure that initially seemed negative, as this system affirmed and maintained white dominance within the alternative cityscape, similar to mundane reiterations of whiteness described by Warren (2003). These views even reflected the politics of resentment described in Chapter 3. However, further investigation uncovered the potential for the appropriation of narratives by non-white users of the site. In many ways this potential for narrative appropriation seemed similar to a process of building bridges between racial communities described by Calafell (2007). We refer to this action—which stems from the diffused intertextual production on the interactive media platforms of the community—as creative narrative appropriation. This is a substrategy of diffused intertextual production that allowed for the transferal of meanings associated with an intertext (or other symbol structure) from one community to another; such transferal was made possible by the poaching and use of narrative components by one community.

On the surface, these two things—discursive closures and construction of bridges—seemed mutually exclusive and incommensurable. How could communities in a city wracked by racial divisions spurred by resentment bridge unruly spaces together while the topics of race or ethnicity were avoided? However, we will demonstrate through the course of this chapter that discursive closure associated with administrative policies utilized within the web community were necessary for the narrative appropriation that constructed bridges between physical communities separated by the hidden geographies within the city.[1] Indeed, we claim that the discursive closures made it possible for people in one of the hidden geographies of the city to draw attention to their physical environment so that members of the DetroitYES! community could observe it. Only through those discursive closures could the connective bridge between the hidden geography and the web community be constructed by way of creative narrative appropriation.

Race in the Contested Cityscape

Race is a difficult subject to explore within the space of Detroit, for a variety of reasons. In many ways, the state of Michigan, and its capital city of Detroit (until 1847), were quite progressive in the early days of the Republic. Michigan entered the United States of America in 1837 as a "free-state," meaning that slavery was made illegal. Because Detroit lay on the border with Canada, it served as a valuable part of the "underground railroad." Many people from Michigan and Detroit volunteered to fight for Union forces in the American Civil War, so as to advance the cause of abolition. After the war was over, Detroit became a major manufacturing and transportation hub because of its position on the Great Lakes; from that point until the 1960s, Detroit became a major political and economic power in the US. It was this period of the city's expanding industrial strength and wealth that formed the basis for nostalgic narratives of a golden age for the city. These were stories about the "peak" of Detroit and its industries, prior to an inglorious decline into bankruptcy and ruin.

Part of the supposed decline of Detroit has often been tied to race related issues in the city during the 1940s and 1960s. After the Second World War, the first racial strains started to emerge and gain widespread notice. In postwar Detroit, the GI Bill, concerns about the coded politics of "urban blight," and often racially unequal subsidies invested in suburbanization, led to the beginnings of "white flight" from the city. By the 1960s these issues led to forms of "urban renewal," grounded in resentment and neoliberal logic that escalated significant alterations to the urban terrain. For instance, a vibrant working-class African American neighborhood on the Near East Side (known as "Black Bottom") was deemed to be "urban blight" and was leveled to make way for the Chrysler Freeway (Farley, Danziger, & Holzer, 2002; Sugrue, 1996). By 1967, the city's notorious police brutality, lack of affordable housing, economic inequality, and urban renewal projects erupted in a final traumatic riot. The explosion of racial and class frustration was triggered by the police raid of an illegal drinking establishment frequented by black Detroiters. The National Guard was mobilized, as was the 82nd Airborne. The city burned and rioters looted for five days, which stood as a "rationale" for the escalating white flight from the city and punctuated a period of malignant indifference that continues to this day (Sugrue, 1996).

Often Detroit is seen as frozen in that post–1967 moment, where arson, crime, unemployment, and property devaluation have remained and become visualized as insurmountable problems. In many ways, these are the same problems that face Flint, which are described in Chapter 3. In the case of Detroit, mainstream images and descriptions of the city tend to focus on dilapidated buildings, crime, and social problems. These images have been the foundation of the perceptions that have made much of Detroit a collection of unruly hidden geographies. In addition, such imagery often reiterates serious racial tensions in the city's past, such as the racially charged riots in 1967. The riots began with the arrest of African-American soldiers who entered an all-white club in the city, and have proven to be particularly important as images of those riots were broadcast around the country. Those images became the foundation of a perception of the city as dangerous, particularly for white people (Farley et al., 2002; Sugrue, 1996). In many ways, those images have played an important role in hiding much of the geography of Detroit from sight and mind. As these mediated images play and replay in American society, people within the city and across the nation have come to ignore large swaths of the physical environment that have gone on to be abandoned or neglected. Those swaths stand as the hidden geographies that are often rediscovered by people when they engage with the city; such sites become understood as unruly and compound feelings of unease created by the overarching narratives of decay, ruin, and conflict.

The alternative cityscape that emerged from the intertextual and interactive texts of the DetroitYES! web community did not seem to challenge these problematic racial images that make the geography hidden from sight. Instead, the virtual tour, the intertext that served as the anchor for the entire community, simply seemed to ignore race and racial tensions in the city's history. The city was depicted as a site that was empty, with no human inhabitants for the most part. The different photographs and commentary provided throughout the tour conjured up images of an unexplored and empty ruined civilization that was destroyed by some great cataclysm, like a volcano or earthquake. Where once great pharaohs/kings/emperors reigned, like Henry Ford and Thomas Edison, only rubble and desolation remained. Such framing conveyed a sense of nostalgia for the cityscape (e.g., Dickinson, 1997), but flew in the face of reality as the city was home to over 600,000 residents, most of which were African-American and working poor. A good example of this could be found in the discussion concerning the Michigan Central Railroad Station in Chapter 7. At the beginning of that exhibit, the commentary read: "Gateway to immigrants and visitors to Detroit for decades, Michigan Central Railroad Station saw millions of people pass through its doors. Now a massive ruin of eerie proportions, it houses a single visitor." The single visitor was a reference to a person that could barely be seen in that photograph in the tour; a man (perhaps homeless) appeared to be standing in the enormous arched entryway. Who is this person? From the perspective of the intertext, they were a savage native of the hidden geography; one of the few descendants of the race of people who survived the cataclysm.

Ultimately, then, the alternative vision that emerged from the web community seemed to be double edged. On the one side, the diffused intertextual production utilized by the community constructed an alternate way of discovering, understanding, and interacting with the hidden geographies within the city; this gave rise to participatory civic identity and Standpoint Performance enacted by community members described in the previous chapters. On the other side, the community seemed to erase the racial tensions that are an important part of the city of Detroit; such erasure seemed to be problematic for any reconciliation that needed to occur in order to move the city beyond the politics of resentment and neoliberal policies that have dominated much of the contemporary space (e.g., red-lining, white flight). In fact, such erasure reinforced the negative dominant narratives about race in the city, which could very well keep many of the spaces of Detroit concealed from sight.

Racial Politics in the Alternative Cityscape

We chose to engage in another inductive qualitative content analysis of threads that involved some discussion about race or ethnicity within the city of Detroit. Within discussion threads on the forums, we searched for references to race or ethnicity, to the race or ethnicity of specific people, or to discussions about people of color who were deemed to be controversial (e.g., Al Sharpton, Kwame Kilpatrick). In addition, we took note of the context of those discussions, and the ways individuals or ethnicity in general were described or discussed by members of the community. The results of our qualitative content analysis concerning race in the forums, along with the grounded theory analysis of the interviews described in Chapter 8, revealed racial politics within the community that have implications for potential appropriation of narratives from the forums. These racial politics took place both online and off. Taken altogether, these concepts stood as the overall racial politics that have emerged over time in the DetroitYES! online community, and are closely tied to the communicative strategy of diffused intertextual production and performance of standpoint. In the following pages, we demonstrate the racial politics online and off, and then explain how they functioned together.

Racial Politics: On the Forums

Our analysis revealed that there were nineteen relevant threads that emerged for examination, out of over one thousand threads posted into the forums over the time period of our research. Of those, seven threads actually focused on the issue of race (either in the title or in the initial posting), while race only came up in the middle of the other twelve threads. Overall, the analysis revealed that there were two common themes concerning race within these threads: silence and idealism. In reference to the first, the small number of threads demonstrated that few people discussed the issue within the forums. In addition, many threads that did delve into race were quite short and only entailed a single post or two. Often, a person found a news story they felt might be of interest to other DetroitYES! members, and posted a link to that story. There may have been a comment or two, but there was no discussion about race, or even the subject matter of the news article. It is interesting to note that outside of the context of our analysis we found a thread in the forum archive devoted to discussion concerning the makeup of the forums and the DetroitYES! community. The thread, entitled "2005 DetroitYES! Stats," was posted by the site administrator, Lowell Boileau, in January of 2006. In that thread, Boileau broke down the community by the following categories: gender, age, favorite ruin, favorite Detroit place, favorite eatery, where the members are from (Detroit, Ann Arbor, etc.). Race or ethnicities as categories were noticeably missing from this statistical breakdown. The lack of any discussion about race or ethnicity in these threads also constituted silence on the matter, and fit within the theme that had emerged from our analysis.

In reference to the second theme, many people who posted on the subject took an idealistic approach to race. They talked about racial relations as if they are currently harmonious, or with racial harmony in mind. For instance, in a thread entitled "Will Detroit Get a White Mayor," one community member stated:

> Church going [black] Detroiters weren't supposed to vote for a gay candidate, but there one sits on city council. Cop hating [black] Detroiters weren't supposed to vote for a cop, but there one sits on the city council. It really wouldn't be that hard for a white person to win a city council seat or a mayoral election in the city of Detroit. The only thing that they would have to do would be to speak to the people with respect and understanding of the problems that Detroit has.

In another thread entitled "Immigrants Add Luster to Metro Detroit," a community member stated the following:

> Immigrants make a city that much better. They help to improve the economy by opening up their own businesses, they bring a different culture to enjoy, different foods, a different understanding of our small world, etc. Welcome them with open arms!

In another thread entitled "Thinking About Moving to Downtown Detroit but Have Some Concerns," one person asked the community if there was racism or racial tensions of which he needed to be aware. In response, one community member stated the following:

> I am a young white male who lives downtown. It's fine. No worries on the race thing. Downtown's residential population is diverse. I haven't had a problem yet other than people assuming I'm from the suburbs (A stereotype I loathe and drastically wish to shed). You may find yourself a minority in some situations, but it doesn't bother me. Black Detroit residents are great people and have a charm/swagger about them that is hard not to like.

In each of these posts, members of the community demonstrated an idealistic notion of race and race relations within the city. African-American people in Detroit looked beyond race and their own community when casting their ballots, immigrants brought opportunities and cultural diversity to cities, and the African-American residents were "charming." This is not to say that all of these things were wrong or incorrect. However, it ignores the fact that race has played a pivotal role in Detroit mayoral campaigns (Farley et al., 2002), and that immigrant communities bring with them social change that is often resisted or resented by dominant groups (Sugrue, 1996). Meanwhile, it would be naïve (and a little patronizing) to think of African-Americans within the city as "charming" characters swaggering about. This is not to say that there were never any critical comments posted in the threads. There were posts within some of the threads that did not take such an idealistic view about race. For instance, in the thread about a white mayor in Detroit, one community member stated the following:

> I just don't agree with those who say that Detroit won't have a white mayor in our lifetimes. We just may, but people have to understand how many in the black majority see white people. There are white folks, and then there are white folks. The former group are generally viewed with hostility (as potentially dangerous given historical and contemporary factors), but the latter as having some common ground or common cause . . . "brothers and sisters from another mother."

Nevertheless, the previous types of comments, along with the silence noted above, were dominant across all of the threads in which race was discussed.

The themes within discussions about race constitute mundane reiterations of whiteness, discussed in previous research by Warren (2003). Working from the perspective of performativity (see Butler, 1990; Fuoss, 1999), Warren built on past research concerning strategic rhetoric of whiteness (see Nakayama & Krizek, 1995) by illustrating certain performative strategies used to negate power discrepancies, and hide white privilege from scrutiny. Such strategies are not so much intentional as they are cultural. Strategies noted by Warren include the construction of sameness, contradictions, stereotypes, and victimhood. The first two strategies expunge race and ethnicity, while the other two implicitly attack anyone who critiques whiteness. Construction of sameness and contradiction were most evident within the postings of several of the community members. The first, construction of sameness, entailed a kind of "color blindness, claiming sameness while ignoring difference" (Warren, p. 87). The second, contradiction, entailed "different messages rubb[ing] against each other in performance in ways that undermine[s] the rhetorical intent claimed by the performer" (p. 95). The contradictions began with sameness, but also entailed value claims that stereotype or objectified people of color; the sameness served as a "friendly" frame to mask claims that order the world in a way that preserves white privilege. This is similar to inferential racism described by Owens Patton (2004), which is the reinforcement of white supremacy through civility utilizing terminology and structure designated by the dominant group. The first of these strategies was evident across all the examples above. Essentially, everyone was portrayed in the posts as colorblind and equal. The projection of such equality erased or downplayed the gross inequalities all throughout the city, and indeed, across the nation. In addition, many postings demon-strated the construction of contradictions; this was particularly true of two of the postings noted above. In one posting, immigrants were equal, but they were also viewed as commodities or objects. Such a view contradicted or even negated, the equality and colorblindness expressed by community member. In the second, the community member tried to express a color-blind view, but that view was contradicted as they discussed those people as "charming" ornaments or window dressing. Overall, such commodification silenced those people whom they were discussing, and shielded white dom-inance from scrutiny.

Racial Politics: Beyond the Forums

The threads on the forums may have downplayed racial politics and tensions within the cityscape of Detroit, but that did not mean that race was not a topic of discussion among members of the DetroitYES! community. Our interviews with the eighteen members of the online community revealed two important concepts: site policies concerning banning and erasure, and controversial views about race held by many white members of the commu-nity. First, we discovered that the site administrator sought to avoid con-troversy in the forums by banishing members of the community who posted inflammatory remarks. For the most part, this was the practice of banning people from the forums for any "uncivil" talk or behavior in the forums that was described in detail in the previous chapter. One issue that was noted in Chapter 8 was that members like the black activist were quickly banned whenever they advocated ideas about the history of Detroit that focused on race relations. This policy, in turn, affected discussions about race within the forums. In our interviews with Boileau, we asked how discus-sions concerning race played out in the forums. We learned that he created an overarching policy for the community in which people were required to treat one another with respect, and that anyone who broke this general rule was banished and their problematic post erased. Inflammatory postings that violated this rule ranged from rude emoticons, to name-calling. According to Boileau, conversations on the forums could often "spiral out of control" and created problems for all of the members of the community. In order to overcome this problem, Boileau resorted to a policy of banning members for controversial comments altogether, and subsequently erased their com-ments from the threads:

In the earlier days [discussions about race were] a little bit more heated at times . . . so things could get a little out of control and then once [people] do that they switch it to name-calling and it breaks down and it loses control and everything. Over time I've improved my moderation skills. I am very strict: no name-calling policy. I am very strict. I throw people out and I don't give them a reason if they get into it now.

For the most part, these policies and their enforcement were described already in the previous chapter. However, because of important implications for the notion of race relations, the policies and people affected by them warrant reiteration here. For Boileau, this was a rule about civility in general, and not an attempt to stifle discussion about race specifically. This policy took on more importance, however, in our interview with the black activist mentioned previously who had been banned from the community on several occasions. That individual often entered the community and began conversations about racism in Detroit and within DetroitYES! Essentially, this activist claimed the city had been plagued by racism for decades, and that several white enterprises (like DetroitYES!) were organized to hide white supremacy in the city. This stood as a performance outside of the intertext constructed through the Fabulous Ruins of Detroit Virtual Tour. During our interview with him, the activist went on to explain to us that he had been expelled and banned from the community by Boileau for his comments on several occasions. He told us that after such reprimands he would simply create a new account and identity in order to gain access again. This story about banishment following racially charged postings was not unique. Another community member, also described in the previous chapter, was similarly banished whenever he brought up the "black holocaust of abortion" and its role in the decline of Detroit. Other members whom we interviewed told similar stories about the banishment of themselves or other people from the community for problematic comments within discussions about race. In fact, most of the stories about banishment associated with the administrative policies discussed in the previous chapter were actually associated with postings that involved controversial comments or discussions concerning race in Detroit. Ultimately, Boileau's banishment and erasure policy did not specifically target race related discussions, but was concerned with civility and tone within all discussions. However, as conversations about race seemed to often become uncivil and devolve into tones that were less than respectful (even according to Boileau), the policy indirectly affected threads that delved into the sensitive, yet important topic of race.

We would like to note that following our first interview with Boileau we found his policy, and its impact on discussions about race on the forum, to be negative and problematic. From a critical theory perspective, any strategies that shut down and erase such discourse about race and racism seemed to be authoritarian and instrumental in protecting white dominance. Even if those conversations created problems in the community, they would be necessary for illuminating and limiting oppressive practices (e.g., Dougherty & Krone, 2000). This policy served as a kind of forced civility—similar to that described by Owens Patton (2004)—that aided in the construction of topical avoidance, a form of discursive closure that often used to suppress conflict (see Clair, 1998; Deetz, 1992). Past research has demonstrated that such discursive closures tend to "distort power relations, disguise inequity, sequester resistant discourses, and ultimately close emancipatory forms of communication" (Clair, 1998, p. 38). From this perspective, then, the DetroitYES! community looked like a site through which mundane reiterations of whiteness (Warren, 2003) and discursive closures (Clair, 1998; Deetz, 1992; Owens Patton, 2004) safeguarded white privilege. It appeared as if the website erased racial tensions and resentment politics in the hidden geographies of the city, as well as in the emergent alternative cityscape constructed through diffused intertextual production. For the most part, these things are not untrue, and it seems as if the black activist discussed at various points in this part of the book was indeed making prescient observations about the web community.

As we interviewed more members of the community, however, our view on this discursive closure changed. We acknowledge that there are definitely problems with such reiterations of whiteness and discursive closures, but during our research we also began to see that there were positive implications for the community as well. In the interviews with several of the white community members, we noted very controversial views concerning race in Detroit. Most notably, many of the white members either engaged in their own discursive closures that blocked any critical discussion about race and race relations in the city, or espoused negative stereotypes about African-Americans in their discussions about race and racial politics in the city. For instance, one community member was asked why nobody seemed willing to critically discuss race on the forums, particularly the role of race in some of the more tumultuous moments in Detroit history (e.g., the 1967 riots). He was a white community member who was often engaged in performances within the intertext, like those noted in the previous chapter. He responded by first discussing the 2010 shooting involving US Representative Gabby Giffords in Tucson, Arizona:

> [The shooting in Arizona] hasn't got anything to do with Rush Limbaugh, Sean Hannity, or Sarah Palin, or any of those talking head fucks. If you want to talk about something talk about mental illness, talk about a lack of … Mental illness, as a society, as a culture, as a people we are fucking freaked out when you run into a schizophrenic. Last month, a friend of mine was murdered in Lafayette Park by his neighbor. His neighbor is a paranoid schizophrenic. The guy went off his nut, killed his father, goes next door and kills my buddy … I don't know if he's white, black, Chinese. I don't know anything about him … People get entrenched in their—you can't see what's a real crime there.

This particular community member essentially conflated the tragic shooting in Arizona and the mental state of Jared Lee Loughner (the shooter) with some of the more tense moments in Detroit history. Such a conflation, then, emphasized the mental state of individuals who commit crimes in Detroit, and ignored any of the racial politics, financial policies, and history involved; crime in Detroit was transformed into irrational actions of unstable people. Essentially, this community member felt that the only people who would emphasize or examine race are those who are biased.

> There are so many times with city council where you'd get the "they don't look like me crowd. We don't want those people in here." You know, the Kwame-ites. They would say that. They don't look like us. We don't want their development going here, we don't want them moving into the neighborhood there.

The Kwame-ites in this instance were the African-American supporters of former mayor Kwame Kilpatrick. Ultimately, for this member, race was only the concern of racists, liberal extremists, or biased black people. The conflations and connection of race as a topic to irrationality stood as a kind of discursive closure that avoided conflict, similar to the avoidance described above. In this particular case, the tactic seemed to be neutralization, in which "value positions become hidden and value-laden activities are treated as if they were value-free" (Deetz, 1992, p. 191). Essentially, this particular member sought to avoid the topic of race by positioning that issue as a value-laden argument. His own position, however, was presented as objective, rational, and value-free, which hid his own values and opinions. This, in turn, neutralized any other position that would seek to truly raise and examine the issue of race in the city.

Shortly after our interview with the individual above, we spoke with another white community member who we call Pearl, who was also briefly discussed in the previous chapter. In our interview with her, she demonstrated a similar discursive closure when faced with questions about race in the city. In that interview, she noted that attitudes of African-Americans in the city of Detroit toward white people were driven by factors that were "ancient history." The riots, the racist attacks on people of color by white police officers, and the notorious era of redlining all happened a long time ago, and had no connection to things going on today. In this way, then, African-Americans were clinging to the past, and could not let those problems go; they used those problems as excuses for why they let the city fall into "decline." Like the community member above, this commentary stood as a discursive closure; in this case, the tactic was naturalization. This tactic of naturalization is a process through which "subjective constructions become made into objects that are treated as fixed and eternal, that is, reified." (Deetz, 1992, p. 190). The subjective construction, in this case the socio-economic status of African-Americans in Detroit, did not have a past; it simply existed as we see it today. Essentially, this tactic closed off the past, so that the production of this "object" became forgotten. Examining the past, then, became irrelevant.

These discussions about race with many of the white community members essentially stood as discursive closures similar to the topical avoidance that emerged from Boileau's policy to ban controversial comments, in that these tactics shut down the potential for conflict in discussions with others. However, the tactics of community members like Pearl were also different from Boileau's, in that they served as postracist political strategy described by Ono (2010) that erase historical problems and imply something wrong with anyone who would engage in such discourse—particularly African-Americans. Such people were framed through the discursive closure as biased, lazy, or worse. Indeed, if anyone (particularly people of color) were to resist against such discursive closures, they would fall into the trap of appearing aggressive, over emotional, or threatening (Calafell, 2010; 2012). Many of those white members who held similar postracist views and engaged in these discursive closures knew that they should not bring such discussions or views into the forums, as they would likely lead to conflict; they would then be at risk for banning from the community.

That is what made Boileau's tactic of discursive closure, then, so important for the racial politics within the alternative cityscape. As uncivil and inflammatory comments were the primary targets for the banning/erasure policy, many of the members of the community felt the need to avoid discussions about race altogether. That subject, then, for the most part, did not exist, or existed in a superficial (albeit inferentially racist) way as demonstrated in the analysis of the discussion threads. There are no implications about community members tied up in this tactic; inflammatory comments based in naturalization or neutralization (and posters who make those comments) just disappeared. People who desired to bring postracist politics into the community were often forced to think twice and reconsider their comments because of the controversy that they might stir. Boileau's policy was something that the community member above who referenced the Arizona shooting acknowledged, and Pearl absolutely loathed. The exclusion of postracist politics, then, helped to foster an online environment that was ripe for creative narrative appropriation by minority people who came into the DetroitYES! community.

Creative Narrative Appropriation

The potential for creative narrative appropriation arose from an interview with an African-American member of the community, while the concept of building bridges came to light through interviews with several of the white members. This is not to say that the before mentioned African-American man is the only black or minority member of the DetroitYES! community. However, this individual, whom we call Guy, had come up with ideas for his beleaguered community by taking part in the posting and reading practices of the DetroitYES! community. His urban garden project was briefly described in Chapter 8, and he presents the best evidence that the racial politics of the forums provided opportunity for the appropriation of narratives and building bridges between communities separated by the unruly hidden geographies of the city created from resentment and neoliberal finance policies.

We learned of Guy from many of the interviews we conducted with white members of the DetroitYES! community. When discussing the issue of how the community members engaged in the physical city, stories would emerge about the Glorious Hope Urban Gardens, an urban farm in the middle of one of the more poverty stricken quarters of Detroit. Most of these individuals noted that they had gone to the gardens to view it personally, and many had even become involved and worked there to some degree. Each person would then tell us the same thing: "You need to talk to Guy." With that, then, we sought out Guy for an interview.

We conducted our interview with Guy at the Glorious Hope Urban Gardens on a cold winter day in February; during the course of the interview he gave us a tour of the grounds. The surrounding neighborhood consisted of many abandoned houses and dilapidated buildings. The structures that could be seen from the streets were falling apart; broken windows, peeling paint, and damaged rooftops stood out to us as we surveyed the area. Many of the other houses and buildings, however, could not easily be seen, as they had been overgrown by shrubs, grasses, and trees of the so-called urban prairie. For the most part, these were some of the most concealed hidden geographies of the city. The gardens, set amongst those hidden sites, included plots for growing vegetables and fruits, a commons area with picnic tables and a playground, and pens for chickens and a goat. In the middle of the area was a single building, which served as the office for the Glorious Hope Cooperative. Within this building was another commons area with a projection screen and DVD projector. Guy explained to us that the building was used to show movies to children before and after school, and also used as a dining space when the organization provided free breakfasts to local children and other people in the neighborhood. He also explained that the building was frequently used as a meeting site by many of the people in the neighborhood.

During the course of our interview, Guy told us that before the gardens were established the city lots all around had only contained burned out abandoned buildings. There were no grocery stores in the area, and most of the residents had a hard time obtaining fresh vegetables and fruits. At that point in time, Guy had only recently moved back to the Detroit area. Around that time, he joined the DetroitYES! community to see if he could garner information about what was going on in the metro areas, and see if he could get some ideas about jobs and work. This was where his urban garden began:

> In February of '08 there was a thread about—after I came out and saw all the garbage—there was a thread about vacant lots, urban prairies, what can be done with urban prairies. That was about the time I came out and saw it. Well I'm going to clean it up and a community garden would be a good thing. Planting food on here would keep people from dumping on it.

As Guy read and engaged on the forums, he discovered discussions about urban farming posted by many of the Indigenous Urban Planners (who were noted in Chapter 7) as they speculated about better uses for abandoned housing and lots in the city. Many of those Urban Planners experimented with growing fruits and vegetables in their own backyards and small plots in their own neighborhoods. Essentially, these were the discussions of post-industrial middle class white people interested in urban farming as a hobby, and they gave Guy the idea to build a garden for his own neighborhood. Within a few months, he bought the burned out plots from the city for a small sum of money. There was just one small problem: he had no idea how to garden or farm. In order to remedy that problem, Guy went back to the forums and notified the community about his project, which garnered him input, advice, and active help from other urban farmers:

> So I put that stuff on there [DetroitYes] and they were like "What are you going to do with it? Community Garden!" This one lady, Christine, got on there and she was like, "They're having a garden resource meeting right around the corner from you tonight at 6:00." And I was like "Cool!" I had no idea how I was going to get this done … Everyday, I was putting stuff on the forum about what I was doing. It went from a couple of months after that, well it wasn't even a couple of months. [A bunch of] people came out and helped me till and map out the plots of where we're going to plant. [Someone] brought out his tiller, he and his wife, we were all tilling and setting up the wood chips and how we were going to plant. That was our first official work day, it came from DetroitYes people.

Our interview with Guy demonstrated the concept of creative narrative appropriation, which in turn creates opportunities for the bridging of communities. Calafell (2007) illustrated such appropriation in her examination of the Mexican-American activist "El-Vez." According to Calafell, Richard Lopez, a musician and activist for immigrant rights, utilizes songs and images of Elvis Presley in order to build a performance that he uses in his activism. Essentially, Lopez dresses up as a Mexican version of Elvis Presley and sings altered versions of old Elvis tunes (i.e., Immigration Times, You Ain't Nothin' but a Chihuahua); those songs contain overt messages about the struggles of Chicano people and the oppressiveness of US immigration policies (which are driven by many of the same logics outlined in Chapters 3 and 4). In this way, then, Lopez appropriates a popular narrative familiar to white middle class people. This Elvis narrative is about a poor southern man who "pulled himself up by the bootstraps" using his talents; the story of Elvis mirrors the so-called "American Dream." By appropriating this narrative, Lopez presents arguments about immigration rights to white audiences who would have likely never given any thought to the subject. Ultimately, Lopez is able to build bridges to other communities appropriating components of a narrative that one particular community valued. In the case of Guy and the DetroitYES! community, a similar process was taking place. Guy had noted that the urban farming concept helped his immediate community:

> I don't know, when I started the garden I had this spiritual thing happen. We always went to church, when I started working in the garden, I have always had this big

heart and wanted to do what I could . . . I knowing what people are going through, some of the stories I have heard in the last couple of years. I couldn't believe it, I was seeing people that you would never think did not have heat in the winter time. Or people didn't have water . . . That's why I wanted to do all of this. In the wintertime if somebody's cold and they don't have heat they can come here. We turn the heat on, we have a kitchen, watch TV, whatever. That's where it started, I wanted a place where we could do stuff in the wintertime. Having something for the kids to do, a place for people to keep warm, I wanted a washer and dryer for people to wash their clothes . . . get a tomato or a bushel of tomatoes or whatever.

In addition, he claimed that the garden also brought attention from white outsiders who would otherwise never pay that hidden neighborhood any mind. As he updated the DetroitYES! community about the progress on the gardens, he found that many of those outsiders took interest and often volunteered to help; Guy was able to recruit labor for his project. One of those laborers was the community member above, who had conflated crime in Detroit with the shooting of Gabby Giffords in Arizona. That particular community member told us about his role in the Glorious Hope Urban Gardens during our inter-view with him: "A bunch of people show up, we start doing the rehab on [the plots of land]. We gut the [buildings], cut out, just dumpsters full of just every-thing." Even Pearl became involved in the gardens to some degree. In this way, then, Guy was able to get white middle class people involved in restoring a predominantly African-American, impoverished neighborhood concealed among the hidden geography of Detroit. What is particularly important to note is that many of these white people, like Pearl, were individuals who uti-lized discursive closures to block or stop any discussion about race or white privilege.

Closures & Bridges

The preceding findings from our interviews and content analysis outlined racial politics that emerged within an alternative cityscape constructed from diffused intertextual production. As stated before, this alternative cityscape allowed for members of DetroitYES! to make sense of the hidden geographies throughout the physical environment of Detroit. The racial politics online and beyond the forums of the DetroitYES! web community were intertwined and ultimately allowed for potential appropriation of narratives and build-ing bridges by minority communities that were concealed by—or within— the hidden geographies of the city. The only themes that emerged from the scattered few discussions about race within the threads on the forum were idealism and silence, which stood as inferentially racist. Such inferential racism emerged in large part because of community members' concerns about being banned for inflammatory comments or stirring up controversy. Public knowledge of Boileau's policies concerning civility led people with negative perceptions about African-Americans or other minorities to curb their postracist politics of discursive closures. This is important, because resistance to postracist politics associated with the politics of resentment became minimal, reducing the trap of irrationality and/or intimidation within the community for people of color. In this way, then, there were both positive and negative aspects to the administrative policy. Essentially, Boileau's policies created a safe place for both white people and minorities to discuss issues concerning the hidden geographies of the city; such policies often enraged some white members (like Pearl). Race was seldom discussed, and issues like urban farming could take center stage. Someone like Guy was then able to enter the community and glean new ideas that they could take back to their neighborhoods and build bridges with other communities outside of their immediate physical environment.

We realize that many readers may dispute our claim that Boileau's policies of banning and erasure opened the alternative cityscape to people of color so that they might enter, appropriate narratives, and build bridges between communities. In fact, many readers probably disputed or rejected our claims in the previous chapter that Boileau's banning practices could give rise to Standpoint Performance; it seems counterintuitive that such practices and limits to communication could foster the construction of a standpoint. Our response to those readers would be to point to one of the competing online communities that has emerged over the years for the purpose of discussing Detroit: Hot Fudge Detroit (HFD). The site was developed by people who had been banned from the DetroitYES! community for violating the administrative rules in the past. In many ways, HFD stood as a kind of shadow extension of the DetroitYES! community—a kind of alter ego. Members who were banned by Boileau often went to this parallel site to continue their discussions concerning the city. The difference is that they engaged in those discussions and interactions with no limits or rules imposed on them. Indeed, the members of HFD frequently engaged in discussions and debates about the DetroitYES! community, venting their frustrations over the sensibilities that guided the threads and postings on that site. One prevalent activity on the HFD forum was a kind of cyber-stalking or virtual bullying of DetroitYES! members. Hot

Fudgers routinely combed through the DetroitYES! forums looking for quotes by individuals they disliked, and ridiculed them within the threads of their own forum. For instance, an ongoing thread that existed in the HFD forums claimed through a vulgar title that one particular member of the DetroitYES! community was "a Miserable Cunt." This thread, which was roughly four years old at the time of our research and growing constantly, followed the posts of an African-American woman who was a prominent member of the DetroitYES! community. Members of HFD (including Pearl, who cross posted between the two forums) regularly decried the woman as conceited, whining, or "cunty." This thread was not unusual, as additional threads followed—or stalked— other members of the DetroitYES! community, ridiculing their subjects in front of the HFD community in extraordinarily venomous and hostile ways.

Another practice that Hot Fudgers adopted was called "cock punching," which entailed creating a new DetroitYES! account and returning to the accompanying forums. Once there, the Hot Fudgers tried to provoke fights and outbursts from members of the community. This was typically accomplished by watching various members closely on the forums, taking note of their personality, likes, dislikes, and role within the DetroitYES! community. Through such stalking, the Hot Fudgers were able to devise ways to bait the unsuspecting DetroitYES! members into arguments that often became hostile, getting both people reprimanded or banned altogether. The offending "cock puncher" then took the entire episode back to the HFD forums to show off through the discussion threads there.

Although Pearl disdained Boileau's tactics, she revealed an important rationale for such administrative actions through her comparison of DetroitYES! with HFD. In this comparison, Pearl noted that HFD was "self-governing" so that banishment and censorship were unnecessary because "wounds heal themselves." However, she recounted a story about a young woman who, like Pearl herself, frequently posted comments on both sites; many members of the HFD disliked this young woman because of her views about the city.

> It's a funny story. Well, it's not a funny story because it's mean. But I laughed anyway ... Maybe you know her. She goes by Mouse on DetroitYES! The guys over in Hot Fudge hate her guts. Somebody over there got her picture and pasted it up on HFD. And it's like, oh! I wouldn't like that! I would be very uncomfortable, and I wouldn't want people to know [who I am].

Members of the other forum diminished the anonymity of someone with whom they disagreed. Pearl herself noted that she would hate to be targeted in such a fashion, and that such tactics had a chilling effect. Within the DetroitYES! forum, such tactics would be punished and corrected immediately by the administrator. Needless to say, the cock punching and cyber-stalking would never be allowed within the forums.

It is our contention that without the policies of erasure and banning— and the impact those policies had on discussions about race—the practices in HFD would be the norm within DetroitYES! Boileau and other community members even noted that before the implementation of the policy, the forum was a hostile site. If that environment had persisted, someone like Guy would never have been able to appropriate the valuable narrative about urban gardens, which simultaneously helped his ailing neighborhood and bridged two different communities. It is entirely possible that the practices of engagement through HFD would allow for the discovery of the hidden geography, and construction of an alternative cityscape; there is clearly the potential for diffused intertextual production as it was described in Chapter 7. It is also entirely possible that such an alternative cityscape could give rise to the construction of standpoint described in the previous chapter. That standpoint, however, would likely be limited to dominant groups. The appropriation of narratives and bridging of communities hidden in the geography, or separated by the hidden geography, would not be possible. The exclusivity of the standpoint fostered through hostile acts and discrimination would not allow for impoverished or marginalized outsiders, who are often concealed or isolated because of the hidden geography, to easily gain access. This is particularly important, as the neighborhood in which the Glorious Hope Gardens was located was very much veiled by the hidden geography of the city. Guy's efforts not only created a garden that produced material resources for his community, but also created a bridge between that a community within the hidden geography and other communities on the outside.

Discussion

Overall, these findings regarding racial politics in the alternative cityscape stand as one of the most important lessons within this book. Many of the so-called hidden geographies that could be discovered were only hidden for those people who lived and moved outside of them. In many cases, these hidden geographies described by Bonnett (2014) are not uninhabited. There are entire communities that exist within these spaces, like in the North Cemetery in Manila. For these people, such spaces are not unruly or wild, but homes where people work, live, and raise their children. The problem, however, is that these unruly spaces are often deprived of the capabilities for hope and dignity described by Sen (2000), or even worse, trapped in cycles of toxicity like in Flint. Such communities already made sense of these sites long ago. In this way, then, the communicative strategy of diffused intertextual production not only allows for outsiders to discover and make sense of these spaces, but can also provide the potential for those who live within them to reach out and create bridges with other communities. However, the case of the DetroitYES! community illustrated the fragile nature of such bridges and engagements. Without the strict rules and administrative policies utilized within the community, the diffused intertextual production would not have had this kind of capacity; the community hidden in the geography would have continued to be concealed and overlooked.

In many ways, the emergence of creative narrative appropriation is what truly differentiated the democratization of space observed in Detroit from that observed in Wildcat Hollow and Germany. In Wildcat Hollow, the mediascape that was constructed through the use of alternative media by particular members gave rise to knowledge and actions that further isolated the trust network. The people in the unruly enclave could only circulate ideas among themselves, and shunned contact with outsiders. There was a degree of democratization in that enclave, but it was for those who were already members of the trust network. What is more, this democratization really only allowed for the members of the trust network to make sense of the unruly enclave in terms of a bygone era. Members of the network interacted with the physical environment largely as their parents and grandparents in the past. In Mannheim and Berlin, mediascapes were constructed that allowed for users of the stadtpunkte and DDR Museum to see the forgotten lost spaces. Those citizens felt empowered to go into the physical environment in order to explore, and build new connections with other people where they could. However, they would likely engage in such exploration alone or in small groups, detached from other people who also engage in such exploration. What is more, the performances and rituals of citizens in Mannheim and Berlin could potentially create enclaves in the physical environment, which would also stand as new, unruly spaces. Essentially, in all of these cases there was a sense of empowerment and engagement in new rituals, but little in the way of reflexivity concerning identity or the alternative views of the environment. The strategies for the communicative democratization of unruly spaces in that site stood as

Carpentier's (2016) sociological participatory engagement, which entails a newfound sense of community that largely placated existing power structures.

In Detroit, diffused intertextual production provided people who lived near or around the hidden geography a way to see those burned out edges in a different way. This new way of seeing allowed members of the web community to move through and interact with those sites, rather than avoiding them altogether. All of this was similar to the sociological participatory engagement associated with Wildcat Hollow and the cities in Germany. However, it is the construction of standpoint and creative narrative appropriation that really made the democratization of unruly spaces in this site stand apart from those other sites. The diffused intertextual production allowed for the members of the web community to voice their concerns with the city—concerns that had developed from a new vision of the hidden geographies and physical environment. What is more, the diffused intertextual production allowed for outsiders to connect with the web community and appropriate narratives that were popular to the predominately white members. In doing so, a bridge was built to new communities concealed by the hidden geography; a more robust form of democratization was taking place in Detroit.

Ultimately, we see diffused intertextual production as a valuable strategy for the communicative democratization of space. This strategy allows for people in communities stricken by problems and perils of austerity to understand in entirely different ways those spaces that have become unruly, and alter their interactions within them—and with them. In the case of Detroit, this strategy allowed a community of people who lived near or in the city to highlight unruly hidden geographies that had made them uncomfortable or frightened, and had come to define the very cityscape at large. Although there were people who are hopeful that a combination of government spending and economic prosperity will lead to structural changes for the city, nobody is naive enough to believe such changes will happen in the immediate future. Conversely, a large segment of the web community was pessimistic that any such government spending or economic prosperity would ever come at all. Whether or not such a change is coming, citizens around Detroit worked together to alter their vision of the existing material environment and change the way that it was experienced. Such alterations have the potential to restore some of the capabilities for hope and dignity described Sen (2000), as well as the qualities and characteristics of communicative cities described by Gumpert and Drucker (2008). The web community itself, through the interactive media platforms used there, stood as a form of vibrant communication—the likes of which had largely withered away over the past decades. In addition, people interacted within physical environments in the city where, in the past, they would not; those unruly spaces became communicative once again. What is more, communities that were closed out or isolated because of the hidden geographies associated with the old cityscape could engage in these communicative practices. Overall, diffused intertextual production holds the potential to tame or domesticate unruly spaces, and allows for ideas and debates to flow more freely in material environments negatively affected by the problems of austerity. In no way does this replace necessary material resources like healthy food or medicine. However, the democratization of unruly spaces and reclamation of communicative qualities of the city empowers the residents to recreate their communities, and begin a process of rebuilding from the grassroots upward.

Note

1. This chapter contains passages adapted from "Racial politics in an online community: Discursive closures and the potentials for narrative appropriation" by J. D. Atkinson, C. Rosati, S. Berg, M. Meier, and B. White (2013), *Journal of Communication Inquiry*, 37, 171–185. https://doi.org/10.1177/0196859913482139

References

Bonnett, A. (2014). *Unruly places: Lost spaces, secret cities, and other inscrutable geographies*. New York, NY: Houghton-Mifflin Harcourt.

Burgin, V. (1996). *In/different spaces: Place and memory in visual culture*. Berkley, CA: University of California Press.

Butler, J. (1990) *Gender trouble*. New York, NY: Routledge.

Calafell, B. (2007). *Latina/o communication studies: Theorizing performance*. New York, NY: Peter Lang.

Calafell, B. (2010). Notes from an "angry woman of color": Academic policing and disciplining women of color in a post (fill in the blank) era. *Journal of Communication Inquiry*, 34, 240–245.

Calafell, B. (2012). Monstrous femininity: Constructions of women of color in the academy. *Journal of Communication Inquiry*, 36(2), 111–130.

Carpentier, N. (2016). Beyond the ladder of participation: An analytical toolkit for the critical analysis of participatory media processes. *Javnost—The Public*, 23, 70–88.

Clair, R. P. (1998). *Organizing silence: A world of possibilities*. Albany: State University of New York Press.

Deetz, S. (1992). *Democracy in an age of corporate colonization: Developments in communication and the politics of everyday life*. Albany, NY: State University of New York Press.

Dickinson, G. (1997). Memories for sale: Nostalgia and the construction of identity in Old Pasadena. *Quarterly Journal of Speech, 83*, 1–27.

Dougherty, D., & Krone, K. (2000). Overcoming the dichotomy: Cultivating standpoints in organizations through research. *Women's Studies in Communication, 23*, 16–39.

Farley, R., Danziger, S., & Holzer, H. (2002). *Detroit divided*. New York, NY: Russell Sage Foundation.

Fuoss, K. (1999). Lynching performances, theatres of violence. *Text and Performance Quarterly, 19*, 1–37.

Gumpert, G., & Drucker, S. (2008). Communicative cities. *International Communication Gazette, 70*(3–4), 195–208.

McMillan, S. (2002). Exploring models of interactivity from multiple research traditions: Users, documents, and systems. In L. Lievrouw & S. Livingstone (Eds.), *The handbook of new media* (pp. 163–182). Thousand Oaks, CA: Sage.

Nakayama, T., & Krizek, R. (1995). Whiteness: A strategic rhetoric. *Quarterly Journal of Speech, 81*(3), 291–309.

Ono, K. (2010). Postracism: A theory of the "post"- as political strategy. *Journal of Communication Inquiry, 34*, 227–233.

Ott, B., & Walter, C. (2000). Intertextuality: Interpretive practice and textual strategy. *Critical Studies in Media Communication, 17*(4), 429–446.

Owens Patton, T. (2004). In the guise of civility: The complicitous maintenance of inferential forms of sexism and racism in higher education. *Women's Studies in Communication, 27*, 60–87.

Sen, A. (2000). *Development as freedom*. New York, NY: Anchor.

Sugrue, T. (1996). *The Origins of the urban crisis: Race and inequality in postwar Detroit*. Princeton, NJ: Princeton University Press.

Warren, J. (2003). *Performing purity: Whiteness, pedagogy, and the reconstitution of power*. New York, NY: Peter Lang.

CONCLUDING REMARKS

The preceding chapters of this book demonstrate that contemporary society is increasingly marked and marred by unruly spaces. In some instances, these spaces create topographical silence, leaving traditional residents feeling isolated and hopeless about the future. In other instances, such spaces leach toxins into the physical environment, taking a tremendous toll on the health and well being of citizens. In all of the cases reviewed in this book, unruly spaces interfere with the flow of communication and segregate communities, creating significant disruptions for the cities and regions examined. As infrastructure degrades and austerity continues to be the dominant solution to the problems faced by governments and cities, unruly spaces will continue to emerge and expand; indeed, the problems of unruliness will only escalate and intensify. What is more, the seemingly never-ending expansion of these unruly spaces across modern globalized society will not only poison citizens or hide communities, but destabilize contemporary democracy. Indeed, we see connections between the recent rise of populist nationalism around the world and the spread of unruliness driven by austerity and neoliberalism. As citizens increasingly see themselves as separate from neighbors and nearby communities, they come to perceive that they are surrounded or outnumbered. Feelings of resentment grow. People call for the construction of walls, or severing ties with longtime economic and political partners.

In Wildcat Hollow, Mannheim, Berlin, and Detroit, global forces like the politics of resentment and post–1970s neoliberal policies have driven an age of austerity that have degraded, or radically altered the physical environments in each. The changes to those physical environments have held a variety of consequences in each region. Despite the varied impacts, however, there is one commonality between all three of these communities: many of the citizens experienced feelings of isolation, and a loss of Sen's (2000) capabilities which give rise to hope and dignity. In each of those cases, the citizenry has no reason to believe that there will be changes to those policies or reversals to the austerity that has impacted their communities. Even in the case of Mannheim and Berlin, in which the federal government of Germany has been far less austere, there is an understanding that changes to the physical environment will take years—if not decades. Nevertheless, we feel that those communities have demonstrated different ways in which citizens can engage in the communicative democracy of such unruly spaces, and take control of them—or at least, facilitate communication within those spaces. Although such a sense of control or creation of new communication does not solve serious problems within the physical environment—like toxic water or authoritarian tactics to stifle dissent—such efforts can, at least, invigorate communicative qualities among the citizens who are forced to deal with such problems. In this way, citizens may, if they engage in the right kinds of democratization of unruly spaces, bridge communities and make voices heard. Such outcomes can dissipate the perceptions of isolation and incursion noted above, and diminish demands for building walls.

The important point here, however, is that the right kinds of communicative democratization must be utilized, lest communities compound the problems stemming from unruly spaces. In the case of Wildcat Hollow, a trust network of traditional residents and families broke the topographical silence constructed from the gentrification occurring throughout the region. However, that democratization isolated those residents even further, leaving the farmers there with only past solutions to solve modern-day problems. To this day, the farms in that region continue to struggle and decline. In Germany, the transformative memory revival and modification observed in Mannheim and Berlin seem to hold the potential to invigorate communicative qualities of those cities and urban spaces. The stadtpunkte and exhibits in the DDR Museum reminded people about the connections of modern spaces to the past, making those unruly spaces interesting and worthy of examination. This form of democratization invited new and engaging ways of seeing the physical environment, as well as people within those environments. However, this form of democratization (like the construction of the trust network noted above) adhered Carpentier's (2016) sociological form of participation, which is more passive and grounded in consumption of texts. The placement of the stadtpunke and organization of the exhibits created performative boundaries, which dictated different kinds of engagement within different parts of the physical environments of those cities. In this way, then, lost spaces were found again, and people made to feel comfortable enough so that they might engage in ways that were probably not possible before. However, the performative boundaries stood as a new kind of unruliness within those cities; enclaves were developed, similar to the enclave in Wildcat Hollow. Where once there was an understanding that people should simply avoid, or rush through, certain areas of those cities, there was the potential for confusion concerning what sites or spaces could (or should) be explored. Performances of engagement and exploration in one part of the city might be welcomed and encouraged, but deemed to be unacceptable in others.

The web community in Detroit offers perhaps one of the most dynamic forms of democratization that we have observed over the years. In that case, the use of diffused intertextual production adhered to Carpentier's notion of political participation, in that citizens were able to engage in the construction of an alternative cityscape, as well as the texts necessary for that vision. Through the interactive web materials, members of the web community could fully participate and engage in dialogue, which fostered the development of participatory civic identity. The diffused intertextual production was manifest in the virtual tour and forums that were the nexus of the community, while the participatory civic identity could be observed through the performances of standpoint by members as they engaged with unruly spaces in the city. The creative narrative appropriation by Guy in his hidden corner of Detroit, however, is probably our most important observation in Detroit. It is with Guy, and his work at the Glorious Hope Community Gardens, that we see the enormous potential of this form of communicative democratization of unruly space. Unlike in Wildcat Hollow or the cities of Germany, our research in Detroit revealed a strategy for democratization that allowed outsiders to become involved in the performances within the intertext. While the traditional residents in Wildcat Hollow shut themselves off from neighbors, and citizens in Germany were invited to simply look and wander, the members of the DetroitYES! community created a space in which bridges could be built between different communities lost in the unruly spaces of the cityscape.

Overall, we feel that there can be merits to each of the strategies described in this book. The discussions about global forces, austerity, and unruly spaces coalesce in the preceding chapters introduce and illustrate the different, emergent strategies of communicative democratization of unruly spaces. Even the construction of trust networks can be valuable, as they allow for the continuation of communal memory. Such a strategy could be useful under the proper circumstances—although it would require a different set of media backdrops and performances. More importantly, however, these insights and discoveries can point researchers and community organizers in new, important directions. With the concepts and strategies demonstrated here, we see the potential for new directions for future research, as well as significant recommendations for practitioners who work to heal divisions that have been fostered in communities by the rise of unruliness around them.

Future Research

The book and findings herein present readers with an understanding of unruly spaces in society, the causes of such unruliness, and the ways in which citizens work together to take control of those spaces (or create the sense of control over those spaces). These findings are important in crafting future dialogue about unruly spaces and their impact on society. However, there are important areas where future research should turn to build on the findings presented here. In particular, future research needs to provide more detailed typology of unruly spaces, explore the limits of democratization described here, and build on the strategies that have been demonstrated through the lived experiences observed in the sites featured in this book.

First, the present book has been based on Bonnett's (2014) rough typology of different unruly spaces discussed in his book *Unruly Places*. Although this rudimentary typology has proven useful in starting discussions like those in this book, the typology still lacks clarity. What is the difference between hidden geographies and lost spaces? On the surface, there seems to be a significant distinction between the two types illustrated in Bonnett's book. Hidden geographies are those built environments that are hidden from people passing by, like the pipelines in Flint, or abandoned houses obscured by the urban prairie in Detroit. Lost spaces are those sites tied to a past that few, if anyone, remembers. One is hidden, while the other might be in plain sight but ignored. However, delving deeper into lost spaces and hidden geographies, like those described in this book, demonstrates significant overlap as well. Both types of unruly spaces are essentially unseen, or invisible—until they are not. When people come to see them, or travel through them, they become uncomfortable or experience anxiety. How can we more accurately draw a true distinction between these two types of unruly spaces? What is more, the nature of spaces of exception and enclaves are still elusive. Both entail the disruption or rejection of rules that governed spaces in the past, like in Cairo and Wildcat Hollow. But what is the real difference between these two? Are spaces of exception simply intentionally constructed enclaves? Or are enclaves something entirely different? Future research needs to build a much more robust and well-defined typology of the different kinds of unruly spaces that people encounter in contemporary society, as well as their impacts on cities and regions around the world.

In addition, future research should examine the limits to the communicative democratization of unruly spaces. The strategies demonstrated in this book have their advantages and drawbacks. In some cases, like the construction of the trust network in Wildcat Hollow, there are significantly more drawbacks than advantages. In other cases, like in the DetroitYES! community, we observed significant advantages that possibly outweighed the drawbacks. For the most part, the advantages and drawbacks described in this book have focused primarily on communication and communicative qualities of cities or regions. But what are the advantages and drawbacks to the physical environment itself? Do these communicative strategies for the democratization actually lead to significant alterations to those physical environments? Are citizens motivated to not only open dialogue with other communities, but also to take up picks and shovels so as to engage in the labor necessary to renovate the materials that make up unruly spaces? The work conducted by white members in the Glorious Hope Community Gardens noted in Part IV would suggest that these changes are possible. But was that an isolated case? These questions should be addressed in future research to assess the limits of communicative democratization of unruly spaces.

Finally, this book demonstrates three distinct strategies for the democratization of unruly spaces: formation of trust network, transformative memory revival, and diffused intertextual production. In addition, there are two substrategies noted as well: transformative memory modification and creative narrative appropriation. Throughout the book, we have provided ample description of these strategies and substrategies, as well as assessment of their effectiveness within the communities in which they were observed. However, are these all of the strategies available to deal with the problems posed by such spaces in contemporary society? What other possibilities exist for the democratization of unruly spaces? Future research should look to other communities that are faced with problems and perils from unruly spaces created from austerity in modern society. Even more, future research should look beyond the United States and Europe. How do people in communities like Cairo or Mexico City deal with the unruliness that has emerged?

Recommendations for Practitioners

The findings in this book also offer activists and practitioners of social change guidelines to aid their efforts to build alternative spaces or transform unruly spaces around them. Through our findings, we are able to put forward five specific recommendations that should be considered before efforts to tame or democratize unruly spaces are pursued. Such recommendations are important, because they can help practitioners to make meaningful changes that might bridge communities and give voice to people who have been made invisible by the unruliness around them. If practitioners simply jump right in and try to imitate the efforts of DetroitYES! or exhibits at the DDR Museum, they may very well create more problems than they solve. They could inadvertently create new unruliness, like spaces of exception or enclaves. For that reason, we recommend the following:

First, it is important that practitioners determine which spaces are unruly, and what it is about those spaces that are problematic. Is a community made invisible by hidden geographies? Are communities becoming enclaves because of shifting or changing rules in the uses of land, or alterations to the physical environment? Or are they spaces of exception because authorities have forced such changes in the rules concerning land use? These questions are important, as they can tell practitioners about the core problems that are keeping communities separate, or hidden from their neighbors.

Practitioners should also assess how unruly spaces have influenced or affected communities. Have the capabilities necessary for hope and dignity been eroded? If so, which ones? Have the communicative qualities of a city been diminished by the unruliness? Has the cityscape been marred by the circulation of images of unruly spaces in mass media? In the case of Wildcat Hollow, the members of the community increasingly felt isolated from neighbors. In Detroit, people felt the need to keep away from the city, or move through as quickly as possible; such perceptions made it impossible to establish connections with people hidden by unruly spaces in the physical environment. Such an assessment will help practitioners formulate goals for communicative democratization of spaces that have become unruly.

Next, practitioners should ask about what has caused the creation of these unruly spaces. Is it natural degradation of the physical environment? Has gentrification played a role in significant changes to the physical environment, or have feelings of resentment and the "enjoyment of violating" driven policies that deprived a community of necessary funding? By asking these questions, practitioners become more aware of the environment, and the growth of the unruly spaces. In all of the cases described in this book, unruliness stemmed from some original policy or sentiment. In Flint, the politics of resentment fueled policies designed to punish the residents for the failures of finance capital and globalization. In Germany, the Second World War left people without homes, and the economy in shambles; the subsequent reconstruction created a physical environment that was inadequate in a variety of ways. Understanding the source of unruly spaces tarnishing cities or regions can inform practitioners much about the communities that need to be interconnected, and citizens who need to gain a voice.

Practitioners should then try to determine which of the available strategies are feasible within particular communities, or within particular spaces. In many ways, this involves surveying the region or city, and engaging in close observations of physical environments. Perhaps practitioners should engage in case studies of the linguistic environment, similar to Papen's (2012) research, as well the research described in multiple chapters of this book. What are the pathways through the city or region? What nodes do people use to congregate and engage in the use of social resources? What capabilities for hope and dignity exist within the community or built environment? Such information will illustrate what is, and what is not, practical for democratizing spaces. Is it possible to construct a museum and bring together exhibits in such a way to revive or modify public memory? Or is that beyond the community's means? Or would it be too disruptive? Finally, practitioners should determine the abilities and means of the citizenry. This will hopefully build on the assessment of possibilities within the environment, and help to illustrate the strategies that can be used within a community or physical environment. Are significant proportions of the community disabled? If so, posting historical markers throughout the region may not work well, as they may be inaccessible to many citizens. Do people have access to interactive media, or understand how to use such media. If not, then the use of diffused intertextual production may prove to be ineffective, or even counterproductive.

Overall, we hope that this book will stimulate further conversations about these important topics, and help scholars and activists alike to make a difference in their communities. As we have noted on multiple occasions, the age of austerity in which we currently live is likely to continue for the foreseeable future. People living in cities like Flint or Detroit, or regions affected by gentrification, have no reason to believe that policies will change in the near future and provide economic relief. Infrastructure will continue to crumble. Community spaces will continue to lie empty. For these reasons, it is vital that people understand that they are not powerless in the face of problems like topographical silence or the invisibility created by their environment. Hidden geographies do not have to be insurmountable. Enclaves do not have to be as isolated as they seem. We look forward to seeing these ideas and concepts bear fruit in the future.

References

Bonnett, A. (2014). *Unruly places: Lost spaces, secret cities, and other inscrutable geographies.* New York, NY: Houghton-Mifflin Harcourt.

Carpentier, N. (2016). Beyond the ladder of participation: An analytical toolkit for the critical analysis of participatory media processes. *Javnost—The Public, 23,* 70–88.

Papen, U. (2012). Commercial discourses, gentrification and citizens' protest: The linguistic landscape of Prenzlauer Berg, Berlin. *Journal of Sociolinguistics, 16,* 56–80.

Sen, A. (2000). *Development as freedom.* New York, NY: Anchor Books.

INDEX

V

Vaizey, Hester 151, 163–164
Visual space 149
Vodafone 92

W

Wark, McKenzie xii
Warnick, Barbara 23, 175–176, 187, 196
Warren, John 218, 224, 227
Wasserturm 129, 132, 134
We the People of Detroit 81

White supremacy 70, 92, 94, 224, 226
Whiteness 218, 224, 227
Wilderson, Frank 70
Williams, Raymond 15, 18, 32, 107, 202–203
Wolle, Stefan 150–152
Woods, Carly 148, 150, 162
World War II 20–21, 105, 123–124, 127, 130–135, 146, 158, 219, 247

Z

Zukin, Sharon 16, 172

POLITICAL COMMUNICATION

FRONTIERS IN

General Editors
Mitchell S. McKinney and Mary E. Stuckey

At the heart of how citizens, governments, and the media interact is the communication process, a process that is undergoing tremendous changes as we embrace a new millennium. Never has there been a time when confronting the complexity of these evolving relationships been so important to the maintenance of civil society. This series seeks books that advance the understanding of this process from multiple perspectives and as it occurs in both institutionalized and non-institutionalized political settings. While works that provide new perspectives on traditional political communication questions are welcome, the series also encourages the submission of manuscripts that take an innovative approach to political communication, which seek to broaden the frontiers of study to incorporate critical and cultural dimensions of study as well as scientific and theoretical frontiers.

For more information or to submit material for consideration, contact:

Mitchell S. McKinney: McKinneyM@missouri.edu
Mary E. Stuckey: mes519@psu.edu

To order other books in this series, please contact our Customer Service Department:

peterlang@presswarehouse.com (within the U.S.)
orders@peterlang.com (outside the U.S.)

Or browse online by series:
WWW.PETERLANG.COM